"Where we choose to live is clearly affecting our politics. George Hawley tells how migration is shaping the vote by explaining why Americans live where they do today."

—Bill Bishop, co-author of *The Big Sort: Why the Clustering of Like-Minded America Is Tearing Us Apart*

"George Hawley has made a major contribution to renewed interest in political demography with his new book. He ably reviews the recent literature that documents some of the most prominent consequences of 21st century demography. Hawley's analysis reveals how major demographic shifts in marriage and family formation, urban-rural divergence, and racial-ethnic population movement are important aspects of these political shifts. He demonstrates there is evidence that, for a growing number of Americans, the desire to live in neighborhoods where their social and political values are congruent with their neighbors is a contributing factor to the geographic polarization that now overlaps with partisan polarization in America. For scholars and citizens interested in the driving forces of political change in the United States, this book is a must-read."

—Richard W. Murray, *University of Houston*

Voting and Migration Patterns in the U.S.

In recent years, political scientists and journalists have taken a great interest in the question of whether the American electorate is "sorting" into communities based on partisan affiliation. That is, there is concern that American communities are becoming increasingly politically homogenous and this is because Americans are considering politics explicitly when determining where to live. Academics have since debated the degree to which this is a real phenomenon and, if it is, whether it has important normative implications. However, little empirical research has examined which factors turned some closely contested counties into Republican enclaves and others into Democratic strongholds.

Examining individual and aggregate data and employing a large number of statistical methods, George Hawley explores the increasing political homogenization of small geographic units and explains the causal mechanisms driving this phenomenon as well as its consequences for individual political attitudes and behavior among residents residing in these geographic units. He argues that some partisans are self-selecting into communities of like-minded partisans, causing some areas to become overwhelmingly Republican and others to become overwhelmingly Democratic. The book also notes that the migratory patterns of Republicans and Democrats differ in systematic ways for other reasons, due to the different demographic and economic characteristics of these partisan groups.

At a time when many studies argue that a large percentage of the electorate is self-selecting into communities based on their political preferences, this bookshelf essential presents a much needed account on the different migratory patterns of Republicans and Democrats and how these patterns are shaping the geography of American politics.

George Hawley is Assistant Professor of Political Science at the University of Alabama. His research interests include demography, electoral behavior, political parties, immigration policy, and the U.S. Congress.

Routledge Research in American Politics and Governance

Voting and Migration Patterns in the U.S.

George Hawley

Routledge
Taylor & Francis Group

LONDON AND NEW YORK

First published 2013
by Routledge

Published 2014 by Routledge
711 Third Avenue, New York, NY 10017

Simultaneously published in the UK
by Routledge
2 Park Square, Milton Park, Abingdon, Oxfordshire OX14 4RN

*Routledge is an imprint of the Taylor and Francis Group,
an informa business*

First issued in paperback 2015

Library of Congress Cataloging-in-Publication Data

Hawley, George (Political scientist)
Voting and migration patterns in the U.S. / by George Hawley.
    pages cm — (Routledge research in American politics and governance ; 10)
    Based on author's doctoral thesis:
    1. Party affiliation—United States.   2. Migration, Internal—Political
aspects—United States.   3. Demography—Political aspects—United
States.   4. Voting—United States.   I. Title.
JF2071.H39 2013
306.2'6—dc23
2013007133

ISBN 978-0-415-83703-3 (hbk)
ISBN 978-1-138-10043-5 (pbk)
ISBN 978-0-203-40335-8 (ebk)

Typeset in Sabon
by Apex CoVantage, LLC

For Kristen

Contents

PART III
A Case Study

Figures

Tables

Acknowledgments

I could not have completed this project without the help of many generous and patient friends and colleagues. Their support has been invaluable throughout this process and I am grateful for all of the assistance they provided me.

I must offer special thanks to Richard Murray of the University of Houston. I began thinking about the issues discussed in this project in 2009 while I was a graduate student taking his course on political parties. It was at this time that I developed an interest in the relationship between demographics and political change. A paper I wrote for that class turned into my first peer-reviewed article. Dr. Murray subsequently served as the chair of my dissertation committee. He continued to provide valuable assistance following my graduation, and I could not have written the chapter in this book on Harris County without his knowledge on the subject and willingness to share data.

Other professors at the University of Houston deserve special thanks. Jennifer Clark and Jeronimo Cortina also served on my dissertation committee and helped me develop many of the ideas present in this book. Their thoughtful critiques allowed me to correct countless errors that otherwise might have found their way into the present text. I am also grateful to James Gimpel of the University of Maryland who graciously offered to read and carefully critique my dissertation. He did this despite the fact that we had never previously met and he had no reason to perform such a valuable service for me.

Other friends and colleagues deserve thanks. Noah Kaplan was a valuable mentor throughout my time in graduate school; I am similarly grateful to Elizabeth Rigby and the late Robert Lineberry. I am grateful to Alan Steinberg for allowing me to add several questions about community satisfaction and migration to a survey he was conducting with university undergraduate students. I am grateful to the Annenberg Public Policy Center of the University of Pennsylvania for sharing with me the county codes for respondents to the 2008 National Annenberg Election Survey; without those county codes I could not have conducted the multilevel analysis using those data that appear in this text.

I am grateful to the editorial staff at Routledge for considering my proposal and helping me through this process. Darcy Bullock and Natalja Mortensen deserve special thanks for their patience with me. I also extend my thanks to the reviewers who read an earlier version of this text and offered helpful critiques and insights.

I am thankful to other University of Houston colleagues who have provided me friendship and support throughout graduate school and beyond, especially Inaki Sagarsazu and Chris Nicholson. A few people employed outside of academia also deserve mention. Steve Vanko, Joe Willis, Stephen Martuscelli, Brady Kornelis, Ryan Byers, Phil Melson, Anthony Wilson, Ryan Cavanaugh, and Zach Marquess have all been supportive and irreplaceable friends.

My family also deserves special thanks. I am grateful to my parents for all of their support. My wife, Kristen, has been my greatest source of encouragement. My son Henry, who was born shortly before I completed this manuscript, provided me the motivation to complete this project as expeditiously as possible. Jasper, my beloved dog-pound parolee, helped me keep my head clear by insisting on multiple daily walks through the neighborhood.

If this book contains any meaningful contributions to the field of political science, credit for those contributions must be shared with all of the preceding people. Any mistakes that appear in the pages ahead belong to me alone.

Introduction

Two years ago a *Forbes* magazine colleague living in San Francisco told me that all her thirty-something friends were leaving town.

"Where is everyone going?" I asked.

"You'd be surprised," she said. "Sacramento. Portland. Boise. Tucson. Smaller places than that, even."

On one level I wasn't surprised. Housing costs in San Francisco had gone to the moon during the 1990s. The dot-com bust that began in mid-2000 had done zippo to slow down housing price inflation. Tiny two-bedroom condos in San Francisco were fetching $600,000. Try paying the mortgage on that without a job. My colleague's friends simply had to leave town. They were running out of money.

Yet on another level I was surprised. People who had lived in a sophisticated city such as San Francisco, I was certain, hold a snob's view of "boonyack" towns such as Boise. It would never occur to fancy urban dwellers to move *there*. Yet they have moved there—in droves.

—Rich Karlgaard, *Life 2.0* (2004)

Americans have always been a mobile people. From the earliest European settlers crossing the Atlantic, to the westward expansion of American pioneers, to the present influx of immigrants from abroad, migration has been a critical aspect of the American narrative. In the coming year, millions of Americans will say goodbye to neighbors, pack moving vans, and move elsewhere in search of a better life. Some of these moves will be across town and others across the country. According to the U.S. Census Bureau, more than 1 in 10 Americans moved in 2010 (Ihrke 2011). These migrations often have enormous personal consequences for the people involved, but in the aggregate they also have tremendous political consequences for American political geography.

Rich Karlgaard was correct to note in the quote above that in recent decades huge numbers of Americans abandoned many large cities in pursuit of better lives elsewhere. Indeed, the focus of his book was how Americans can best accomplish this. Millions have also abandoned small towns and the countryside in favor of life in big cities. This is certainly not a new phenomenon. Karlgaard did not mention, however, that although people may have fled cities like San Francisco "in droves," most of these cities have not emptied out. In fact, in the 1990s, San Francisco experienced a net gain of more than 20,000 people entirely via migration—though many of those migrants were from abroad, rather than elsewhere in the United States. Although there is substantial variation among metropolitan areas in the United States regarding migration rates (Bogue, Liegel, and Kozloski 2009), with the exception of distressed industrial cities like Detroit, most of America's major metropolitan areas have not suffered a significant net loss of population in recent decades. As some people move out, others move in. Moreover, communities' in-migrants and out-migrants tend to differ ethnically, financially, and politically. This book focuses on that final characteristic. The different migratory patterns of different groups of Americans have rapidly reshaped the geographic partisan landscape of the United States.

American political scientists and political historians have always been aware of geographic differences in political attitudes and behavior—the American Civil War, after all, can be attributed to regional differences in political preferences. Regional political disputes continue to this day. After Obama's successful reelection in 2012, many conservative residents of Republican states such as Texas began to make half-hearted suggestions that they secede from the union. At least one northern liberal has suggested that everyone will be better off if they do so (Thompson 2012). When Republicans had the electoral advantage following the 2004 election, a number of American liberals suggested a new map of North America to include new nations called "The United States of Canada" and the derisively titled "Jesusland." Few would suggest these proposals have any realistic prospects, but that does not mean there are not intense regional (and even within-state and within-community) cultural and political disputes. Migratory patterns are exacerbating this trend.

Increasingly, political scientists have turned their attention to an important development in the United States: geographic political segregation. That is, Republicans and Democrats have been moving away from each other physically, and an increasing number of geographic units provide landslide victories to candidates belonging to one of the two major political parties. In the 1976 presidential election, just slightly over 26 percent of the American electorate lived in "landslide" counties—defined by Bishop and Cushing (2008) as counties in which one party won by 20 percentage points or more. By 2000, the percentage of the electorate living in such counties reached 45 percent.

According to Bishop and Cushing, the "Big Sort," as they call it, can be ascribed to the migratory patterns of Americans:

> Over the past thirty years, the United States has been sorting itself, sifting at the most microscopic levels of society, as people have packed children, CDs, and the family hound and moved. Between 4 and 5 percent of the population moves each year from one county to another—100 million

Americans in the past decade. They are moving to take jobs, to be close to family, or to follow the sun. When they look for a place to live, they run through a checklist of amenities: is there the right kind of church nearby? The right kind of coffee shop? How close is the neighborhood to the center of the city? What are the rents? Is the place safe? When people move, they also make choices about who their neighbors will be and who will share their new lives. Those are now political decisions, and they are having a profound effect on the nation's public life. (Bishop and Cushing 2008, 5)

This theory is analogous to those made by sociologists and demographers who argued that migratory patterns in the United States changed in fundamental ways during the 1970s. During its first two centuries as a nation, internal migration in the United States was almost entirely driven by the pursuit of work. As the Industrial Revolution progressed, migrants exited rural America for the jobs available in the major urban centers. However, in the postindustrial United States, migratory patterns often are increasingly likely to be driven by the preferences of consumers rather than the need to find a well-paying job (Easterlin 2000; Garkovich 1989; Long 1988; Long and DeAre 1988; Long and Nucci 1997; Schachter 2001). These scholars did not, however, emphasize the aggregate political consequences of consumer-preference-driven internal migration.

Discussion of geographic differences in politics and culture in the United States runs counter to some conventional wisdom. After all, globalization was supposed to usher in a "flat world" where geography does not matter because communication technology and air transportation connects everyone while multinational corporations have penetrated every community (Cairncross 1997; Friedman 2005). To a certain extent, those arguing the position that the United States is a country on the road to complete homogenization have a point. One could drive Interstate 90 from Puget Sound to Boston Harbor and eat and sleep exclusively at chain restaurants and hotels, listen to the same AM radio talk show hosts and Top 40 songs, and watch the same television programming throughout the entire trip. We furthermore have much less local and regional variation of the political parties than was once the case, and the two major political parties are more unified in opposition to each other than ever (Therialt 2005; McCarty, Poole, and Rosenthal 2006). While this economic and political homogenization is not entirely superficial, it masks important underlying differences between communities (Weiss 1988). Different communities have different proclivities to host a Whole Foods rather than a Walmart, a bookstore rather than a gun shop, and your address determines the probability that your neighbor is a member of MoveOn.org rather than the Tea Party (Chinni and Gimpel 2010). These differences matter to individuals. As Florida put it:

The place we choose to live affects every aspect of our being. It can determine the income we earn, the people we meet, the friends we make, the partners we choose, and the options available to our children and families. People are not equally happy everywhere, and some places do a better job of providing a high quality of life than others. Some places offer us more vibrant labor markets, better career prospects, higher real estate appreciation, and stronger investment and earnings opportunities. Some places offer more promising mating markets. Others are better environments for raising children. (Florida 2008, 5–6)

It cannot be denied that many moves are motivated by a desire to maximize income. This is, after all, one of the most important theories of international migration (Massey and Zenteno 1999). However, within the United States, the decision to move is clearly driven by more than just income maximization. This is not to say that migration is more common now than it was during other periods. In fact, the number of recent movers declined in recent years: between 2007 and 2008, 11.9 percent of the U.S. population changed residences, the lowest percentage since at least the late 1940s (Frey 2009; Cohn and Morin 2008). However, according to the March 2000 Current Population Survey conducted by the United States Census Bureau, just 16.2 percent of all movers in the United States from 1999 to 2000 said they moved primarily for work-related reasons (Schachter 2001), though the more recent Pew Mobility Survey found that 44 percent of movers (categorized as those who had moved at any point in their lives, not just recent movers) named work as a "major reason"—they could name more than one—for the move (Cohn and Morin 2008). Even the Pew survey, however, found that large percentages of the population moved for family reasons (35 percent), to live in a good place to raise children (36 percent), cost of living (24 percent), climate (18 percent), recreational or outdoor activities (17 percent), and cultural activities (10 percent).

In comparison to earlier periods in American history, Americans have an unprecedented ability to move to where they will be happiest, which frequently means that individuals choose to live among like-minded people. The theory that people "vote with their feet" (Tiebout 1956) is certainly not novel, but it has not been applied specifically to the issue of political landslide counties and other geographic units in the United States.

This book will examine the relationship between migration and political change, specifically considering the trend toward uncompetitive geographic units. It will make a number of arguments. The most important argument is that some of this is deliberate. That is, some Republicans and Democrats are intentionally self-selecting into communities of like-minded partisans. All other things being equal, strong partisans prefer a community where their neighbors' political yard signs have the same party label as their own.

There is anecdotal evidence suggesting that this occurs. In an online article for *U.S. News & World Report*, Emily Brandon (2008) compiled a helpful list for the supposedly growing number of Americans who want to retire to a community where their political values are shared: "There's nothing quite like the warm bath of expressing your political views in public and knowing they are wholeheartedly embraced by the majority of your neighbors. 'Pretty much when you meet people you can assume they are on the same political wavelength that you are,' Ashleigh Evans, 69, says about San Mateo, Calif. 'If a plumber comes to the house, you can pretty much assume he is a Democrat and feels the same way about most things that I do.' " The article went on to recommend that Republican retirees consider Idaho Falls, Idaho, and Fort Worth, Texas, as destinations, and that Democratic retirees take a look at cities like San Mateo, California, and Chicago, Illinois.

Self-selection is not the only migration-related catalyst for this change, however. A number of variables that predict specific migratory patterns (such as race, occupation, and marital status) are also correlated with party identification. A non-Hispanic white Evangelical Protestant who wishes to live among other non-Hispanic white Evangelical Protestants is most likely a Republican, and so are her preferred neighbors. A bohemian artist who wishes to live among other artists is most likely a Democrat, and her most-preferred neighborhood is probably solidly Democratic. If a community possesses characteristics that have nothing to do with politics per se but are nonetheless attractive to people belonging to a racial or economic group that, on average, votes for Democrats, then that community will become more Democratic. This work will accordingly focus on a number of important community elements, drawing on past literature on the urban-rural divide (Gimpel and Karnes 2009) and the rural brain drain (Carr and Kefalas 2009; Artz 2003), the marriage gap (Plissner 1983; Gershkoff 2009), racial/ethnic political gaps and foreign immigration, and the political preferences of the urban professionals (Judis and Teixeira 2002), a group that largely overlaps with the more recently identified "Creative Class" (Florida 2002).

In making this argument, this work draws heavily from literature in political science, economics, and demography. It considers both aggregate and individual data, as well as more qualitative analyses. It sheds new light on American political geography and contributes to the ongoing discussion of polarization in the United States.

Beyond examining these specific questions and attempting to contribute to our knowledge of migration and politics, this book has an additional motivation. Although political scientists have demonstrated an increasing interest in these issues, when examining recent political science research studying these kinds of questions we often see an unfortunate dearth of citations to relevant literature outside the field of political science. There is a rich literature examining migration written by sociologists and economists that is too often neglected by political scientists. While this book by no means provides an exhaustive list of all important studies of migration, and there are surely some important works I unfortunately neglected, I believe this book provides a useful summary of some of the most important works on the subject of migration.

Part I

Migration and Partisan Self-Selection

In recent years, political scientists have expressed an increasing interest in the question of geographic polarization the United States. The number of competitive states is apparently on the decline, and the number of small geographic units such as counties that consistently give overwhelming victories to one of the two major parties is also apparently increasing. There are concerns that this trend is leading to a more politically polarized electorate and is even threatening the unity of the nation.

Some scholars examining this phenomenon have posited that at least some of this can be explained by migration and partisan self-selection. That is, some Americans are deliberately moving to be among the politically like-minded or to get away from communities in which they are a small political minority. The idea of politically motivated migration is not new for Americans. In fact, it is part of the nation's foundational myth—Americans continue to celebrate the arrival of the Puritans who sought to escape religious persecution by governments in Britain and Europe. Many early American Mormons moved west in the face of conflict with their neighbors. African Americans migrated in large numbers out of the South in the early twentieth century in search of work and to escape Jim Crow laws of the South. More recently, a small number of American libertarians have been moving to New Hampshire under the auspices of the "Free State Project," seeking to establish a state with a comparatively limited government.

That being said, it has not been definitively demonstrated that Republicans and Democrats are deliberately moving away from each other and some scholars argue that the trend toward geographic polarization has been overstated. This section will provide a brief summary of trends in American political geography, showing that geographic polarization is on the rise in the United States. It will also briefly examine the characteristics of those counties that have become overwhelmingly Republican and overwhelmingly Democratic in recent years. It will then provide an overview of recent trends in American migration, as well as the leading theories of migration. Based on the existing literature on residential mobility, the forthcoming chapters will argue that the hypothesis that Americans are moving for political reasons is not an implausible. There is an extensive literature on "homophily"—the love of the same—and migration, and there are strong reasons to believe that many Americans are happiest when living among the politically similar.

It is insufficient to argue that this hypothesis is merely plausible, however. If American partisans really are happiest when living among co-partisans, and they will take the local political distribution into consideration when determining where to live, then there should be evidence for this in individual survey data. Chapter 3 will examine survey data in order to determine whether there is a relationship between community satisfaction and politics. The chapter will demonstrate that, for some Americans, there is a meaningful relationship between the relative congruence of their personal political views with their communities' aggregate political characteristics and their satisfaction with that community. I will further demonstrate that there is a relationship between a community's political attributes and a partisan's willingness to move to that community.

Although politics is surely not the primary motivating factor for most migratory decisions, this section will demonstrate that it is a nonnegligible consideration for many people. These findings bolster the argument that geographic polarization in the United States is at least partially due to politically motivated migration.

1 Geographic Political Segregation in the United States

1.1 INTRODUCTION

This chapter surveys the existing literature on geographic political segregation in the United States at both the state and county level, demonstrating that Americans increasingly live in states and communities that regularly provide landslide victories to one of the two major parties. This chapter also provides an overview of the kinds of communities that tend to become overwhelmingly Republican and Democratic as well as the kinds of people you tend to find in such communities. It also surveys the literature indicating that this trend will have important consequences for American democracy.

1.2 THE DISAPPEARING SWING STATES

Because of the Electoral College, states are the most important geographic units in national elections and are a primary focus of pollsters in the months prior to any presidential election. To make the case that geographic polarization is increasing, it is useful to consider the issue of "swing states," also known as "Battleground States." In the 2012 presidential election, the number of states for which there was any doubt regarding the outcome was exceptionally small. Although there were a few moments when Republican candidate Mitt Romney appeared within striking distance in a few states once considered solidly Democrat, for most of the election only eight states were seriously in play: Colorado, Florida, Iowa, Nevada, New Hampshire, Ohio, Virginia, and Wisconsin. After the election was over, it was revealed that many of these so-called swing states did not have the razor-thin margins that some analysts predicted. Barack Obama beat Romney by more than five points in Wisconsin, New Hampshire, Iowa, and Nevada. The two presidential candidates were within 5 percentage points of each other in only four states in 2012.

This is a significant change from previous elections. Several states considered in play as recently as 2008 (such as Indiana, Pennsylvania, and New Mexico) were viewed as solidly Republican or solidly Democrat in 2012.

The transition of New Mexico, which was shockingly close in 2000 and 2004 into the solid-Democrat category, is particularly remarkable—and can largely be attributed to demographic changes in that state resulting from migration. As recently as the 2000 election, Western states such as Washington and Oregon were considered competitive. In the 2012 election, Obama won both by big margins—Obama won Washington by more than 14 percentage points.

In recent years, we have seen the number of states won by narrow margins continue to shrink.[1] In 2012, only sixteen states were won by fewer than 10 percentage points. In 2000, twenty-two states were won by a margin of less than 10 percent. In 1996, twenty-four states were won by a margin of less than 10 percent. That last number is particularly impressive because Bill Clinton's popular vote victory over Bob Dole was much larger than Obama's popular vote victory over Romney. Looking farther back, in 1976 a remarkable thirty-one states were won by 10 percentage points or less. Although both parties have been relatively competitive in all national elections in recent years, this is increasingly not the case at the state level. It is possible that these state-level changes are entirely the result of attitude change and generational replacement, but given the extensive literature suggesting that party affiliation is relatively stable for most Americans and strongly correlated with parental party affiliation (Campbell et al. 1960), it would be a mistake to immediately discount the possibility that migration between states is playing an important role in this trend.

1.3 THE RISE OF LANDSLIDE COUNTIES

This story becomes more remarkable when we look at smaller geographic units. To make their case that Americans are sorting themselves out along party lines, Bishop and Cushing (2008) relied primarily on county-level data. Figure 1.1 shows the distribution of Republican landslide counties in the 2008 elections—Republican landslide county is defined as a county in which John McCain beat Obama by 20 percentage points or more.

In Figure 1.1 we see a huge swath of dark-shaded counties running through the center of the United States. If we knew nothing about the distribution of the population throughout the United States, we might infer from this map that John McCain won the election handily. For comparison's sake, Figure 1.2 shows the distribution of Republican landslide counties in the 1976 election. Comparing the two figures, we see that the tremendous Republican dominance of the rural counties in the West, parts of the Midwest, and the South is a relatively new phenomenon that requires an explanation.

Figures 1.3 and 1.4 show the distribution of Democratic landslide counties in 2008 and 1976. From these figures, if we were to again disregard the issue of population distribution throughout the United States, we could infer that the regions of Democratic dominance have actually shrunk in recent

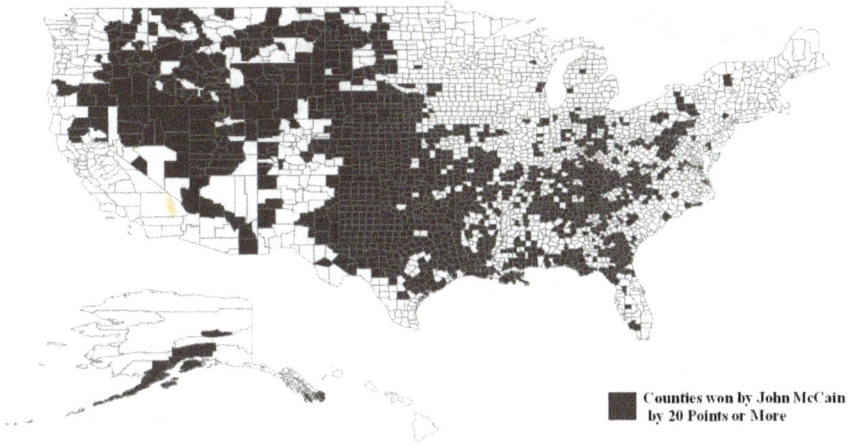

Figure 1.1 Landside Republican Counties, 2008

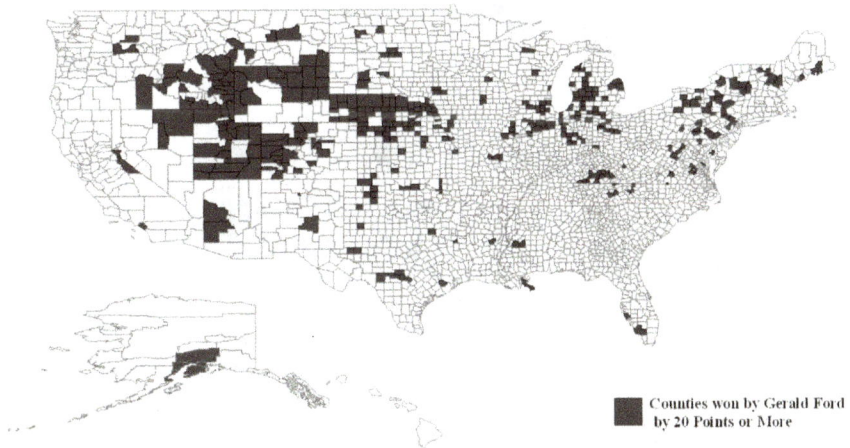

Figure 1.2 Landslide Republican Counties, 1976

decades. From a purely geographic standpoint, this is true. However, the new Democratic citadels are predominantly major population centers.

As we will see shortly, the Democrats not only have an advantage in urban areas, but win the overwhelming majority of votes in many of these urban centers. Although the urban–rural divide in American politics is certainly not a new development (Gimpel and Karnes 2009), these figures demonstrate that Democratic dominance over the densely populated counties on the Pacific coast, around the Great Lakes, and in the Northeast is a new development.

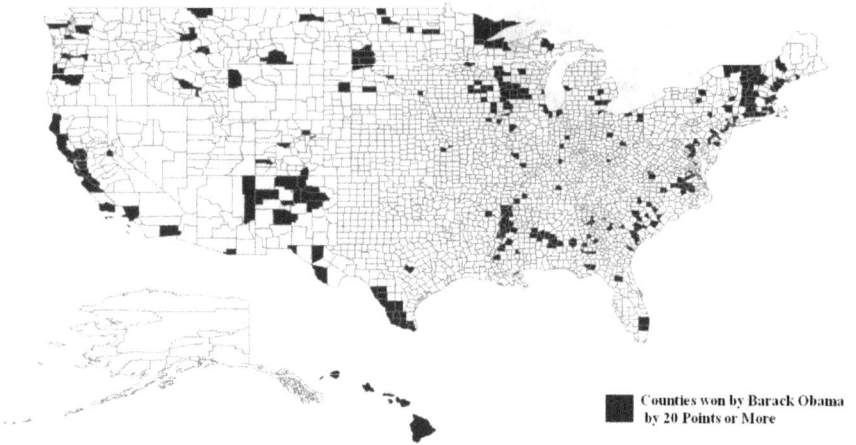

Figure 1.3   Landslide Democratic Counties, 2008

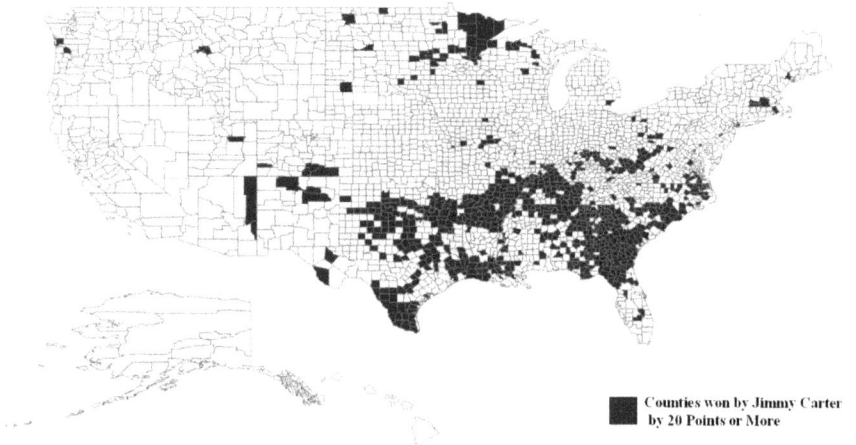

Figure 1.4   Landslide Democratic Counties, 1976

1.4 ALTERNATIVE EXPLANATIONS FOR THE INCREASE IN LANDSLIDE COUNTIES

Bishop and Cushing (2008) posited that the increase in the number of uncompetitive counties can be explained by migration. They further suggested that these migrations were actually motivated by political concerns. However, migration is not the only plausible explanation for the growth of landslide counties. It is worth considering alternative explanations for this phenomenon, and pointing out possible flaws in these alternative hypotheses. Generational replacement, voter mobilization, and partisan conversion are also strong candidates for an explanation. In some cases, particularly in those Southern states that swung dramatically from the landslide Democratic to the landslide Republican camp, conversion and generational replacement likely do explain a great deal of the political change witnessed in recent decades.

Partisan conversion may be a result of "neighborhood effects." That is, some evidence suggests that people tend to be politically socialized by their local social interactions (Baybeck and Huckfeldt 2002a, 2002b; Miller 1977). As Miller (1977: 65) put it, "people who talk together, vote together." It could be that, after a community begins, in the aggregate, to lean toward one political camp, the rest of the community tends to join the bandwagon. Over time, this may lead communities to vote overwhelmingly for candidates of a particular party and ideology. A problem with this hypothesis is that, for it to be a plausible explanation for geographic partisan sort, one would first have to explain why such neighborhood effects were stronger in 2008 than in 1976. If anything, they should be weaker. With the dawn of the Internet and the increasing ease of long-distance communication, people now have an easier time communicating across great distances. Therefore we should expect individual communication networks to be more spatially dispersed now than in the past—though some evidence suggests that the Internet supplements, but does not decrease, local, face-to-face interactions (Wellman et al. 2001).

If we hold to the theory that vote choice is driven by voters keeping a "running tally" of policy outcomes (Fiorina 1981), then perhaps we could speculate that Republican legislators, governors, and presidents lead to categorically better policy outcomes in some geographic locations, and likewise for Democratic legislators and executives in other areas. Over time, these different outcomes will lead to different voting patterns among residents of these different locations. This may not be entirely off base, but proving that this explains the increase in uncompetitive geographic units would require a demonstration that voters reward and punish politicians and parties based on objective, measurable criteria and that one party or the other tends to provide better policy outcomes for certain communities. At present, much evidence suggests voters are actually not very good at holding their legislators accountable for the economic growth or stagnation they oversee (Bartels 2008), and it seems unlikely that Republican politicians are categorically bad legislators in urban and minority-dominated districts, while Democrats lead to demonstrably worse outcomes in rural and suburban districts.

We may also posit that there is something specific about the physical geography of certain areas that nudges them into one partisan camp or the other. Williamson (2008) noted that aggregate party affiliation tends to track the built environment. He found that younger housing stock and longer commuting times are associated with greater Republican support. To a certain extent, this argument is not incongruent with the one being made here. Certain aspects of the built environment may cause a community to be viewed more favorably by Republicans than Democrats, and vice versa. Williamson's argument, however, built on that made by Bickford (2000), suggests that aspects of the built environment actually *shape* political views—with gated communities tending to lead to more exclusionary attitudes and political conservatism, whereas those in crowded urban centers are gently nudged into holding more egalitarian and liberal attitudes. Whatever the validity of this argument, it cannot sufficiently explain the nation's geographic sort unless it is first demonstrated that the built environment has also changed dramatically; after all, many of the new Democratic landslide counties are in urban areas with very old housing stock and the built environment has changed relatively little. Thus, to make this argument successfully one would have to explain why many of these areas were not such strong Democratic enclaves thirty years ago.

Another possible explanation is that, due to improved technology, political campaigns are now better able to "microtarget" very specific communities and even individuals. That is, whereas campaigns in the past tended to carpet bomb huge swaths of the country with campaign material, fund-raising appeals, and get-out-the vote efforts, they are now better able to focus their resources on very specific counties, precincts, and even individual voters (Hillygus and Shields 2008; Cho and Gimpel 2007). As a result of this trend, microtargeting may actually reinforce the degree to which a community votes strongly for candidates of a particular party; if a party effectively writes off a community and does not bother to campaign there, that community may transition from simply leaning toward the other party to offering that party overwhelming support. There are reasons to be skeptical that this theory explains the dramatic geographic sorting phenomenon witnessed in the United States. Although campaigns clearly now focus more energy on highly targeted efforts, there has not been a corresponding decrease in more traditional, less-targeted forms of campaigning such as television advertisements (Ridout 2009). Further, while microtargeting was discussed with great interest following the 2004 presidential election, the failure of the Republican Party's sophisticated microtargeting techniques in subsequent elections suggests that its overall importance to aggregate political trends was always overstated (Fiorina and Abrams 2008).

It might also be objected that the speed with which some types of counties transitioned from competitive to highly uncompetitive suggests that migration could not be the primary cause of these aggregate changes. This critique seems particularly appropriate when we consider rural counties. As the figures showing the distribution of county types demonstrated, rural counties were overrepresented in the landslide Republican category. However, as McKee (2008), pointed out, Bill Clinton was relatively competitive in rural counties as recently as 1996. This is an important point, though the migration hypothesis can survive this challenge. To begin with, although Bill Clinton performed better in rural counties than did Al Gore, John Kerry, or Barack Obama in subsequent elections, he did lose among rural voters by a substantial margin; in 1996 Clinton won 43 percent of the rural vote. Based on Bishop's classification of uncompetitive counties, a county split of 57–43 would already be skirting the landslide classification, and only a relatively modest rate of migration would be necessary to move such a county into the uncompetitive category.

It is also important to note that aggregate partisan changes in rural counties were not uniform throughout the United States, and here we also see substantial differences in counties experiencing substantially different migration patterns. Figure 1.5 was generated by calculating the population percentage change in those counties classified as rural from 1990 to 2000. The mean change was 5.96 percent growth, with a standard deviation of 13.37 percent. This figure shows how the county Republican vote change differed for rural counties experiencing different levels of growth. While it is true that, on average, those counties that experienced only a very small population change during the 1990s became slightly more Republican, the real explosive growth in Republican support came in those rural counties experiencing substantial population loss. Meanwhile, those rural counties that grew quickly during these years experienced virtually no change, and the fastest-growing rural communities actually became slightly less Republican.

It is interesting that those rural counties that experienced high levels of growth also experienced, on average, virtually no aggregate political change, at least in terms of presidential voting. This suggests that migrants who move to rural communities are not monolithically Republican. This seems to represent a challenge to the hypothesis that migration is leading to political change in rural America. It is equally important to note, however, the

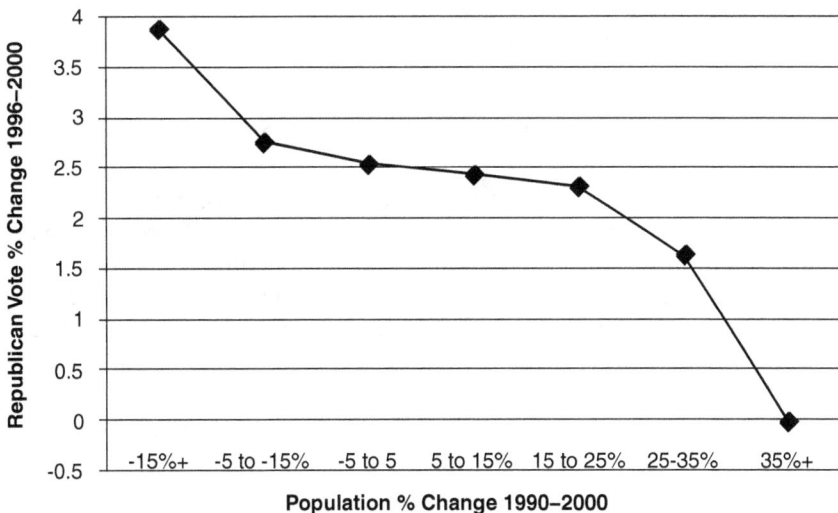

Figure 1.5 Rural Population Change and Rural Vote Change

political changes in rural counties that experienced a substantial net loss of population. These counties tended to become much more Republican. We can therefore infer that, although those who move to rural communities are not overwhelmingly Republican, those who *leave* rural counties are disproportionately Democratic. This is not surprising, as in recent decades the migrants who departed rural counties were typically younger and with higher average levels of education than those who remained (Carr and Kefalas 2009), and those traits are associated with a greater probability of Democratic Party affiliation.

Brown (1988) examined the political consequences of migration, and found that migrants do not consider politics when determining where they will live, but they do tend to become politically socialized to their new environments, though it can be a slow process—taking a decade or more for the new community to unravel a migrant's previous political identity. Brown's conclusions were at odds with Converse's (1966, 10) finding that, "partisan preferences of individuals do tend to survive change in residence very admirably, even when the voter migrates into strongholds of the opposition," and Campbell et al.'s (1960, 449) claim that, "[T]he movement of an extremely Democratic group into a relatively more Republican environment appears to have resulted in virtually no individual change or dilution of Democratic allegiances." It should be noted, however, that the time period Brown primarily examined in his study, the 1970s and 1980s, was prior to the sorting of the electorate as measured by Bishop and Cushing and that this period exhibited lower levels of partisan loyalty than were present in the 1990s and beyond (Bartels 2000). In Chapter 3, I recreate aspects of Brown's research using more recent data, in an attempt to demonstrate that the current generation of migrants is more likely to self-select into communities with certain political attributes than the migrants during the period Brown considered.

1.5 THE SOUTH AS A CHALLENGE TO BISHOP AND CUSHING

Comparing Figure 1.1 and Figure 1.4 reveals an important issue that is potentially problematic for Bishop and Cushing's theory. We see that many counties that provided John McCain a landslide victory in 2008 also provided a landslide victory to Jimmy Carter in 1976. If migration is the primary reason counties transition into the "landslide" camp, then there must have been truly massive migrations into, or out of, these counties. This is clearly not what occurred.

The story here is fundamentally different from the story behind other kinds of landslide counties, and migration did not play the primary role. Throughout this book I argue that migratory patterns are nudging some counties and other geographic units in one partisan direction or the other. While migration was certainly at play in the South, there is also a well-documented story of generational replacement and individual partisan change. This story will receive little attention here, first because a county that flips from landslide Democrat to landslide Republican creates no net increase or decrease in the total number of landslide counties, and second because this work deals with more recent trends than the Southern Realignment, such as the movements of professional class workers and differences in family formation patterns.

The partisan realignment of Southern whites has received much attention by historians and political scientists (Aistrup 1996; Carmines and Stimson 1989; Bullock, Hoffman, and Gaddie 2005). As recently as the 1940s, the Southern states were monolithically Democratic (Key 1949). As the Democratic Party turned sharply left on issues of civil rights and segregation, Democratic support among Southern whites eroded. The GOP made breakthrough gains in the South in the 1964 presidential election, despite losing badly in most of the country, and in 1972, Richard Nixon won every Southern state. Southern votes were still up for grabs in presidential elections at that point, however, and in much of the South, Jimmy Carter, himself a Southern governor, Evangelical Christian, and moderate Democrat, won by a landslide in 1976. This Democratic Southern resurgence in national elections was short-lived, and Southern whites continued their exodus into the Republican Party in subsequent elections.

This rapid change in the South cannot be solely attributed to migration. Many Southerners were actually changing their partisan preferences during these years. However, even here there is an important story of migration. Brown (1988) noted that during the 1950s, migrants from the North into the South were predominantly Republican, and when they arrived in the South, they remained Republican. These newcomers played an important role in weakening Democratic hegemony in the Southern states.

Although the Southern Realignment is not a primary concern of this project, it is important to note that more recent migration has changed the electoral fortunes of the two parties in the South. Whereas Southern immigrants of the 1950s were predominantly Republican, the new migrants into states such as North Carolina and Virginia are now less Republican than residents born in those states. In fact, Obama's narrow victory in North Carolina in 2008 has been attributed to the influx of people from south of the Rio Grande and north of the Potomac (Hood and McKee 2010), rather than opinion change among lifelong North Carolina residents.

1.6 THINKING SMALLER THAN COUNTIES

More than any other, the work of Bishop and Cushing (2008) was responsible for bringing the issue of geographic political segregation to public and scholarly attention. In their analysis, they relied almost exclusively on counties as the unit of analysis. They did so because of the large amount of quality data available at the county level. However, counties may not be the most useful geographic unit to consider this issue.

The use of counties may substantially *underestimate* the trend toward geographic sorting. Even if a county, in the aggregate, is politically hetero-geneous, it may actually be remarkably segregated, politically or otherwise. In the South, for example, there are a substantial number of counties con-taining communities that are overwhelmingly black or white. Although these counties may appear evenly divided politically in the aggregate, the disproportionately Republican whites and the overwhelmingly Democratic African Americans may actually rarely interact and live in geographically separate neighborhoods.

Even in demographically homogenous counties, the appearance of politi-cal heterogeneity may be masking underlying segregation. In Whatcom County, Washington, which is 88 percent non-Hispanic white, the voters in the large city of Bellingham, home of Western Washington University, overwhelmingly support Democratic candidates; however, the surrounding agricultural communities in that county vote disproportionately for Repub-licans. The average resident of Whatcom County will likely live her life just as politically segregated as a resident in any landslide county.

Another problem with counties relates to variations in population size. In a rural county with a tiny population, even a modest change in party iden-tification can cause dramatic aggregate political change. Indeed, one could argue that the impressive maps showing the growth of Republican landslide counties are almost entirely due to growing Republican strength in sparsely populated rural areas.

For these reasons, Chapter 7 of this book will take a closer look at quanti-tative electoral and demographic data from the nation's largest swing county: Harris County, Texas. This chapter reveals that, even though a county may appear competitive, a closer look reveals a remarkable dearth of competitive communities and neighborhoods. In fact, looking at the smallest geographic units within this swing county, political segregation is exceptionally high. Harris County Republicans tend to have Republican neighbors, and Harris County Democrats tend to have Democratic neighbors. From the analysis of this county we could infer that Bishop and Cushing's analysis of political segregation actually underestimates this phenomenon because of their reli-ance on counties as the primary unit of analysis.

1.7 DESCRIPTIVE DATA FROM THE COUNTIES

Despite the potential concerns with counties as a unit of analysis, much of this book will rely on examinations of county-level data. This deserves some explanation. While the decrease in the number of competitive states is important and interesting, most migrations occur over shorter distances—that is, most moves occur within the state. While congressional districts have some appeal, and have been examined to consider the question of geographic sorting (McDonald 2011), they are also problematic. Congressional districts lack fixed boundaries, and these boundaries are furthermore the result of partisan gerrymanders.

Smaller geographic units such as census tracts could potentially be used for this kind of analysis. However, the only meaningful data readily accessible for census tracts are those provided by the Census Bureau, and a large number of other important community traits would have to be excluded from the statistical analysis—most important, reliable election data. Accurate precinct-level data is available for some major municipalities, which is why the case study in Chapter 7 supplements this book's other findings, but there is not a database of precincts nationwide that includes presidential election results. Counties are therefore the smallest geographic unit for which a large amount of reliable data can be gathered from multiple sources for all U.S. states and thus are employed to usefully explore this issue. Counties are furthermore important political units, typically with their own government, which is not true of census tracts. In rural counties, the position of county commissioner is frequently the most powerful local elected office. If further justification for an examination of counties is needed, I can point out that other scholars examining related questions have focused primarily on counties for several decades (Miller 1956; Putnam 1966; Brown 1988; Bishop and Cushing 2008; Chinni and Gimpel 2010; McVeigh and Sobolewski 2007).

Accurate county-level data is available via the Inter-University Consortium for Political and Social Research (ICPSR) study, "County Characteristics, 2000–2007" (ICPSR study number 20660), from the ICPSR study, "Historical, Demographic, Economic, and Social Data: The United States, 1790–2002" (ICPSR study number 2896), directly from the United States Census Bureau, and from the Department of Agriculture's Economic Research Service. County-level election data was also collected from the Congressional Quarterly Voting and Elections Collection.

Although President Obama won the 2008 election by a significant margin, it is important to note that there were wide swaths of the country in which he performed quite poorly. As we saw in the figures in the introduction, John McCain won the majority of the rural counties in the center of the country by landslide margins.

When looking at that great swath of red through the center of the country, it bears noting that a great majority of those staunchly Republican counties are sparsely populated, whereas many of the Democratic citadels are major population centers. Table 1.1 provides basic descriptive statistics of these counties, taken from the ICPSR file, "County Characteristics 2000–2007," as well as the data from the Department of Agriculture. Taken together, they show a number of key differences between Republican and Democratic landslide counties.

These data drive home the degree to which densely populated urban counties are disproportionately likely to swing into the landslide Democratic camp, and sparsely populated rural areas make up the lion's share of the landslide Republican counties. In 2008, John McCain defeated Barack Obama by a margin of more than 20 percentage points in 44.44 percent of all counties. Obama defeated McCain by such a margin in only 10.09 percent of all counties. The mean total population (as of 2005) of the landslide Obama counties was 284,991.40 persons, whereas the mean population of all counties was 94,368.16 and the mean population of landslide McCain counties was only 37,161.08. Put another way, the average landslide Obama county had more than seven times the total population of the average landslide McCain county. In total, a little more than 50 million Americans lived in landslide Republican counties during the 2008 election, whereas more than 90 million Americans lived in landslide Democratic counties.

We also see some important regional differences in the distribution of landslide counties. After breaking down the United States into its nine census regions, we see that the most lopsided region is New England (which includes Maine, Massachusetts, New Hampshire, Vermont, Rhode Island, and Connecticut). In thirty-seven of this region's sixty-five counties, Barack Obama defeated John McCain by more than 20 percentage points. McCain won by a landslide in zero New England counties. In contrast, in the West-South-Central region (which includes Texas, Oklahoma, Arkansas, and Louisiana), McCain defeated Obama by twenty points or more in 364 of the region's 469 counties, and Obama won by a landslide in only 21 of the region's counties.

These regional differences have important consequences for electoral politics at the national level. The Democratic Party presently has an advantage in terms of states that are all-but guaranteed to give their votes to Democratic presidential candidates and elect Democratic representatives to Congress. While the realignment of the Deep South has received tremendous attention from scholars, the degree to which the electorate in New England has become solidly Democratic in recent decades is equally remarkable. This is particularly interesting because New England was once the most strongly Republican region in the United States. In the first three decades of the twentieth century, New England gave the overwhelming majority of its votes to Republican presidential candidates in all election years except 1912, when the Republican Party was split. Even though Roosevelt won a majority of New England states in 1932, New England remained the most Republican region of the country during that period. In 1936, the only two states in the nation that gave a majority of their votes to Republican presidential candidate Alfred Landon were in New England (Maine and Vermont). The Republican Party remained dominant in presidential elections in New England until 1960, when Kennedy won three New England states with a large percentage of Catholics. In his nationwide landslide victory, Lyndon Johnson carried the entire region. Democratic strength in the region has continued to strengthen, and the party has been particularly dominant since 1992 (Abramson, Aldrich, and Rohde 2010); the Democrats won every New England state in 1992, 1996, 2004, 2008, and 2012. The only exception during this entire period was 2000, when George W. Bush won New Hampshire. The decline of the Republican Party in New England has been ascribed to the decline of the liberal wing of the Republican Party (Rae 1989). Although the Republican Party's move to the right, particularly on social issues, may have helped it in other regions of the country, it has devastated the party in New England.

The decline of the Republican Party in the Mountain West is also an important trend, although the total number of electoral votes within that region is still relatively small. Although there is a large number of landslide Republican counties in this region, in the aggregate the Republican Party has weakened in this part of the country in recent decades. Between 1952 and 1984, Democratic presidential candidates succeeded in carrying any mountain states only twice, in 1960 and 1964. Republican strength in the region weakened during the 1990s, but George W. Bush performed well in the region in 2000 and 2004 (winning the entire region in both elections, with the exception of New Mexico, which he lost in 2000). Since 2008, the Democratic Party has experienced a surge in support from the region, winning New Mexico, Colorado, and Nevada in both 2008 and 2012. Much of this can be explained by changing demographics in the region; the growing Latino population in these states is a particularly important political development. The dominance of the Democratic Party in California can also be largely credited to the large Latino population within that state.

Although aggregate numbers are suggestive of the degree to which these differences represent the urban–rural divide, we have other measures of the degree to which a county was primarily urban or rural. The United States Census Bureau categorized counties with regard to whether they contain a Core Based Statistical Area (CBSA). Each CBSA must contain at least one urban area with at least 10,000 people. CBSAs are then broken down further in Metropolitan Statistical Areas and Micropolitan Statistical Areas. The former contain an urban area of more than 50,000 people, and the latter contain an urban area of more than 10,000 but less than 50,000 residents. We see in Table 1.1 that 51.72 percent of all the Republican landslide counties were classified as not containing a CBSA, compared to only 30.6 percent of all Democratic landslide counties. In contrast, 51.42 percent of all Democratic landslide counties were classified as Metropolitan Statistical Areas, whereas only 27.01 of all Republican counties received such a classification. For another measure, the 2000 United States Census provided what percent of each county can be classified as rural.

Other big differences appear also to be a function of the degree to which the landslide divide is largely an urban–rural divide. Landslide Democratic counties have, in comparison to the national county average, higher crime rates and higher housing costs. They are also demographically different, containing larger percentages of Hispanics and African Americans and a lower median age, as well as a higher percentage of the population possessing a bachelor's degree or higher.

Table 1.1   Basic County Descriptive Statistics

	Landslide Republican	Landslide Democrat	All Counties
Percent of All Counties*	44.44	10.09	100
Mean Total Population (2005)	37,161.08	284,991.40	94,368.16
Net Total Population (2005)	51,876,862	90,342,258	296,410,404
Median Total Population (2005)	18,949.50	56,023.00	25,235.00
% of Counties That Lost Population	42.69	41.01	42.92
% Not in CBSA	51.72	30.60	43.20
% in Metropolitan Statistical Area	27.01	51.42	34.70
Mean Total Population Change 1980-2005	9,966.54	45,812.75	22,022.26
Mean Total Population Change 2000-2005	2,450	6,516	4,759.56
Mean % Population Change 2000–2005	2.26	1.34	2.45
Mean % of Population Age 65+ (2005)	15.49	12.84	14.91
Mean County Median Age (2005)	39.10	36.33	38.61
Mean % Hispanic (2005)	7.23	12.39	7.08
Mean % Black (2005)	5.85	21.232	8.99
Mean Unemployment Rate (2005)	6.02	5.00	5.41
Mean Index Crime Rate, per 100,000 persons (2004)	2,505.36	3,623.28	2,771.43
Mean County Median Home Value (2000)	$72,123.91	$114,797.40	$83,835.27
Mean County Median Household Income (2000)	$31,079.90	$33,106.41	$32,526.40
Mean County Median Household Income (2008)	$42,239.39	$45,817.15	$44,006.70
Mean County Median Home Value-Median Income Ratio (2000)	3.26	2.30	2.52
% Females Married: Age 25–29	80.86	57.91	74.52
Mean Percent of Population with BA or greater (2000)	22.30	14.62	16.49
Mean Percent of Population Claimed as Members by Religious Organization	57.28	49.13	52.99

(Continued)

Table 1.1 *(Continued)*

	Landslide Republican	Landslide Democrat	All Counties
Mean Percent of Population Belonging to an Evangelical Church	24.99	9.88	18.40
ERS Policy Type: Low Education	0.22	0.28	0.20
ERS Policy Type: Low Employment	0.12	0.26	0.15
ERS Policy Type: Persistent Poverty	0.09	0.28	0.12
ERS Policy Type: Population Loss	0.18	0.20	0.19
ERS Policy Type: Retirement Destination	0.16	0.09	0.14
Census Region: Pacific	29	28	132
Census Region: Mountain	157	24	283
Census Region: West-North Central	291	37	618
Census Region: East-North Central	68	35	354
Census Region: West-South Central	364	21	469
Census Region: East-South Central	222	31	364
Census Region: South Atlantic	230	70	588
Census Region: Mid-Atlantic	21	23	149
Census Region: New England	0	37	65

* All descriptive statistics exclude Alaska.

The Economic Research Service within the Department of Agriculture also divides counties into different dichotomous variables. We see that a greater percentage of the landslide Democratic counties were categorized as experiencing "persistent poverty" than the average U.S. county. They are also more likely to experience "low education" and "low employment." It is important to keep in mind, however, that the landslide Democratic counties tend to fall into three categories: the densely populated urban areas, the rural counties along the Mississippi Delta and the Southern Coastal Plains, and the border regions of the Southwest. The strong Democratic voting patterns in the latter two categories can be attributed to their poverty and large minority populations, and the former are not necessarily poor or overwhelmingly minority. The metro Democratic counties have, overall, much more population than the rural Democratic counties, and these descriptive statistics do not control for population size.

The worship–attendance gap, or "God gap," is a much-discussed phenomenon both in political science literature and in the popular media. Those who attend a religious service at least once a week also have a high probability of voting Republican, whereas those who never attend a worship service have a high probability of voting Democratic (Olson and Green 2009). President Bush's reelection in 2004 was largely credited to his enthusiastic support from conservative Christians. Therefore, it is important to find some useful measure of aggregate religious-attendance variable to include in this study. Unfortunately, finding reliable data on this subject is problematic. The United States Census has not asked the religious affiliations of its respondents for many decades.

The best available estimates for county-level religious attendance data comes from the Glenmary Research Center, which publishes county-level data on religious congregations and their memberships (Jones et al. 2002). The Glenmary data provide membership information of every major religion and denomination in every U.S. county.[2] One potential variable of interest is simply the percentage of each county that is formally a member of a religious institution.

We see from the descriptive statistics, however, that the difference in these different county types for total congregation membership is relatively modest. In landslide Republican counties, the mean percentage of the county population belonging to a religious congregation was about 57 percent. In Democratic counties, that number was 49 percent. In all counties that number was 52 percent. Looking at all congregations, however, masks the important political diversity of different Christian denominations (Beatty and Walter 1988; Brooks 2002; Brooks and Manza 2004). We know, for example, that Evangelical Christians are considerably more Republican on average than mainline Protestants or Catholics. For this reason, I also calculated the percentage of each county that belongs to a religious congregation that can be classified as Evangelical. Here we see more dramatic differences. In the landslide Republican counties, the mean percentage of the population belonging to an Evangelical church is 24.99 percent. In landslide Democratic counties, however, the mean percentage of the population belonging to such congregations was less than 10 percent. Given this large difference, the Evangelical population will likely be a more useful variable for this analysis than the total percentage of a county belonging to any kind of religious body.

One of the most dramatic differences between the overwhelmingly Democratic counties and the overwhelmingly Republican counties is the rates of marriage for young women. Whereas more than 80 percent of women between the ages of 25 and 29 in the landslide Republican counties have been married, this was only true of 57.91 percent of women of that age in landslide Democratic counties. Because the marriage gap is so important to American political geography, an entire chapter will be devoted to this subject.

1.8 "TYPES" OF LANDSLIDE COUNTY

It is important not to place too much emphasis on the distinction between landslide Democratic counties, competitive counties, and landslide Republican counties. There is obviously a great deal of variation within these three categories. After all, from a demographic, cultural, and economic stand-point, Tunica County, Mississippi, and Lane County, Oregon, are about as different as two U.S. counties can be. The former is approximately 70 percent African American and has a median annual family income of approximately $25,000; the latter is 90 percent non-Hispanic white, with a median income of approximately $45,000. Both of these counties, however, voted overwhelmingly for Barack Obama in 2008. Although not all land-slide Republican and landslide Democratic counties are identical, or even very similar, there are certain attributes of counties that make them much more likely to fall into one of those categories. The rest of this section will focus on different common types of landslide counties.

According to Chinni and Gimpel (2010), there are really three charac-teristics that suggest a county will go into the landslide Republican camp: a high concentration of non-Hispanic white Evangelical Christians, a high concentration of Mormons, and rural areas in which non-Hispanic whites are a clear majority of *voters*,[3] if not a strong majority of total residents.[4] It should be noted that counties that exhibit these characteristics are not par-ticularly wealthy. Although there may be some religious hostilities between Evangelicals and Mormons, the voting patterns of white Southern Baptists and white Mormons are largely indistinguishable—a Republican on the bal-lot will probably get their votes. These county types are also not mutually exclusive. There are many rural counties in the South and Midwest that are also dominated by Evangelical Christians, and many rural counties in the Mountain states in which the population is overwhelmingly Mormon. What you will not find anywhere, however, is a large urban center in which the Republican Party enjoys a lopsided advantage. Even those counties Chinni and Gimpel (2010) categorized as "Monied Burbs," which one might expect to exhibit Republican voting habits due to economic conditions alone, gave on average more votes to Obama than McCain.

Democratic counties also tend to fall into a few broad categories, though they can be rural or urban. First, any county in which racial or ethnic minor-ities are a strong majority of voters is generally going to give Democratic candidates a strong majority of its votes, though there is not an obvious linear relationship between the size of the minority population and aggregate vot-ing habits. Many racially diverse counties are also diverse politically because non-Hispanic whites in those counties vote overwhelmingly for Republi-cans and blacks and Hispanics vote overwhelmingly for Democrats. The racially diverse counties where you do see overwhelming majorities given to Democrats are those metropolitan counties where both minorities and non-Hispanic whites give strong support to Democratic candidates—we see this in cities like San Francisco, Washington, D.C., and Chicago. These commu-nities often exhibit high levels of economic inequality along racial lines, but despite different economic interests, all major groups tend to lean toward the Democratic Party, on average. There are a few counties that exhibit neither large minority populations nor high population density but nonethe-less vote overwhelmingly for Democrats. These counties are often the home of a major research university, such as Middlesex County, Massachusetts, which is home to Harvard University and gave Barack Obama more than 60 percent of its votes, or Lane County, Oregon, home of the University of Oregon, which was previously discussed. Other such counties include major resort communities, such as Teton County, Wyoming, and Pitkin County, Colorado; these counties that are rich, white, rural, and strongly Democratic, however, are exceptionally rare.

Not surprisingly, the characteristics of landslide partisan counties mirror the characteristics of strong partisan individuals. Landslide Democratic counties have, on average, a larger minority population, a younger median age, are more urban, and have a larger percentage of the population possessing college degrees—all characteristics that also predict that individuals will vote Democratic. Similarly, landslide Republican counties are typically more rural, older, more non-Hispanic white, and have fewer college-educated residents within their borders. Not all attributes that predict individual partisanship predict aggregate partisanship in the same direction. While higher incomes are associated with individuals voting for the Republican Party, landslide Democratic counties actually have a meaningfully higher median income than landslide Republican counties. This phenomenon has been examined by other scholars in the past (Gelman et al. 2008), and will be further explored in later chapters of this work.

1.9 GEOGRAPHIC PARTISAN SORTING: DOES IT MATTER?

The causes of this apparent geographic partisan sort provide an interesting intellectual puzzle. In order to justify serious study by political scientists, there should first be compelling evidence to suggest that this trend has important consequences for American political behavior and election outcomes. There is a rich literature suggesting that changing political contexts can lead to meaningful changes in individual political attitudes and behavior.

To begin, I should note that there are some reasons to discount the argument that geographic sorting is having a negative influence on American politics. Although an increasing number of communities may not be politically competitive, this does not necessarily mean that American politics in the aggregate is no longer competitive. Provided the overall support of both political parties remains relatively static, the clustering together of co-partisans does not necessarily advantage one party over another. Nor will it necessarily have any influence on the competitiveness of presidential contests.

One might plausibly argue that a geographically polarized electorate will also tend to produce a more polarized Congress. For example, in a district in which the overwhelming majority of voters identify as Republicans (Democrats) then the primary elections may actually be more competitive and important than the general election, thus Republican (Democratic) candidates in these counties may be more concerned with placating the conservative (liberal) base of the party in order to successfully win the primary election, secure in the knowledge that a primary victory will ensure a victory in the general election. Such candidates may have little incentive to moderate their positions in order to reach out to Democrats (Republicans) and political independents, and thus we should expect members of Congress from "safe" districts to be more ideologically extreme. However, Brunell (2006a; 2006b) demonstrated that members of Congress who win by large margins are not typically more ideologically extreme than members from competitive districts. McCarty, Poole, and Rosenthal (2009) also failed to uncover any evidence that uncompetitive elections are to blame for higher levels of polarization in Congress. If these findings continue to hold, we should not be concerned that a continuation of the sorting process will lead to more extremism in Congress. Brunell (2008) further noted that uncompetitive elections are actually good for American politics, as voters are more satisfied with election results when the person they voted for actually won, and they are furthermore going to be more satisfied with how they are represented; uncompetitive congressional elections, either as a result of migration or gerrymandering, increase the percentage of Americans who are represented by someone for whom they voted and should therefore be encouraged.

Even if we cannot necessarily predict that a geographically polarized electorate will produce a polarized Congress, we may plausibly predict that individual voters will become more ideologically extreme as a function of this trend. Before considering the issue of whether or not the electorate is influenced by the local political context, we should first be confident that voters actually know the political composition of their neighborhood. Most Americans surely do not carefully examine county- or precinct-level returns after each election to determine the extent to which their views are congruent with their neighbors. And yet, they can nonetheless reasonably estimate the degree to which they are in the political majority or minority. Through their personal observations of political expressions such as yard signs and bumper stickers, as well as their interactions with others, they can make reasonable approximations of the local partisan climate (Huckfeldt 1986; Books and Prysby 1991).

Many political scientists have long believed that local political context can influence individual attitudes. Berelson, Lazarsfeld, and McPhee (1954) argued that the stability of political preferences is a function of how much social support individuals have for those preferences. Thus, as the local community becomes increasingly supportive of one political viewpoint in the aggregate, individuals who may otherwise have held dissenting opinions should increasingly conform their views to the views of the majority, and those already sharing the majority opinion may become even more ideologically calcified. As a result of this sorting process, we may see an increasing number of people supporting a political party at odds with their interests or holding views more extreme than would necessarily be predicted based on their individual attributes.

Berelson et al.'s (1954) findings have been reexamined since the initial publication of their work. MacKuen and Brown (1987) also found that local context shapes individual views. They found that individual attitudes toward parties and politicians were heavily influenced by their neighbors' attitudes, though they did not find that partisan affiliation was similarly sensitive. Lyons (2011) found that partisans who are members of the majority in a county are less likely to change their party identification than those who are in the minority; thus, if the percentage of Americans living in communities where they belong to the partisan majority continues to increase, we should also see a decrease in the number of Americans who switch political parties.

Local context also plays an important role in the development of individual communication networks. Putnam (1966) found that the partisanship of friendship groups was largely related to the aggregate party affiliation rates in a community. Huckfeldt (1983) also found that our friendship networks are heavily determined by the local context, a finding confirmed by other scholars (Mollenhorst, Völker, and Flap, 2008). We should not overstate this, however. Even when a community is overwhelmingly Republican or Democratic, individuals who are political minorities at the local level will nonetheless often be able to seek out and befriend those who are like-minded politically. Finifter (1974) studied friendship groups among predominantly Democratic Detroit autoworkers. He found that Republican autoworkers tended to congregate together and thus created a protective social group for themselves. In spite of this caveat, it is clear that Democrats (Republicans) in predominantly Republican (Democratic) communities will have more Republicans (Democrats) in their social networks than would be the case in a different social context.

This matters because it has been demonstrated that social networks have consequences in regard to political attitudes. On the positive side, Krassa (1990) demonstrated that political "deviants," that is, those whose views are different from the local majorities', tend to be better informed politically than other members of their communities. This is likely because those who face regular political disagreement in their daily lives need to have better information in order to overcome the constant barrage of contrary information. Thus we should not necessarily view belonging to the political minority in a landslide community as categorically negative. On the other hand, Huckfeldt, Morehouse, and Osborne (2004) found that politically heterogeneous social networks tend to increase ambivalence toward politics. That is, those with a social network that contains a wide variety of political attitudes should become more conflicted in their own attitudes. Therefore, we may expect political minorities in landslide counties to be highly ambivalent about politics and more likely to withdraw from political participation. In contrast, those in the majority in landslide communities likely have highly homogenous discussion networks and are less ambivalent in their political attitudes. Similarly, Mutz (2002) found that cross-cutting social networks tend to discourage political participation. That is, people who are in a politically heterogeneous social network may avoid engaging in any sort of political activity because they do not want to endanger any of their social relationships. Thus we should expect to see more political activity on the part of residents in landslide communities if their views are in the majority, and less if they are a minority. While this research suggests that political minorities living in landslide counties are at a disadvantage and are less likely to participate politically, in the aggregate, the trend toward more landslide communities may actually be a boon for political participation, as an increasing number of Americans presumably have politically homogenous social networks and are therefore not subject to cross-cutting pressures.

Forms of participation such as voting may also be influenced by the geographic partisan sort. Evidence suggests that uncompetitive races tend to suppress voter turnout (Gilliam 1985; Gey 2006; McDonald 2006). Thus the increasing clustering of partisans likely lowers voter turnout. Republicans in particular are less likely to turn out and vote if they are in an area that is heavily Democratic (Dyck, Gaines, and Shaw 2009). The geographic sorting process may therefore appear exaggerated in many heavily Democratic areas; Republicans may live there, but they do not vote. Primary participation may be particularly sensitive to the local context. We might expect, for example, that those belonging to the majority party in an uncompetitive context may feel more social pressure to show up for the primary election (Gerber, Green, and Larimer 2008). In a community in which nearly everyone votes for candidates of a single party, we may expect showing up for the primary election to be considered a more important social act than is the case in a more politically heterogeneous community—that is, the sense that participating in a primary is an important part of one's civic duty (Blais 2000) may be stronger in uncompetitive counties.

Other forms of participation may suffer as a result of this clustering, as it also appears that donating money to political campaigns is dependent on context, though local political competition does not seem to be one of the more important determinants of campaign donations (Gimpel, Lee, and Kaminski 2006; Brown, Powell, and Wilcox 1995). It is hard to say how the trend toward geographic partisan sorting will influence aggregate giving patterns, as the dearth of close races may depress the desire to give, but the growth of geographic clusters of strong partisans may also make it easier for campaigns to target communities for donations.

In a forthcoming article (Hawley 2013), I argued that higher levels of attitude polarization can be found among partisans living in counties where they are in the overwhelming political majority. This was confirmed using a number of different measures. Compared to partisans living in other contexts, partisans in the majority in landslide counties were much more likely to have polarized attitudes toward the major presidential candidates. They were also more likely to strongly identify with their political party and to be highly ideological. These effects were consistent and highly statistically significant despite the potential problems caused by the use of relatively large second-level units (counties). If we explore smaller geographic entities, such as neighborhoods or census tracts, the results would likely have been even stronger.

It is important to note that not all political scientists believe context plays an important role in political behavior, particularly vote choice. Gary King (1996), one of the most celebrated quantitative methodologists in political science, has argued that many political scientists have overstated the importance of contextual effects:

> Consider two voters. Both are conservative, poor, white men who identify with the Republican Party, prefer more defense spending and insist that the federal government balance the budget immediately. They are each afraid that someone will take their guns away, hope to end welfare as anyone knows it, and think Rush Limbaugh should be president. The only difference is that, after being raised as twins in Utah, they were separated. One moved to Lancaster County, Pennsylvania amidst many other voters like himself. The other settled in Brookline, Massachusetts, with Michael Dukakis and many other Liberal Democrats.
>
> Now suppose Bill Clinton runs for re-election against Phil Gramm in 1996. Both voters would obviously vote for Graham. Academics know this with a reasonable degree of certainty from extensive research in political science, political geography and related fields. Politicians know this from district surveys, studying precinct election returns and talking with constituents. This might not have been so obvious without the last hundred years of quantitative and qualitative scholarly research, but is plainly obvious today. But how much does context matter? How long did the context of liberal Brookline, Massachusetts cause the second voter to consider voting Democrat? To be more precise, how much did the probability of voting Republican differ between the two voters? The answer is pretty clear from the scholarly literature: not much. (King 1996, 160)

In spite of King's objections, political scientists continue to study contextual effects on political attitudes and political behaviors such as vote choice, and continue to uncover substantively and statistically significant effects. The importance of contextual effects in political science is beyond the scope of this book, though I contend that the preponderance of evidence suggests contextual effects can be substantial. If they do not matter, however, then predicting the political consequences of migration is somewhat easier. If a Democrat will forever remain a Democrat, even if she moves to an overwhelmingly Republican community, then her migration will permanently change the partisan distribution of her new community. On the other hand, if, as Brown (1988) suggested, she eventually becomes politically acclimated to her new community and her voting patterns come to resemble those of her neighbors, then her migration will not have changed her new community's political characteristics.

1.10 CONCLUSION

This chapter provided a brief overview of the trend toward geographic polarization in the United States. As Bishop and Cushing (2008) noted, the number of uncompetitive counties has increased substantially in recent years. We also see a relative dearth of competitive states now compared to what we saw as recently as the 1990s.

An examination of descriptive statistics from the uncompetitive counties revealed some important differences between uncompetitive Republican and uncompetitive Democratic counties. We see that the urban–rural political divide is a key determinant of the trend toward geographic segregation in the United States. We also see important regional differences, such as the political differences between New England counties and Southern counties. The dramatic differences in marital patterns are also worth noting, and an entire chapter of this book will be devoted to this subject.

Although examining the political consequences of this trend toward greater geographic polarization is beyond the scope of this book, the existing literature gives us strong reasons to believe that local political context shapes our political beliefs and behaviors. There are particularly compelling reasons to believe that polarized opinions in the electorate are at least partially the result of geographic polarization.

On the other hand, we should not discount the possibility that the causal arrow points in the other direction. That is, what if geographic polarization is the result of partisan and ideological polarization in the electorate? Perhaps, if Republicans and Democrats dislike each other to an increasing degree, they are now actually moving away from each other. If this is the case then we should expect the higher levels of partisan loyalty and ideological extremity found in uncompetitive areas to be at least partially the result of self-selection and migration. That is, strong Republicans and strong Democrats may be deliberately moving to communities where their views are a majority. As a result of these moves, these communities become even more strongly Republican or Democratic. The next two chapters will explore this possibility. They will argue that there is a strong case to be made for partisan self-selection and migration in the United States. If this is the case, we have strong reasons to believe that geographic polarization is here to stay.

2 A Theory of Geographic Partisan Sorting

2.1 INTRODUCTION

This chapter will provide an overview of the existing literature on migration, considering different theories of migration, noting the varying weight given to variables such as economics and community satisfaction in different models of migratory behavior. It will continue with a brief examination of contemporary trends in migratory behavior in the United States. To build the case that politics is now a consideration of many potential migrants, it will survey the most recent literature on political polarization in the U.S. electorate. It will also discuss how political scientists have studied migration and discuss the existing research on politics, migration, and geographic sorting. It will conclude by arguing that the political science and demography literature provide a compelling argument for politically motivated migration and partisan segregation.

2.2 THE STUDY OF MIGRATION: AN OVERVIEW OF THE LITERATURE

To understand social change within a municipality, state, or nation, the study of migration is vital. That being said, it is often difficult to assign causal arrows with any certainty when studying migration. Migration is both a consequence and a cause of societal changes. It has a myriad of potential causes, both individual and contextual, and the justifications for migration vary from person to person. The causes of migration are furthermore not static; changing economic and social conditions may drastically change the catalysts for migration and aggregate migration patterns. Scholars of migration are aware of a significant array of push and pull forces that attract or repel people from a community. Despite the miscellany of justifications for migration, certain patterns do emerge, and some generalizations are consistent across time and space. Most broadly, the traditional model of migration suggests migration for most people can be partitioned into three steps: the decision to move, the search for possible alternatives, and the evaluation of various alternatives (Brown and Moore 1971).

Compared to other fields of social science, the systematic study of migration is relatively young. E. G. Ravenstein is considered by many to be the father of modern migration analysis. In 1885, he published his groundbreaking work, "The Laws of Migration" in the *Journal of the Statistical Society of London*. Ravenstein subsequently published another article of the same name in 1889. Based on his analysis of census data in Britain, Europe, and North America, Ravenstein posited a series of generalizations about migration. These generalizations were as follows: (1) most migrants only travel a short distance; (2) migration proceeds step by step;[1] (3) migrants who travel a long distance tend to move to a major center of commerce or industry; (4) currents of migrants will spur a compensating counter current; (5) people who live in towns are less mobile than people who live in cities; (6) within their own nation, women are more mobile than men, but men are more likely to move beyond national boundaries; (7) most migrants are adults; (8) the growth of towns is driven more by migration than natural population increase; (9) as industries become more developed and transportation improves, the migration rates increase; (10) the main direction of migration is from rural agricultural areas to urban commercial and industrial areas; (11) migration is primarily motivated by economic concerns.

Ravenstein's contribution to the study of migration was enormous, and subsequent research confirmed many of his most important insights (Grigg 1977). In the decades following Ravenstein's pioneering work, scholars of migration increasingly took for granted his contention that migration is motivated by economic consideration. The common economic explanation for migration was succinctly stated by J. R. Hicks: "differences in net economic advantages, chiefly differences in wages, are the main causes of migration" (1932, 76). According to this theory, potential migrants select the location that they suspect will maximize their earnings.

This parsimonious model of migration apparently performed quite well during Ravenstein's time and the decades that immediately followed. It provided a particularly cogent explanation for the exodus of migrants out of the countryside and into the cities that occurred in the United States and abroad in the latter part of the nineteenth century and into the twentieth century. Farmers abandoned the countryside and shuffled into great urban centers looking for work, not because cities offered other attractive amenities.

Scholars eventually began to reconsider the simplest economic models of migration. Everett Lee (1966) modified Ravenstein's hypotheses, and argued that there were four types of factors involved in migratory decisions: (1) factors associated with the area of origin; (2) factors associated with the area of destination; (3) intervening obstacles; and (4) personal factors. Lee further asserted that we cannot expect the decision to migrate to always be purely rational, nor can we assume that everyone who migrates necessarily had a say in the decision. Rossi (1955) emphasized the importance of considering life-cycle transitions when studying migration.

There is no doubt that economic considerations, particularly employment opportunities, continue to play a key role in migration (Odland 1988; Barff 1989, 1990; Blanchard and Katz 1992). It seems intuitive that higher levels of unemployment in a region will necessarily lead to higher rates of out-migration, and communities with plentiful jobs will experience an influx of new migrants. On the other hand, some empirical studies indicate that the relationship between unemployment and migration is not as clear as it seems. DaVanzo (1978) noted that higher unemployment rates do influence out-migration rates, but only for those people who are actually unemployed. Given that, even during economic downturns, the vast majority of Americans remain employed, only a relatively small number of people will be motivated to move based on the local unemployment rate. Pekkala and Tervo (2002) provided evidence suggesting that migration is not actually a very effective means for the unemployed to find employment. This is consistent with other research indicating that displaced workers who move actually have greater difficulty finding employment (Nord and Ting 1991).

Demonstrating a causal relationship between unemployment and migration is also more problematic than it seems because unemployment rates are not necessarily a reliable indicator of the probability an individual will find a job in a particular community. Unemployment rates also disregard those individuals who have given up looking for work, but would work if more jobs became available (Cadwallader 1992). This is not necessarily an argument against economic models of migration; rather, this simply suggests that accurately measuring the economic variables that spur potential migrants may be more difficult than it first appears.

In recent decades, there has been a serious move on the part of migration scholars to think beyond obvious economic variables when considering the issue of migration. In particular, more attention has been given to the issue of community satisfaction (Michalos 1996). We may not just move to increase our earning potential; cultural and recreational amenities, crime, pollution, and other determinants of quality of life may induce migrations. This new emphasis on noneconomic variables does not necessarily indicate that earlier scholars were wrong to place such a heavy emphasis on economics. Instead, people may now be looking at other community attributes when making migratory decisions precisely because American society has reached such a high level of affluence. In his important contribution to the study of quality of life and migration, Liu (1975) noted:

> Recently, more and more people have been commenting on the paradoxes of affluence. Discontent with the quality of life in the United States seems to have increased proportionally with technological advancement and growth in material wealth. Environmental quality, individual equality, economic opportunity and status, and a host of other forces that

combine to shape the quality of life of the individual, are now major considerations in any public policy decisions. (329)

Liu went on to note that an index of quality-of-life measures proved to be a statistically and substantively significant predictor of migration patterns. Speare (1974) argued that residential satisfaction was an important predictor of whether an individual would consider moving. One reason quality-of-life measures have taken on an increased level of importance relates to the increasing lifespan of Americans and the destinations of retirees. Americans, on average, live much longer now than they did a century ago and often live for several additional decades after they stop working. Retirees who move are obviously less concerned with employment opportunities and income maximization than other potential migrants, and will be inordinately concerned with quality-of-life issues.

Although they are difficult to measure in large-N quantitative studies, scholars also note that family and other social connections can be an important determinant of migration. All other things being equal, migrants are more attracted to communities where they already have an established social network, as this can assist them with any problems they may have with adjustment (Choldin 1973).

Related to the issue of family and friendship connections in migrant-receiving committees is the issue of *homophily* (McPherson, Smith-Lovin, and Cook 2001)—or "love of the same"—which is an issue that directly relates to a key subject of this book. People tend to cluster together with others like themselves. There are multiple characteristics people may actively seek out when building their social networks. Residential segregation by race is a particularly well-documented and studied phenomenon in America (Lieberson 1980; Massey and Denton 1993; Charles 2003). While legal racial segregation ended decades ago, de facto racial segregation remains a fact of life in American metropolitan areas—a typical pattern is one in which blacks dominate the urban centers and whites live in the outlying suburbs. It is difficult to prove that racial hostility is the primary cause of this segregation, as few people will tell pollsters that they chose not to move to a community specifically because it contained too many members of a specific racial or ethnic group. There are alternative explanations; Bajari and Khan (2005) argued that the migration of whites to the suburbs was largely driven by their preference to own their own single detached housing units. The lower interest among blacks for such community attributes can be explained by their lower average incomes, educational attainment, and marriage rates. However, it is worth noting that Bayer, Ferreira, and McMillan (2007) found evidence that all racial groups tend to prefer to live among people who share their race, and they are willing to pay more money to do so. Beyond segregation along racial lines, there is also evidence of residential segregation by educational attainment (White 1987; Wright 1997) and by religion (Hershkowitz 1987; Brimicombe 2007).

There are theories suggesting a relationship between partisan politics and migration, though that relationship is indirect. Charles Tiebout (1956) pioneered a theory that differences in local public goods will lead to different migration patterns. Tiebout argued that communities will offer different bundles of goods and services, and people will choose communities that are most congruent with their preferences. A potential migrant with children may be particularly interested in a municipality that spends a great deal of money on public schools; others may be more interested in high-quality parks and beaches; others may be concerned about police protection; some migrants may have virtually no interest in public goods and instead prefer the community that offers the lowest tax rates.

Again, this theory does not directly relate to partisan politics. However, if the preference for different bundles of public goods and local tax rates differs systematically between members of the two major political parties, and communities with different distributions of Republicans and Democrats tend to offer systematically different types of public goods, this may lead to a partisan sorting of the electorate at the local level. Caution should be exercised before concluding a strong relationship between local partisan distributions and municipal policies, however. Compared to state and national levels of government, local government tends to be more pragmatic than ideological (Warner and Hebdon 2001). The differences in outcomes between a municipal government dominated by Republicans and a municipal government dominated by Democrats may not actually be particularly conspicuous.

Another potential indirect relationship between partisan politics and migration in the United States comes from the theory of "welfare magnets" (Peterson and Rom 1990; Hanson and Hartman 1994). A welfare magnet is a state or municipality that attracts poor migrants, or is more likely to keep its current poor residents in place, because it has policies that are attractive to the poor. This became a particular issue of concern in the 1990s when welfare reform at the national level (specifically, The Personal Responsibility and Work Opportunity Reconciliation Act of 1996) provided states with greater discretion to determine their own welfare policies. There was concern that, because states wanted to discourage the in-migration of new welfare recipients and encourage the out-migration of current recipients, states would engage in a "race to the bottom" in terms of support for poorer residents. Some states also attempted to implement residency requirements to ensure that new migrants did not immediately join the ranks of welfare recipients, though these policies were declared unconstitutional by the Supreme Court in *Saenz v. Roe* (1999), as it violated the constitutional right to travel.

If migrants move in search of welfare benefits, then this could exacerbate a partisan sorting of the electorate. Presumably, majority-Republican states will offer less generous welfare benefits than majority-Democratic states, leading to an out-migration of poorer residents—these residents, because of their socioeconomic status, are also more likely to be Democrats. These Republican states would then become even more strongly Republican, and the new locations of these poorer migrants would become even more strongly Democratic.

Although the subject of welfare magnets sparked heated debates at the state level, the empirical evidence supporting this hypothesis is weak (Clark 1992; Hanson and Hartman 1994; Walker 1994; Levine and Zimmerman 1995; Allard and Danziger 2000). One problem with the welfare magnet hypothesis is that it may make unrealistic assumptions about the ease with which poorer Americans can migrate. Migration can be costly, and the marginal benefits of slightly increased welfare benefits likely do not outweigh the economic and social costs associated with moving across state lines. However, Borjas (1999) did present evidence suggesting that poor, welfare-receiving immigrants are more likely to settle in high-benefit states compared to both immigrants who do not receive welfare and native-born Americans, suggesting that poor immigrants do consider welfare benefits when determining where they will settle.

On the subject considered by Borjas, developing theories of domestic migration within the United States is further complicated by the issue of foreign immigration. By an enormous margin, the United States receives more immigrants than any other nation in the world. The massive influx of newcomers since the 1960s has fundamentally changed the political, demographic, and economic landscape of the United States, and therefore any consideration of the relationship between migration and politics will have to account for foreign immigration.

Like the study of migration in general, for most of its early history the study of immigration relied on assumptions from classical economics (Lewis 1954; Ranis and Fei 1961). Whereas purely economic models of migration within the United States may be problematic because of the nation's relative affluence from coast to coast, economic theories of international migration remain as valid as ever. While the economic differences between major American metropolitan areas may be relatively small, the difference between the economic conditions in virtually all regions of the United States and those of developing countries remains enormous.

Scholars attempting to model international migration using insights from neoclassical economics rely on a small number of assumptions. First of all, they contend that the main cause of international migration is differences in wage rates in different countries. That is, individuals move in substantial numbers from low-income countries into high-income countries until equilibrium is reached between those countries. Because of this, these models do not predict any mass international movement in the absence of different wages rates. The theory assumes that workers with different skill sets may not show the same migratory patterns; in fact, the flow of highly skilled workers and unskilled workers may even be in the opposite direction. Assuming these propositions are correct, the way for governments to influence patterns of migration is to influence labor markets in either the sending or the receiving countries (Massey and Denton 1993).

Later theorists also attempted to model international migration from an economic perspective, but did so using a more sophisticated model than the basic expected-income hypothesis. More recently, scholars have posited a "new economics of migration," which does not assume migration is driven exclusively by individuals attempting to maximize their incomes (Stark and Levhari 1982; Stark and Bloom 1985). This newer model is typically based on households rather than individuals, which is why it provides a more realistic view of how migration decisions are made, and also incorporates decisions from the perspective of relative risk. It furthermore does not necessarily assume that every member of a household migrates—under this model it often makes sense for one individual within a household to migrate in order to diversify a household's earnings and provide those who stayed behind in the country of origin with remittances.

Another economic theory suggests that developed economies require a certain amount of migration (Piore 1979). This is known as "segmented labor-market theory." According to this theory, modern, developed economies have two major segments: the sector for well-paid and secure work and the sector for insecure and low-paid work. This theory suggests that modern economies will always produce jobs that native-born citizens will refuse to do at the rate employers are willing to pay, thus there will always be demand for cheap labor provided by foreign laborers. Beyond low wages, these jobs typically involve unpleasant conditions, little job security, and very little chance for advancement. This theory considers employers the key driver of mass immigration from the developing world into developed countries and suggests that the only way to influence migration levels is to influence employer behavior in the receiving countries.

In general, once countries begin to experience a stream of immigrants, that stream tends to continue and grow over time because each new arrival increases the size of the migrant network (Massey and Zenteno 1999). The first arrivals in a country have few friends and neighbors with whom they share a common language and customs. As their numbers grow, large enclaves within the immigrant-receiving countries are considered hospitable for others considering international migration. Those in immigrant-sending countries are much more likely to emigrate if they have friends and family within the country of destination. These social networks provide potential migrants with better prospects for employment as well as other sources of social capital for the migrants once they arrive. Each new arrival subsequently makes it more likely that more migrants will follow, and the social networks for potential migrants rapidly increase in size. Large numbers of migrants lead to new institutions that support incoming migrants as they acclimate to their new surroundings and fight for new economic and political rights for migrants.

The failure to incorporate these dynamic feedback effects typically leads to demographic forecasts that dramatically underestimate the total number of immigrants a nation will likely receive (Massey and Zenteno 1999). The United States Census Bureau, for example, tends to use static rather than dynamic models when predicting the future demographic makeup of the United States. It is for this reason that the Census Bureau tends to predict fewer migrants entering the country than is actually the case.

From the above we see problems with attempts to make a parsimonious model or theory of migration. Although migration may have been purely motivated by economic concerns at the dawn of the Industrial Revolution, the same cannot be said today, at least when it comes to domestic migrants. Potential migrants must take into account a wide variety of considerations when making migratory decisions and the relative weight each consideration will receive will vary between individuals. Before making the argument that partisan politics is a direct determinant of migration patterns, an overview of migration trends in the United States will be helpful.

2.3 CURRENT TRENDS IN U.S. MIGRATION

Americans have always been a mobile people, and this remains the case today. It is important to note that this is actually less true now than it once was. Internal migration rates in the United States have been on a long-term decline (Rogers and Rajbhandary 1997). Before 1960, twenty Americans out of every one hundred moved every year; in 2006, that number dropped to fourteen of every one hundred Americans (Bogue, Liegel, and Kozloski 2009). This is nonetheless a large percentage of the population. Americans have become even less mobile in recent years as a result of the recent crash in home values and recession; potential movers had difficulty selling their current homes, potential home buyers had difficulty financing such a purchase, and dearth of quality jobs limited the likelihood of migrating for the sake of work (Frey 2009). As I write this, the United States is no longer in a recession, but the economy remains sluggish and migration remains somewhat depressed.

Rosenbloom and Sundstrom (2004) noted that internal migration rates in the United States have followed a U-shaped pattern since 1850, falling until about 1900 and then rising steadily until about 1970. The migration rate subsequently declined again. A number of theories attempt to explain why migration rates vary across time. The relationship between generation size and economic fortunes is one possible explanation. It has been argued that people in large generations, such as the Baby Boomers, face greater labor market competition (Freeman 1979; Easterlin 1980; Rogerson 1987). These economic difficulties may depress their ability to migrate. This theory is increasingly problematic given that the generations subsequent to the Baby Boom were dramatically smaller, yet the migration rate has continued to decline. Another theory suggests that mobility has declined due to the rise in two-earner households (Van Ommeren, Rietveld, and Nijkamp 1998). In a household in which only one adult member works, it is easier to move and find a job for that single earner; in households in which both adult members work, a move would require both members to find new jobs. For this reason, dual-earner households are more likely to stay in one place.

Regardless of the explanation for decreased mobility, it is a demonstrable phenomenon. Nonetheless, high percentages of the U.S. population move in great numbers every year. All Americans are not equally likely to move in any given period; some people are more mobile than others. The rates of migration, as well as the distances migrants travel, varies systematically by economic and demographic groups.

One of the most important predictors of migratory behavior is age. Young people, those in their late teens and early twenties, have by far the highest migration rates. Whether they are leaving to go to college, to look for work, to get married, or just to live on their own, the overwhelming majority of Americans will move at some point during this stage of their lives. As people age, they become increasingly less mobile; as they become established in their careers, get married, buy houses, and have children, Americans become less likely to move. This trend reverses as they approach retirement age and the propensity to migrate again increases. The next chapter of this book will more thoroughly discuss the migratory patterns of young Americans.

Bogue et al. (2009) examined recent census data and provided a useful breakdown of migration rates for other groups. They showed that non-Hispanic whites are less likely to migrate, though the higher rates of migration for minority groups was largely due to local (within-county) moves. Those with a college education are more likely to move than those without. The single are more likely to move than the married, and divorce is a strong predictor that an individual will move. There is not a clear linear relationship between income and mobility. The poorest Americans are not particularly mobile, neither are the wealthy. The probability of migration peaks at a household income of about $30,000 per year.

Migration rates also vary dramatically by state. Prior to the most recent recession, Florida received, by far, the most migrants, though the rate of in-migration to Florida seems to have slowed. Other migrant-receiving states include Texas, Arizona, North Carolina, Georgia, and Nevada— though the migration rates to these states, particularly Nevada and Arizona, dropped off significantly in recent years as a result of the recent economic downturn (Medina and Tavernise 2011). States that have experienced significant out-migration in recent years include New York, California, Illinois, Massachusetts, Louisiana, Michigan, and Ohio.

Thinking larger than states, different regions of the country experience different migration patterns. The regions of the country where the recent housing "bubble" was the greatest, particularly the Inter-Mountain West, experienced the most in-migration prior to the housing market crash.

These regions subsequently experienced a substantial drop in their rate of in-migration. The market crash has actually slowed the out-migration of native Californians to other states, which for some time was losing many domestic residents via migration—though the state was still growing because of immigration. For many years, the New England states have lost more people than they gained (Agrawal 2006), and New England migrants move in greatest numbers to the Southwest and South Atlantic regions of the United States.

While scholars are in wide agreement that migration rates in the United States today are lower than they were several decades ago, some have argued that this migration slowdown has been exaggerated. Kaplan and Schulhofer-Wohl (2010) argued that much of the apparent decline in mobility in the United States is due to a change in the Census Bureau's imputation procedures. Although the downward trend in American mobility has continued in recent years, there has not actually been a major decline in migration rates since 2006.

While this book argues that all kinds of migrations have potential political consequences, it is important to pay special attention to the issue of foreign immigration to the United States, as this has had extraordinary political, economic, and demographic consequences for the country. The United States has received a large number of immigrants throughout most periods of American history. Until relatively recently, the majority of American immigrants originated in Europe. This changed rapidly in the 1960s following the Immigration and Nationality Act of 1965. This act opened the door to migrants from Latin America, Africa, and Asia. The United States has also witnessed a dramatic increase in its number of illegal immigrants, predominantly from Mexico, since the 1960s. As a result of these new immigrants, the demographic complexion of the United States has changed remarkably. By 2011, only a minority of children born in the United States were non-Hispanic white.

More recently, immigrant destinations have changed. As Massey and Capoferro (2010) noted, some regions of the United States, which have not historically been popular destinations for immigrants, began to receive a large number of newcomers in recent years. As noted earlier, immigrants tend to settle in regions that already possess a large immigrant network. For this reason, for much of U.S. history, particular states (New York, Texas, California, New Jersey, Florida, and Illinois) and particular cities (Los Angeles, Miami, New York City, Chicago, and Houston) experienced a disproportionate amount of immigration. This has changed. New states, with no history of large-scale immigration in living memory, have become major immigrant destinations. These states include Virginia, North Carolina, and Georgia. Because new immigrants overwhelmingly come from Latin America, large Latino communities have now formed in states where they never existed before.

Immigrants are not the only American minorities whose migration patterns have changed in recent decades. The new migratory destinations of African Americans are both interesting and politically important. The migratory patterns of African Americans have long differed from those of whites. The "Great Migration" of blacks out of the South and into northern states during the twentieth century was a significant demographic event. A large percentage of these African Americans were former sharecroppers who moved because of agricultural distress, but many also departed from urban areas in the South to urban areas elsewhere (Marks 1989). As a result of this migration, the South lost a dramatic percentage of its native-born black population. By 1950, 2.5 million blacks born in the South were living outside the region; by 1980 that number reached 4 million (Tolnay 2003). This great migration eventually waned, starting in the 1960s, and by the mid-1970s the trend actually reversed; more blacks moved to the South than left the South—though some were still leaving. Black mobility patterns within municipalities also began to change following the end of legal segregation. As an increasing number of whites were moving to the suburbs, many blacks moved into less-segregated neighborhoods that were also more desirable (Taueber and Taueber 1965). Blacks also began to move to the suburbs, but the suburbs they inhabited tended to be closer to city centers and suffer higher levels of poverty and crime than the suburbs predominantly occupied by whites (Tolnay 2003).

Because the rise of uncompetitive Republican counties has occurred disproportionately in rural areas, migratory trends in rural America deserve special attention. From the descriptive statistics in the previous chapter, it appeared that much of the gap between the landslide Republican counties and the landslide Democratic counties is actually the political gap between urban and rural America (Gimpel and Karnes 2009; McKee 2008).

Urban–rural migration in the United States has long been a subject of scholarly interest and political concern. From the 1890s to the 1970s, the United States witnessed a steady exodus from the countryside to the cities. This abruptly turned around in the 1970s during what was dubbed the "Rural Renaissance" (Frey 1987; Fuguitt 1985). This rebound was short-lived. By the 1980s, the trend reversed and migration once again began favoring metropolitan areas. There was one more brief reversal during the 1990s, but by the early 2000s, the movement of large percentages of the population from the countryside to the cities, particularly by younger Americans, was treated by some scholars as a major crisis in rural America (Carr and Kefalas 2009). Indeed, rural areas have a particularly difficult time attracting and keeping college-educated young people, and the only nonmetropolitan communities that experience a major increase in their educated population are college towns (Winters 2011). The differing migration patterns of the college-educated and those who do not attend college may also be leading to changes in the geographic distribution of party support.

2.4 POLARIZATION OF THE U.S. ELECTORATE

In order to plausibly argue that Americans demonstrate political homophily in their migratory patterns, one must first successfully argue that Americans have strong positive feelings toward their co-partisans or a strong dislike of those who identify with the opposing party. Is this a plausible hypothesis? The literature on polarization in the American electorate suggests that it is. The pages ahead will provide an overview of the state of the literature on partisanship and polarization that argues Americans form strong affective attachments to their parties. This literature suggests the distribution of party identifiers in a community is likely a consideration of many Americans when making migratory decisions.

The basic theory driving this book is heavily influenced by the "Michigan model" of political behavior (Campbell et al. 1960), which emphasizes attitude stability and the importance of party attachment. This view built upon the findings of the earlier "Columbia Studies" that began in the 1940s (Lazarsfeld, Berelson, and Gaudet 1944; Berelson, Lazarsfeld, and McPhee 1954), which found that vote choice was more a function of "brand loyalties" and attitude reinforcement from interactions with friends and colleagues than a rational examination of candidates and issues:

> For many voters political preferences may better be considered analogous to cultural tastes—in music, literature, recreational activities, dress, ethics, speech, social behavior. . . . Both have their origin in ethnic, sectional, class, and family traditions. Both exhibit stability and resistance to change for individuals but flexibility and adjustment over generations for the society as a whole. Both seem to be matters of sentiment and disposition rather than "reasoned preferences." While both are responsive to changed conditions and unusual stimuli, they are relatively invulnerable to direct argumentation and vulnerable to indirect social influences. Both are characterized more by faith than by conviction and by wishful expectation rather than careful prediction of consequences. (Berelson, Lazarsfeld, and McPhee 1954, 310–11)

This view of voter behavior focuses heavily on the relationship between social identity and partisan affiliation. As Green, Palmquist, and Schickler (2002) described partisan affiliation, people are aware of "what kind of person" they are; they are also aware of "what kind of person" affiliates with a political party. Most people then align with the "correct" political party based on those two characteristics, rather than through some rational calculation of expected utility or carefully considered ideological position. A set number of individual characteristics (race/ethnicity, education levels, vocation, income, cultural values) can therefore be used to reliably predict partisan preferences for most people. Partisanship is not an ephemeral social identification that regularly changes with the fortunes of a single political campaign, and it is a strong predictor of vote choice (Bartels 2000, 2002; Green et al. 2002; Goren 2005; Johnston 2006).

This line of research suggests party identification is highly stable for most people, and it relates to important questions of personal identity. It is questionable as to whether people identify with their political party nearly as strongly as with their race, class, or religious group. However, a large body of evidence within the political science literature suggests the electorate has become much more politically polarized in recent years, which implies that the strength of party attachment is increasing for many people.

There is not a consensus within the political science literature on the issue of polarization. In fact, the question of polarization is one of the most hotly debated questions in political science. Scholars continue to argue as to whether polarization is occurring in any meaningful way, and, if so, what causes it. One problem with the polarization literature is that there may be multiple definitions and measures of polarization. As DiMaggio, Evans, and Bryson (1996) noted:

> Given polarization's prominence in contemporary political discourse, the literature provides strikingly little guidance in defining it. Perhaps the best place to begin is with what polarization is *not*. Polarization is not noisy incivility in political exchange, although the two things may (or may not) be associated empirically, polarization refers to the extent of disagreement, not to the ways in which disagreement is expressed. Nor is polarization reducible to the responses between agreement with survey items (except in limited cases of two-point scales). It is in the extremity of and distance between responses, not in their substantive content, that polarization inheres. (692–93)

One point on which most political scientists agree is that polarization is a measurable reality at the most elite levels of American politics. The two major parties are exceptionally divided in Congress, as measured by the extraordinary number of party-line votes (Poole and Rosenthal 1997, 2001). The parties now also exhibit a greater ideological divide than any time in recent memory (Stonecash, Brewer, and Mariani 2003). It is less clear whether polarization extends to the mass level.

One variant of the theory of mass polarization insists that there exist two Americas; between these two camps there is a significant ideological divide, created by fundamentally different views regarding the nature of reality. The bases of these different ideological standpoints are fundamentally metaphysical in nature, and therefore these differences cannot be resolved by dispassionate debate over substantive policy issues.

James Hunter (1991) wrote an influential early text in this genre. Hunter argued that there was a substantial divide between those he deemed "progressive" and those he described as "orthodox." Citizens who believe that authority in a society is derived from human beings belong in the progressive category. The orthodox, according to this taxonomy, tends to believe in a transcendent source of societal authority.

A different variant of this idea was developed by Thomas Sowell (2002), who argued that the divide was between those who held a "constrained" or an "unconstrained" *Weltanschauung*. The constrained vision of society, according to Sowell, accepts the imperfections of human nature as being fixed. Therefore, a well-ordered society attempts to channel human traits such as self-interest in positive directions—capitalism being one method whereby natural human greed is put to good use by society because individuals must produce wanted goods in order to accumulate wealth for themselves. Sowell argued that Adam Smith and American Founders such as James Madison were early articulators of this constrained vision—and that this is reflected in the multiple checks and balances in the United States Constitution. In contrast, Sowell said that the unconstrained vision argued that human nature was not necessarily fixed, and that society could ultimately expunge traits such as selfishness from society. According to Sowell, William Godwin and Marquis de Condorcet were early proponents of this unconstrained vision, as they believed they could use the state to fundamentally alter human nature. While Hunter and Sowell clearly laid out quite different taxonomies, both works suggest that the ideological divide in the United States, which closely corresponds to the partisan divide, is deep and not bridgeable via calm utilitarian arguments about different policy proposals. This view of polarized American ideologies suggests that liberals and conservatives have fundamentally different, and irreconcilable, views about the world.

A problem with this argument is that it is difficult to verify empirically, and determining whether a policy was built on a constrained or unconstrained vision is not always as easy as it seems. Was the invasion of Iraq in 2003 the product of a constrained worldview, as conservatives like Sowell would argue, because it was based on a tragic view of human nature in which war is inevitable? Or was it the result of an unconstrained vision because it assumed that the U.S. military could profoundly change the social structure of a foreign country in a manner most favorable to American interests?

How you measure polarization will largely determine whether you can find evidence for it in the electorate. Perhaps the most famous salvo launched against the ideological polarization hypothesis was that of Fiorina, Abrams, and Pope (2005). They argued that there was not a deep or wide ideological chasm between different partisan groups in the electorate. On a number of important policy issues typically described as being on the frontlines of the American "culture war"—abortion, gun control, and gay marriage—there is actually not a large ideological divide in the United States. They found that most Americans subscribe to relatively moderate views on all of these issues. Far from holding ideologically rigid positions on these hot-button issues, most Americans are actually rather pragmatic, according to this view. The real ideological divide is found only among political elites, and if the electorate appears polarized, it is because they are only given two polarized political parties to choose from. This view has a long history in political science. Philip Converse (1964) argued that most voters actually have relatively few ideological constraints, and only a small fraction of any population develops a coherent and consistent ideology.

Other scholars have challenged Fiorina, Abrams, and Pope's (2005) conclusions. Abramowitz and Saunders (2008) presented evidence that Americans are increasingly polarized along party lines, geographically, and politically; this conclusion was further buttressed by Jacobson (2012). Layman, Carsey, and Horowitz (2006) noted that, while there have always been major differences between the major parties, mass coalitions divided along ideological lines and on multiple policy issues are a more recent phenomenon and they are increasing. Bishop and Cushing (2008) stand by their conclusion that the geographic segregation of the United States along partisan lines is a clear indication of increased polarization.

Using the existing polarization literature is potentially problematic for this particular study. Fiorina, Abrams, and Pope may be correct that there is widespread agreement within the United States on policy issues, and the public, on average, prefers the moderate position in most debates. Whether or not this form of polarization exists is not necessarily relevant to this study. Rather, what matters for our purposes is whether there is a growing dislike among members of political parties for those who belong to the opposite party.

Liberal commentators snickered at the angry Tea Party protesters who declared, "Keep your government hands off my Medicare" (Cesca 2009). Medicare is, of course, a government program beloved by liberals. In fact, it was a centerpiece of President Johnson's Great Society program. Possible hypocrisy aside, attitudes like this may reveal an important attribute of American politics. Conservatives in the electorate may not be the limited-government fanatics they (and their liberal opponents) think that they are. This does not mean that they do not loathe Democrats, both at the elite and the mass level. It is furthermore quite likely that this hostility is mutual.

Turning to the literature, is there evidence that Republicans and Democrats dislike each other, and that this dislike has grown? There is. People who like Republicans tend to dislike Democrats (Green 1988). Mason (2013) noted that Fiorina and others are correct to note that the public is largely moderate on policy issues; however, partisans are nonetheless becoming increasingly biased and angry toward each other. In other words, it is possible to become polarized over nothing, or at least very little. Although DiMaggio et al. (1996) demonstrated that the public is becoming less polarized when it comes to feelings on racial groups, those in poverty, and gender, they did demonstrate partial polarization in attitudes toward conservatives and liberals. Examining similar data at a more recent date, Evans (2003) reached similar conclusions, and found that this was especially true of the politically active.

Cassese (2007) argued that the "culture war" in the United States could largely be explained by social identity theory (Tajfel 1978). A meaningful percentage of the electorate strongly identifies with key social groups, including political social groups. Those who strongly identify with their political groups will have strong affective attachments to those groups, and be especially hostile to those in opposing groups when they feel their group interests are threatened. By thinking about polarization as a form of identity politics, rather than as disagreements about policy issues, we may be able to reconcile the evidence indicating a more polarized electorate with the evidence suggesting Americans tend to be moderates on most important issues.

Although debates continue on the issue of polarization, the preponderance of evidence suggests that polarization—at least as it matters for this study—is a reality in the United States. Although there is only limited evidence for polarization on policy issues, there is significant evidence suggesting that partisan Americans have strong affective attachments to their parties, and their dislike of their political opponents is growing.

2.5 THE CASE FOR POLITICALLY MOTIVATED MIGRATION

Although the American people are somewhat less mobile now than in the past, a substantial percentage of the population will move every single year. Although migratory decisions may have been exclusively driven by economic considerations in the past, this is certainly not the case today. Quality-of-life concerns and levels of community satisfaction are now important determinants of migrant destinations. There is also compelling evidence that migrants demonstrate homophily when determining where to live— notably along racial, class, and religious divisions. If migrants examine the religious affiliations, racial categorizations, and educational attainment of their potential neighbors when they determine where they will settle, might they also be interested in the distribution of political affiliation in a community? If their party identification is a strong part of their social identity, they might.

The literature on political polarization suggests that many Americans have strong affective attachments to their political parties. Strong partisans are furthermore likely to have an intense dislike of those who identify with the opposing party—even if they disagree on policy only at the margins. For this reason, we can anticipate that many Americans are, indeed, sorting themselves out along party lines.

This is obviously not the first work to consider this question. In *The Big Sort* (2008), Bishop and Cushing made exactly this argument. Bishop and Cushing did not, however, demonstrate statistically that the Big Sort was the result of migration rather than some other mechanism. They simply inferred it from the growing political homogeneity of many American communities. Other scholars have considered this question and reached similar conclusions. Seabrook (2009) analyzed county-level data and concluded that there is a great amount of geographic clustering by vote choice in the United States, though this clustering did not seem to increase between 2004 and 2008. Abramowitz (2010) also concluded that the United States is increasingly polarized geographically.

The finding that Republicans and Democrats have different migratory patterns is also not new. When examining the increasing suburbanization of the American people in the 1950s, Campbell et al. (1960) found that 71 percent of Democrats who were raised in cities continued to live there, but only 46 percent of Republicans did so. Gimpel and Schuknecht (2001) found that Republicans tend to stay in one place for shorter periods than Democrats, even after controlling for other economic and demographic variables. In a more recent study, Cho, Gimpel, and Hui (2009) examined voters who moved between 2004 and 2006. They noted that, although it varies by region, Republican movers tend to avoid heavily Democratic neighborhoods. McDonald (2011) examined migration flows across congressional districts, finding that the destinations of migrants were more ideologically congruent than the location from which migrants departed.

In a forthcoming article, Myers (2013) examined geographic polarization trends within the state of Texas. This study used Voter Tabulation Districts (VTDs) rather than counties; VTDs have the advantage of being much smaller units of analysis than counties, and allowed Myers to see geographic polarization trends at the smallest geographic units. He concluded that Texas was becoming more geographically polarized over time, and argued that his findings provided support for Bishop and Cushing's (2008) thesis.

These findings are suggestive, but they do not definitively demonstrate that political homophily was the cause of this phenomenon. To make the case that migrants are deliberately self-selecting into politically like-minded neighborhoods, it must first be demonstrated that living among like-minded partisans leads to higher levels of community satisfaction—or that being a political minority leads to higher levels of dissatisfaction. The next chapter will examine individual-level data to make this argument.

Although they are constrained by economic and family considerations, Americans have a great deal of discretion in terms of where they will live. This becomes increasingly true at the smallest geographic units such as neighborhoods. Because American partisans are exhibiting high levels of polarization (at least in terms of their attitudes toward their political friends and foes, if not in terms of policy), then neighborhoods, municipalities, and states dominated by those who belong to the opposing camp will be considered undesirable; similarly, communities dominated by co-partisans will be attractive. Politics will therefore be both a "push" and a "pull" sufficient to explain the growing number of uncompetitive geographic units.

It may still be objected that politically motivated migration remains an implausible theory. After all, given the costs associated with moving, it is hard to imagine someone calling a realtor because a yard sign with the wrong party label appeared down the street. However, it has been previously argued that even relatively minor preferences for similar neighbors can lead to high levels of segregation. Thomas Schelling (1971) demonstrated that widespread segregation can come about even when people simply have a preference not to be part of a tiny minority within a neighborhood; that is, a person may not have any problem with diversity, they just do not wish to be the only African American, Methodist, or Republican in a neighborhood. Over time, however, most communities will reach a "tipping point" leading to an exodus of local minorities:

> Whites and blacks may not mind each other's presence, may even prefer integration, but may nevertheless wish to avoid minority status. Except for a mixture at exactly 50:50, no mixture will then be self-sustaining because there is none without a minority, and if the minority evacuates, complete segregation occurs. If both blacks and whites can tolerate minority status but there is a limit to how small a minority the members of either color will be—for example a 25% minority—initial mixtures ranging from 25% to 75% will survive but initial mixtures more extreme than that will lose their minority members and become all one color. And if those who leave move to where they constitute a majority, they will increase the majority there and may cause the other color to evacuate. (148)

Schelling further argued that segregation can come about even if members of only one of the groups exhibit preferences for neighbors with similar characteristics. While Schelling's work and subsequent research by other scholars was primarily concerned with racial segregation, these theories could be just as easily applied to other social categories such as religious affiliation or party identification. Thinking specifically in terms of politics, we could see high levels of political segregation even if only Democrats or only Republicans prefer politically similar neighbors, but members of the other political party do not care about their neighborhood's political composition. This is actually what we find in the forthcoming chapter—Republicans are apparently more sensitive to the local political distribution than Democrats when it comes to community satisfaction.

I argue that partisans will be less satisfied with their community when they are in the political minority. Because of this dissatisfaction, they will be more willing to move away. I further argue that there is a direct relationship between the politics of a potential destination and a partisan's willingness to settle in that potential destination. Although the existing literature suggests that this is a plausible hypothesis, a close examination of individual-level data is necessary. The next chapter considers this issue.

3 Geographic Partisan Sorting
Empirical Evidence from Individual Data

3.1 INTRODUCTION

The previous chapter made the case that the political characteristics of a community are meaningful determinants of migratory behavior. We now know that migration within the United States is not determined exclusively by economic considerations—though economics remains an important constraint, as people will not move to communities where they cannot make a living. Migration can also be motivated by quality-of-life concerns, one of which is the homophilous tendency of migrants—the desire of people to live among others like themselves. This has been demonstrated along a number of different individual attributes, race being the most studied of them.

We have also seen that many Americans are highly polarized in their attitudes toward their own party and the competing party. When we combine this knowledge with the finding that many American communities and neighborhoods are exhibiting little political heterogeneity, particularly in their presidential voting patterns, we can plausibly argue that Americans are actively moving away from those who oppose them politically and toward those who share their political values. To demonstrate this, however, we must turn to individual data. This chapter will examine data from a random, national survey on migratory behavior. Specifically, this chapter will rely heavily on the 2009 Pew Mobility Survey conducted by the Pew Research Center. This survey asked 2,260 randomly sampled adults in the United States questions concerning their attitudes about their current residence and why they moved there. This will be further buttressed by an examination of a survey of undergraduate students conducted at the University of Houston in 2012.

3.2 BROWN'S FINDINGS REVISITED

Brown (1988) made the case that partisans were not self-selecting into like-minded partisan communities. To demonstrate this, he examined the correlations between individual party identification of migrants and the political environment in which migrants currently lived. He used data from 1970 and 1980. To ensure that any correlation was not the result of migrants acclimating to their new environments and embracing the views of their neighbors, he restricted his sample to those who had moved within the last five years. In both years, he found no evidence for self-selection. In 1970, the Pearson's r correlation was a miniscule 0.014. In 1980, the correlation was not only small, but in the opposite direction—the Pearson's r was -0.061. Did the same pattern hold in 2009? The Pew Mobility Survey suggests otherwise. In 2009, the correlation coefficient had increased to 0.20. This is still a relatively small correlation, but the correlation is statistically significant at $p < 0.01$, which is a sharp break with Brown's findings from 1970 and 1980. Thus, it is clearly no longer possible to dismiss the idea that migrants are self-selecting politically, and Brown's conclusion must therefore be updated. However, although there is now a clear correlation between partisan identification and the political context of migrant destinations, this does not necessarily demonstrate that individuals are moving for political reasons.

3.3 PARTISANSHIP, COMMUNITY SATISFACTION, AND POLITICAL CONTEXT

Respondents to the Pew Survey were asked for their partisan identification. Respondents were initially asked if they were Republicans, Democrats, Independents, members of third parties, or had no preference. Those respondents who identified as Independents were subsequently asked if they "leaned" toward one of the two major parties. For the purposes of this study, Independents who lean toward one party are counted as partisans, as self-described Independents who nonetheless lean toward a particular party are often at least as partisan in their political behavior as those who openly proclaim themselves supporters of one of the major parties (Keith et al. 1992). True Independents were dropped from the statistical analysis because the movement of those with no partisan affiliation whatsoever would presumably not tip the partisan balance in a community in one direction or the other. In the Pew Mobility Survey, 15.27 percent of all respondents were true Independents.

It is important to note that this survey asked respondents whether they preferred to live among the politically like-minded. Specifically, they were asked if they preferred to live in "[a] place where most people share your political views." Relatively few respondents claimed that they wanted to live among the politically similar rather than a place where there was a mix of political affiliations. Only 23 percent of all respondents said they preferred to live among those who shared their political beliefs. However, there were differences among different political groups. A little more than 30 percent of Republicans said they preferred to live among other Republicans, but only 20.28 percent of Democrats made this claim. We see stronger results when we break it down by ideology. The survey asked respondents to place themselves on a five-point ideological spectrum from "very conservative" to "very liberal." Among those who described themselves as very liberal, a significant 35.09 percent said they preferred to have liberal neighbors. Of the very conservative, an impressive 50.98 percent said they preferred conservative neighbors.

These findings may underestimate the real percentage of the population that prefers politically homogenous communities. Some respondents may prefer not to admit to pollsters that they do not want those with whom they disagree as neighbors. These numbers do suggest that Republicans, particularly conservative Republicans, demonstrate the highest level of political homophily when determining residential satisfaction. Rather than trust that respondents have provided honest and accurate answers, it may be more useful to see if there is a relationship between levels of community satisfaction and the actual political makeup of the respondents' communities.

The Pew Mobility Survey helpfully provides the county Federal Information Processing (FIP) codes for each respondent, allowing each respondent to be placed in his or her county. Before conducting a more sophisticated statistical analysis of these data, a glance at the distribution of community satisfaction rates among different partisan groups in different county political "types" will be useful. Bishop and Cushing's (2008) classification was used to determine levels of competitiveness. Counties that gave one of the two presidential candidates more than 60 percent of the vote in 2008 where classified as "landslide" counties, whereas other counties were classified as being competitive. It is important to note the limitations of county data. Much of this sorting process is likely taking place well below the level of county; for this reason, a more detailed examination of residential patterns within a more competitive county will be examined in a later chapter. However, counties are sufficiently small to warrant an investigation.

Respondents to the survey were asked to rate their communities along a five-point scale, from "Excellent" to "Poor." Table 3.1 provides different rates of community satisfaction for different partisan groups in different political contexts. Among Republicans, 40 percent of those currently living in a landslide Republican county described their local community as excellent, but only 23 percent of Republicans living in a landslide Democratic county described their community as such. Perhaps more interesting is the fact that these data suggest Democrats were not sensitive at all to the local political context when thinking about their feelings toward their local community.

There are limits to what we can infer from these basic statistics, of course, as the preceding table provides no control variables. It does suggest, however, that individuals are happiest when living among the like-minded, and Republicans are more likely to express positive feelings about their community if their political party is a local majority; Republicans living in landslide Republican counties were almost twice as likely to rate their community as

Table 3.1 Individual Partisanship, Local Political Context, and Views about Community

	All Counties				
	Excellent	*Very Good*	*Good*	*Only Fair*	*Poor*
Republican (840 observations)	32%	38%	22%	6%	1%
Democrat (1,075)	23%	34%	29%	11%	3%
Independent (345)	26%	37%	24%	10%	3%
	Landslide Republican Counties				
	Excellent	*Very Good*	*Good*	*Only Fair*	
Republican (206)	40%	33%	19%	6%	0%
Democrat (166)	22%	35%	30%	11%	1%
Independent (75)	36%	33%	21%	5%	4%
	Landslide Democratic Counties				
	Excellent	*Very Good*	*Good*	*Only Fair*	*Poor*
Republican (152)	23%	44%	26%	7%	1%
Democrat (359)	23%	33%	28%	12%	3%
Independent (87)	22%	33%	24%	16%	5%

excellent as Republicans living in landslide Democratic counties. However, this phenomenon appears to be true primarily for Republicans. Thus, this initial glance at the data provides further evidence that this geographic sorting process is primarily driven by the migration patterns of Republicans.

It is possible that these findings are spurious. It is conceivable that, although Republicans and Democrats, on average, value different community attributes, the local partisan political composition is not a relevant determinant of feelings toward one's community. To more thoroughly examine the possibility that local political context influences partisans' opinions about their community, I performed a regression using the Pew Survey question about views on the local community as the dependent variable. As noted above, the question asks respondents how they would rate their community on the following scale: "poor," "only fair," "good," "very good," and "excellent." It would have been possible to treat this question as a continuous variable and perform a least-squares regression. However, given the variable's categorical nature, I instead performed a logit analysis, with "excellent" taking a value of 1, and other answers taking a value of 0. This categorization was made because only a tiny percentage of either group classified their communities as "poor" or "only fair." The "excellent" category also exhibited the most dramatic differences for the different partisan groups.[1]

The independent variables included both individual- and aggregate-level characteristics. In the forthcoming models, I controlled for respondent gender, age, marital status, the presence of children under the age of eighteen, whether the respondent was a homeowner, whether the respondent attended a religious service at least once a week, and household income. I also included county-level variables in these models. Community-level variables included whether the county was classified as rural, suburban, or urban (with rural excluded as the base category), the percent of the county that was African American, the percent of the county that was Hispanic, the median household income and median home values, the mean January temperature, the percentage of the county vote that went to Barack Obama in 2008, and an interaction between respondent political affiliation and the county vote for Obama.

Although the relationship between these independent variables and individual views toward the local community can be examined using a straightforward logit model, this is somewhat problematic given that I used both individual and contextual independent variables. Failing to deal with this hierarchical structure could therefore lead to the estimation of incorrect standard errors (Steenbergen and Jones 2002). Specifically, we can plausibly expect positive cluster correlation, which will make standard errors too low and increase the risk of a Type I error. For this reason, I estimated a three-level multilevel model in which individuals were nested in counties that were nested in states. Compared to alternatives, multilevel models are the most appropriate statistical method for this analysis. Instead of relying on multi-level modeling, one could simply assume that this clustering did not matter, and use a single-level model (a method sometimes referred to as "naïve pooling"). However, in this case the model explicitly assumes that contextual variables are influencing individual behavior. Thus the very assumptions of the model suggest that completely pooling that data is inappropriate. In contrast, we could also assume that the actions within each group (in this case, each set of observations in each county) are completely unrelated to each other, and thus completely separate models should be estimated for each county. This is surely an implausible assumption, and furthermore would require the estimation of an absurd number of models. Multilevel modeling represents a compromise between these two options (Gelman and Hill 2007, ch. 12).

It is important to note that the use of multilevel models in this case may be somewhat problematic given the relatively small number of observations per second-level unit—in a few cases there was only one person surveyed in a county. When a multilevel model calculates a regression line for a group, the line is always closer to the overall regression line than it would be if the groups were examined completely separately ("shrinkage"). The degree to which the group-level regression line is moved closer to the overall regression line is a result of a number of factors. If there are very few observations at the group level and/or the group-level variance is large, but the overall variance for the entire population is relatively small, the estimates for the group will be calculated as being closer to the overall regression. Conversely, if the overall variance for the entire sample is large, but there is very little group-level variance, then the estimate for the group will not move much closer to the overall regression line (there will be little shrinkage). All of this is to say that it is more difficult to accurately estimate group-level parameters when there is a relatively small number of observations per group.

A problem with fitting a multilevel model with relatively few observations in the higher-level units is that it will have larger standard errors. Nonetheless, it is possible to estimate multilevel models even if there are only one or two observations in the higher-level units, and this estimation is still preferable to ignoring data's hierarchical structure (Gelman and Hill 2007, 275–76). Furthermore, while it would have been possible to create a model in which only those counties with some arbitrarily high number of observations were included, doing so would have led to a serious underrepresentation of rural respondents, as sparsely populated rural counties were overrepresented among those counties with a small number of respondents. The results of these three-level multilevel logit models can be found in Table 3.2.

From Table 3.2, we see statistical and substantive significance from a number of variables worth noting. Controlling for all other variables, we see that race and ethnicity were not statistically significant determinants of community satisfaction. It is also worth noting that the size of the black and Hispanic communities within a county had no apparent relationship with community satisfaction. Those with a bachelor's degree were more satisfied, on average, than those who did not hold a degree. We also see that, although there was a positive relationship between home values and satisfaction, owning a home did not make respondents any more likely to rate their community highly.

From this table we also see that Republicans are more likely to be highly satisfied with their community, even controlling for all other individual attributes. However, the interaction between partisanship and local political context demonstrated that, on average and controlling for all other variables, Republicans became less likely to rate their community highly if a large percentage of that county voted for Obama. Looking at the maximum effect of this variable when holding all other variables equal, we see that a change from the minimum to the maximum percentage of Democrats led Republicans to be 26 percent less likely to give their community a high rating. This was furthermore statistically significant at the $p < 0.05$ level. There was no similar finding for Democrats—there was no evidence that Democrats were sensitive to the political context at all. This is important because it is congruent with Cho, Gimpel, and Hui's (2009) discovery that Republicans tended to avoid heavily Democratic neighborhoods when migrating.

The above finding regarding political context and community satisfaction is important because, as noted in the last chapter, previous scholarship

Table 3.2   Multilevel Logit Model of Likelihood Respondent Viewed Community as "Excellent"

	Model 1	Std. Error	Prob. Change min– > max
Individual Characteristics			
Constant	–1.93	(0.54)*	
Republican	1.16	(0.42)*	0.23
Female	0.08	(0.11)	0.02
Black	–0.41	(0.22)	–0.07
Hispanic	0.23	(0.22)	0.05
BA	0.28	(0.12)*	0.05
Married	0.16	(0.13)	0.03
Children under 18	–0.20	(0.15)	–0.04
Own Home	0.20	(0.16)	0.04
Frequently Attend Religious Services	0.05	(0.12)	0.01
Age 31–45	0.10	(0.20)	0.02
Age 46–60	0.05	(0.18)	0.01
Age 60 +	0.43	(0.19)*	0.09
Income Quartile 2	0.44	(0.19)*	0.09
Income Quartile 3	0.17	(0.19)	0.03
Income Quartile 4	0.77	(0.20)*	0.16
Income Unknown	0.47	(0.20)*	0.10
Contextual Characteristics			
% Democrat, 2008	0.00	(0.01)	–0.07
Urban	–0.40	(0.16)*	–0.07
Suburban	0.01	(0.13)	0.00
Unemployment Rate, 2009	–0.04	(0.02)	–0.16
% Black	0.00	(0.01)	0.00
% Hispanic	–0.01	(0.01)	–0.13
Median Income (Divided by $10,000)	0.07	(0.07)	0.08
Median Home Value (Divided by $10,000)	0.02	(0.01)*	0.36
Mean January Temperature	0.01	(0.01)	0.06

(Continued)

Table 3.2 *(Continued)*

	Model 1	Std. Error	Prob. Change min– > max
Interaction			
Republican X % Democratic, 2008	–0.02	(0.01)*	–0.24
Number of Observations	1901		
Number of Counties	852		
–2 X Log Likelihood	2088.733		

* $p < 0.05$

has established that the decision to migrate is partially driven by community satisfaction (Speare 1974; Bach and Smith 1977; Landale and Guest 1985; McHugh, Gober, and Reid 1990; Stinner and Van Loon 1992). If Republicans are less likely to report high levels of community satisfaction when they live in strongly Democratic counties, they are also more likely to subsequently migrate. If political context plays a role in choosing their community of destination, then their migrations will, in the aggregate, leave their counties of origin with fewer Republican voters, and their destinations with more.

This finding undermines the long-established position that migration within the United States is not driven by politics (Brown 1988). Previous scholars have shown that white migrants typically prefer to move to be among other whites (Farley et al. 1994; Massey and Denton 1993; Gimpel 1999), a trend which has political consequences because of the degree to which whites are more likely than other groups to vote Republican. This view typically ignores the possibility that political change is actually at the beginning of the causal story, rather than the end. The evidence presented so far in this and the preceding chapters points to a causal mechanism whereby increases in the Democratic share of the vote at the county level lead to lower levels of satisfaction with their local community among Republicans. If this subsequently leads Republicans to migrate elsewhere, this will actually speed up the process by which a county switches from being competitive to being categorized as landslide Democrat.

This story is still missing one more important piece of evidence. The previous table demonstrated that Republicans are, on average and controlling for all other variables, less likely to provide their local communities the highest possible ratings as the percentage of the local vote going to the Democratic presidential candidate goes up. It did not, however, demonstrate that this dissatisfaction increases the probability that they will move to a new community.

3.4 PARTISANSHIP AND THE POLITICAL CONTEXT OF RECENT MIGRANT DESTINATIONS

Previous sections of this chapter demonstrated that there was a statistically significant correlation between the county political context and the partisan attachments of recent migrants. To more thoroughly examine this issue, I created a least-squares regression model in which the political context, as measured by the percentage of the county-level vote in the 2008 presidential election, of migrant destinations was a function of individual attributes. The model is restricted to those who moved within the last five years. Individual partisanship is the key independent variable in this model, broken into three dummy variables, with Democrats serving as the base category. The results of this analysis can be found in Table 3.3.

The results demonstrate that, on average and controlling for all other variables, the counties of recent Republican migrants provided 3.56 fewer percentage points to Barack Obama in 2008 in comparison to recent Demo-

Table 3.3   Support for Obama in Migrants' Counties of Destination

	Model 2	Std. Err.
Republican	−3.56	(1.72)*
Black	5.58	(2.17)*
Hispanic	2.88	(2.17)
BA	2.72	(1.66)
Married	0.41	(1.80)
Children under 18	−1.59	(1.93)
Own Home	−4.00	(1.81)*
Frequently Attend Religious Services	−1.35	(1.66)
Age 31–45	−3.10	(2.20)
Age 46–60	−2.86	(2.13)
Age 61 +	−5.87	(2.43)*
Income Quartile 2	−0.16	(2.31)
Income Quartile 3	2.66	(2.30)
Income Quartile 4	2.56	(2.57)
Income Unknown	5.34	(2.66)*
Constant	55.75	(2.02)*
Observations	369	
Adjusted R-Squared	0.07	

* $p < 0.05$

cratic migrants. We also see that migrants who subsequently purchased a home moved to counties that gave less support to Barack Obama; this is likely due to the fact that many of the counties that provided Obama his largest margins of victory were also counties in which homes were prohibitively expensive for many Americans.

These findings provide yet more evidence in favor of the hypothesis that partisans, particularly Republicans, are self-selecting into communities that, in the aggregate, share their partisan preferences. Caution should be exercised, as the data do not indicate how far the migrant moved (we know that a majority of moves are over a relatively short distance [Bogue, Liegel , and Kozloski 2009]), nor does it indicate the degree to which their counties of origin leaned toward Republicans or Democrats. Unfortunately, the county of origin for migrants was not provided in the Pew data set. We can, however, compare the political context of respondents' current states with states to which they would most like to move.

3.5 PARTISANSHIP AND THE POLITICAL CHARACTERISTICS OF RESPONDENTS' PREFERRED STATE

The Pew Mobility Survey asked respondents, "[i]f you could live anywhere in the United States that you wanted to, which state would you most prefer to live in?" From this question we can examine whether Republicans and Democrats differ in their preferred destinations. I therefore conducted a regression analysis (not shown) in which the dependent variable was the percentage of the vote earned by Barack Obama in 2008 in the states respondents claimed they would most like to migrate into. Again, partisanship was broken into a dummy variable, where Republicans were classified as 1, Democrats were classified as 0, and true Independents were excluded. The results demonstrated that the most preferred states of Republicans were, on average, more Republican than the most preferred states of Democrats. This was statistically significant at the $p < 0.05$ level.

One must note a caveat before drawing strong inferences from this finding. Such an analysis tells us nothing about the state in which respondents currently live. It may be that Republicans and Democrats already live in Republican or Democratic states, respectively, and their preferred states are other Republican or Democratic states. In that case, even if they migrate to their preferred destination, they are not moving to a different political climate and would not contribute to geographic sorting.

It is more useful to note whether Republicans wish to move to a state that is *more* Republican than the state in which they currently live, and likewise for Democrats. To determine this, I generated a variable indicating whether the most preferred state of the respondent was more Republican than the state in which they currently live. Among all respondents, only a minority said they wanted to live in states that were more Republican than their current state—41.26 respondents were so classified. This is largely due to the large number of respondents who said their ideal state was California or Hawaii, states that have exceptionally pleasant climates. Nonetheless, there was variation within different partisan groups. Among Democrats, only 38 percent chose a most-preferred state that was more Republican than their current state. Among Republicans, 45 percent named a state that was more Republican than their current state as their most-preferred destination.

An additional regression analysis of determinants of the political characteristics of respondents' most preferred state will be useful to determine whether politics plays a role in determining Americans' ideal state of residence. I created this variable by subtracting the support for Obama in 2008 in their current state from the support for Obama in their most-preferred state. Among all respondents, the support for Obama in their most preferred state was about 2 percent higher than the support for Obama in their current state. However, Table 3.4 shows that this differs by partisan group.

Table 3.4 Difference in Democratic Support: Current State—Most Preferred State

	Model 3	Std. Error	Beta
Republican	−0.02	(0.01)*	−0.07
Black	0.03	(0.01)*	0.07
Hispanic	0.01	(0.01)	0.01
BA	0.02	(0.01)*	0.05
Married	−0.01	(0.01)	−0.04
Children under 18	−0.01	(0.01)	−0.03
Own Home	0.01	(0.01)	0.04
Frequently Attend Religious Services	0.00	(0.01)	−0.02
Age 31–45	−0.02	(0.01)*	−0.07
Age 46–60	−0.03	(0.01)*	−0.10
Age 61 +	−0.03	(0.01)*	−0.09
Income Quartile 2	−0.01	(0.01)	−0.02
Income Quartile 3	0.02	(0.01)*	0.08
Income Quartile 4	0.03	(0.01)*	0.07
Income Unknown	0.03	(0.01)*	0.07
Constant	0.03	(0.01)*	
Observations	1717		
Adjusted R-Squared	0.0236		

* $p < 0.05$

We see from Table 3.4 that, even after controlling for many other individual-level characteristics, the preferred states of Republicans are slightly less Democratic than the preferred states of Democrats. That being said, it is important to note that this model only explains a very small amount of the overall variation. Obviously, other considerations—such as where family members live—will play a more important role in determining ideal states of residence than politics. Nonetheless, this does suggest that Republicans and Democrats differ systematically in terms of their desired migratory behavior.

This reveals other interesting findings. The wealthiest Americans are more likely to prefer to live in a more Democratic state, as are those with a college education, but older Americans are more likely to prefer a more Republican state—perhaps this latter finding is due to comparatively high levels of Republican strength in states that are desirable for retirees, such as Arizona and Florida.

3.6 CITIES, POLITICS, AND WILLINGNESS TO MIGRATE

Thus far, this chapter has focused primarily on counties and states. It will be equally useful to examine metropolitan areas as potential locations for migrants. The Pew Mobility Survey asked a question that allows us to consider this issue. Specifically, the survey asked respondents the following question: "As I read through the following places, just tell me your first reaction—Would you want to live in this city or its surrounding metropolitan area or NOT want to live there?" The list of cities the survey offered as options differed a great deal politically, from relatively conservative (Houston, Phoenix) to extraordinarily liberal (Washington, D.C., Detroit).

Measuring the overall partisan distribution of a city can be somewhat tricky, as counties, rather than cities, are the primary small unit for aggregating votes in presidential elections. However, the Bay Area Center for Voting Research (2005) aggregated presidential vote totals within every major city in the United States in order to estimate the degree to which it was conservative or liberal, finding that Provo, Utah, was the most conservative city in the United States, and Detroit, Michigan, is the most liberal.[2] Using these data I examined the relationship between the political attributes of a city and the willingness of potential migrants to move there.

To determine whether the political attributes of a city would make a potential migrant more or less likely to consider a community attractive, I examined the correlation between the percentage of respondents of each party willing to move to a city and the political attributes of that city. Among Democrats, there was not an apparent relationship between the politics of a city and their willingness to move to that city—the correlation coefficient was weak and actually in the wrong direction. Among Republicans, however, there was a strong negative relationship between a city's liberalism and their willingness to relocate to that city (Pearson's $R = -0.68$).

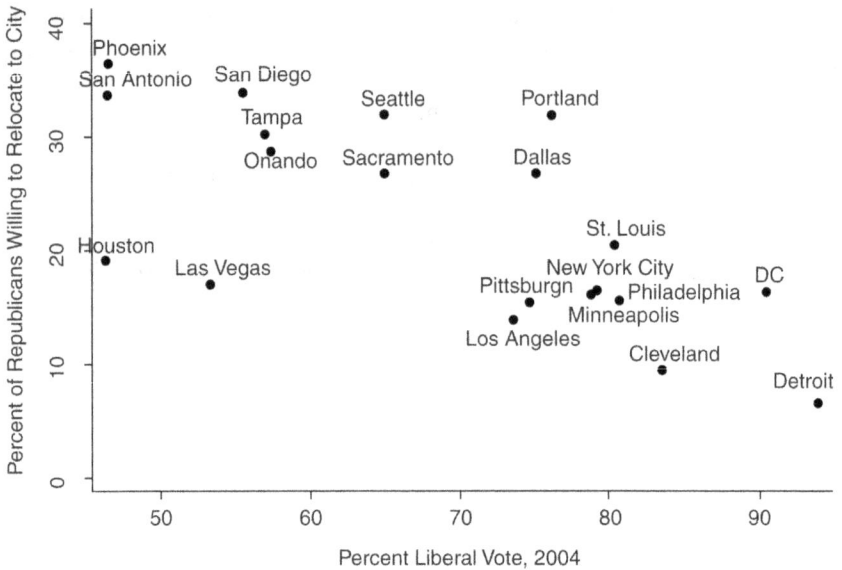

Figure 3.1   City Liberalism and Republican Willingness to Migrate

Figure 3.1 shows the relationship between the percentage of the vote going to liberal candidates (either John Kerry or a member of a liberal third party) in the 2004 presidential election and the percentage of Republican respondents who would consider living in that city. We see a linear relationship between a city's aggregate liberalism and Republican willingness to live in that city. If Republicans are unwilling to move to cities that are dominated by Democrats, then that Democratic domination is unlikely to change in the near future. Interestingly, because Democrats are apparently more willing to move to heavily Republican cities, then strongly Republican cities may eventually become more Democratic as a result of Democratic migration.

Because all of the evidence presented so far suggests that Republicans are quite sensitive to political context when determining their overall levels of community satisfaction and their willingness to relocate to a community, but Democrats are less sensitive, we should expect large and growing Democratic communities to be quite politically stable—if only Democrats will relocate to such cities, then they should remain Democratic indefinitely unless the voters living there change their party affiliation in large numbers. On the other hand, if a heavily Republican community is a nice place to live, then it should draw both Republicans and Democrats—eventually leading to greater political competition. There is some evidence for this. Of those large metropolitan counties (more than 200,000 people) that experienced above-average growth rates from 2000–2009 and gave Bill Clinton a landslide victory in 1996, 81 percent of them also gave Barack Obama a landslide victory in 2008.[3] We see different patterns for large Republican counties; of those large and growing counties that gave Bob Dole a landslide victory in 1996, only 44 percent gave McCain a landslide victory. However, Republican counties that are not growing tend to stay Republican counties. Of all landslide Republican counties in 1996 that experienced below-average levels of growth in the subsequent decade, 82 percent were still landslide Republican counties in 2008. This suggests that large, prosperous, and overwhelmingly Republican cities are politically unstable because of in-migration from Democrats, but large Democratic cities, regardless of their levels of economic or other success, are likely to remain monolithically Democratic.

This finding potentially places Republican-elected officials in municipal governments in a quandary. Although a community may be overwhelmingly Republican now, if it enjoys economic or other forms of success and experiences significant in-migration, its new migrants are as likely to be Democratic as Republican, and the community may cease to be overwhelmingly Republican. Apparently, the best way for a heavily Republican community to remain Republican is to flounder economically and be an unattractive destination to new migrants.

This finding may help explain the political transformation of states such as Colorado in recent years. Colorado was once an overwhelmingly Republican state until quite recently. Its political complexion has changed dramatically, largely as a result of migration (Robinson and Noriega 2010). Apparently, Colorado's reputation for political conservatism did not stop Democrats from considering it an attractive location. The significant influx of Democratic migrants—many attracted to the natural amenities available in the Mountain West (Rupasingha and Goetz 2004)—from states like California has been slowly changing the politics of states such as Colorado—which provided its electoral votes to Barack Obama in 2008 and 2012 after supporting Bush in 2000 and 2004. We do not see similar trends elsewhere for Republicans. That is, there is not presently a strongly Democratic state that is drawing large numbers of Republicans who are turning it into a Republican state.

3.7 PARTY IDENTIFICATION AND IDEAL COMMUNITY TYPE

It is well established that the interiors of major metropolitan areas are often overwhelmingly Democratic, suburbs are usually more Republican—though Republican dominance of the suburbs is waning—and rural areas and small towns are some of the most Republican areas of the country. It is therefore worth knowing if Republicans and Democrats have a different willingness to live in these different community types.

It is not entirely clear that these differences are due to partisan self-selection into these types of communities, or if some demographic, economic, or cultural differences account for the voting differences we see in these community types. Most rural areas remain overwhelmingly white and religiously observant; inner cities tend to have large minority populations; and suburbs tend to be a more representative cross-section of America (McKee and Shaw 2003). Rural areas also have a hard time attracting and keeping college-educated young people (Carr and Kefalas 2009). Demographics are not the only possible explanation for the urban–rural divide, however. Gimpel and Karnes (2009) noted that rural areas tend to foster a more individualistic ethic and have higher rates of homeownership and self-employment. Although rural areas are often poor, they are also more likely to experience labor market out-migration during times of economic distress; during periods of high unemployment, many people suffering the worst economic hardships will abandon rural areas and move to cities.

The Pew Mobility Survey categorizes respondents as living in urban, suburban, and rural communities. We do see meaningful differences between Republicans and Democrats in terms of the communities in which they live. Only 22.74 percent of Republicans lived in cities, 27.5 percent lived in suburbs, 27.74 percent lived in small towns, and 21.19 percent lived in rural areas. Of Democrats, 32.37 percent lived in cities, 28.37 percent lived in suburbs, 25.67 percent lived in small towns, and 13.12 percent lived in rural areas. This tells us that Republicans and Democrats are about equally likely to live in suburbs and small towns, but Democrats are more likely to live in cities and Republicans are more likely to live in rural communities.

Beyond where partisans live now, however, it is important to know the type of community in which they want to live in the future. Here we see more dramatic differences. The survey asked respondents the following question: "If you could live anywhere in the United States that you wanted to, would you prefer a city, a suburban area, small town or rural area?" Here we see some substantial differences between partisan groups. Again, Republicans and Democrats were about equally likely to express a desire to live in suburbs and small towns. However, 25.24 percent of Republicans expressed a desire to live in a rural area, compared to 16.28 percent of Democrats; 26.23 percent of Democrats expressed a desire to live in cities, compared to only 15.6 percent of Republicans.

Perhaps this is due to people wishing to stay in communities similar to the communities in which they currently reside. Indeed, we do see that residents currently living in cities are more likely to wish to remain in cities than residents currently living elsewhere. That being the case, there is a meaningful difference between partisan groups. Of Republicans currently living in cities at the time of the survey, 38.74 percent said they wished to continue living in a city. Of urban Democrats, 47.13 percent wished to continue living in cities. We also see that only 35.96 percent of Republicans living in a rural area wish to live in a different community type, but 46.1 percent of Democrats living in rural areas would rather live in a small town, a suburb, or a city. Thus, if Americans continue to move to communities where they will be happiest, we should continue to see the urban–rural political divide grow.

The Pew Mobility Survey provided a useful starting point for this analysis. However, the survey did not ask several questions that would have been useful for considering these questions. For that reason I supplemented these findings with a survey of undergraduate college students, a demographic group that is playing an important role in this geographic sorting process.

3.8 AGGREGATE MIGRATION DATA FOR YOUNG AMERICANS AND RESULTS FROM A STUDENT SURVEY

To further consider the issue of political context and community satisfaction, I conducted a survey of undergraduate students at the University of Houston, one of the most racially and ethnically diverse universities in the United States. This university was also an ideal setting for this survey because of the comparatively small percentage of students living on campus. The University of Houston does not require freshmen students to live in dormitories, and 85 percent of all students live off campus. To encourage student participation, the students were offered extra credit points on their final grade by their respective professors.

In such surveys there is always the question of external validity. I do not make the claim that the findings for this group are generalizable to the entire U.S. population. However, there are reasons to be particularly interested in the migration patterns of young, college-educated Americans. Young Americans are not only politically distinctive (being more Democratic, on average, than the nation as a whole), but they also have distinct migratory patterns. It is well established that young Americans are, by far, the most geographically mobile demographic group in the United States. They also tend to have different destinations compared to other Americans.

Before turning to their distinct migratory patterns, a brief discussion of the politics of young Americans may be helpful. The partisan "age gap" in the American electorate is a well-documented—if perhaps not well understood—phenomenon. In the 2008 presidential election, those aged eighteen to twenty-nine provided Obama a strong majority of their votes; in fact, according to exit polls, Obama beat McCain by a remarkable 66 percent to 32 percent among voters under thirty (Fisher 2010). With very few exceptions (Nixon in 1960 and Reagan in 1980), young voters have been more Democratic than older voters in presidential elections for several decades (Sokhey and Djupe 2009). The generation gap should not be overstated, as strong evidence suggests that early political socialization, particularly parental influence, plays a substantial role in party affiliation throughout individuals' lifetimes (Campbell et al. 1960; Jennings and Niemi 1981; Jennings and Markus 1984). However, if parental influence is the sole determinant of partisan affiliation, then we should see no (or virtually no) generation gap in electoral politics, unless there are vastly different birth-rates between Democrats and Republicans.

There are two primary explanations for the partisan age gap: period effects and life-cycle effects. The former holds that a generation's important shared experiences during early adulthood years will shape its subsequent voting patterns for the rest of that age-cohort's movement through the life cycle (Converse 1976). The generation that spent its formative years during the Great Depression, for example, remained strongly Democratic all the way into the 1990s (Erikson and Tedin 2005). The life-cycle hypothesis, which borrows heavily from the demographic concept of "family-life cycles" (Loomis and Hamilton 1936), notes that people tend to become more conservative as they age. As young people age, their incomes typically increase and they move into higher tax brackets, they become more likely to own property, and they are increasingly likely to get married and begin to raise children. All of these changes can lead to changes in political orientation, and, indeed, some evidence suggests individuals do tend to become more conservative as they age (Jennings 1987), though this ideological age gap has not always been present, and we cannot assume that it will continue indefinitely into the future.

Because the politics of young Americans are so distinct, their migration patterns can be a powerful catalyst for political change if their destinations are substantially different from the destinations of older Americans—even if they vote at lower levels. Unfortunately, detailed breakdowns of the migratory patterns of different age cohorts at the county level in the United States during the first decade of the twenty-first century have not yet been provided by the United States Census Bureau. However, given that the distribution of landslide counties has been fairly consistent in recent elections (Bishop and Cushing 2008), a look at migratory patterns during the 1990s may provide some illumination.

Data for Figures 3.2, 3.3, and 3.4 were created by Voss et al. (2004) using data from the U.S. Census Bureau and vital statistics from the National Center for Health Services. Both figures provide two lines, one for landslide Democratic counties in the presidential election of 2000, and one for landslide Republican counties in that same election—landslide counties were again categorized using Bishop and Cushing's (2008) definition as counties that gave more than 60 percent of their votes to one presidential candidate. Along the *x*-axis in both figures, the population is broken up into five-year increments.

In Figure 3.2, we see the mean net migration for different age groups in the two categories of counties. As expected, during these years landslide Democratic counties were magnets for millions of young people within the United States. The mean landslide Democratic county gain, through migration, was 3,335 people between the ages of twenty and twenty-five during the 1990s. The mean landslide Republican county gain, however, was only forty such people. The trend reverses, however, for movers over the age of

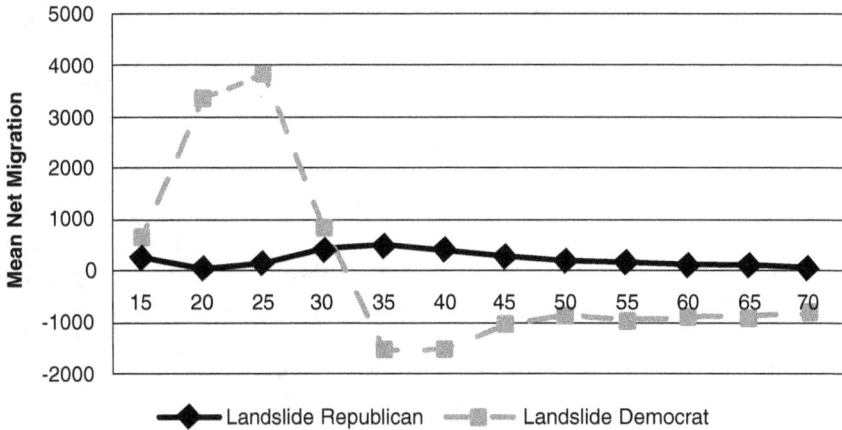

Figure 3.2   Mean Net Migration by Age and County Type during the 1990s

thirty-five. Republican landslide counties gained an average of 512 residents between thirty-five and forty via migration, whereas landslide Democratic counties hemorrhaged these residents, losing 1,542 people in that age cohort on average via migration.[4]

It bears repeating that the baseline populations for the average landslide Democratic and landslide Republican counties were quite different—there are a large number of sparsely populated landslide Republican counties, and a small number of densely populated Democratic counties. To clarify the differences in the migratory patterns, Figure 3.3 provides the *total* net migration of different age cohorts in all landslide Republican and all land-slide Democratic counties. In this figure we see that the Democratic counties

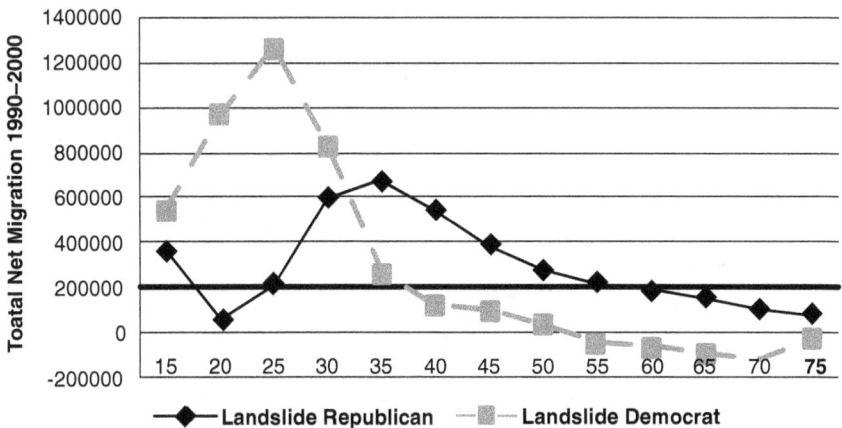

Figure 3.3   Total Net Migration by Age and County Type during the 1990s

gained an impressive 2,191,928 residents between the ages of twenty and thirty-five entirely via migration, whereas the Republican counties gained only 872,892 such residents. Among those over thirty-five, however, we again see the trend reversed. Landslide Democratic counties actually lost 2,478,740 residents over the age of thirty-five entirely through migration during the 1990s, whereas the Republican counties gained 2,652,983 older residents during that same period.

There is a problem with using these findings to draw strong inferences how the migratory patterns of different age cohorts is driving a geographic partisan sort. In the United States, age and race/ethnicity are correlated, with the average non-Hispanic white American being considerably older than the average black or Hispanic American. This may not be an age gap in migratory patterns at all, but instead a race/ethnicity gap. Immigration further complicates the issue, as without foreign immigration (which is overwhelmingly nonwhite or Hispanic white) it would not have been possible for all county types to gain young people entirely from migration. To address this issue, Figure 3.4 specifically examines the migratory patterns of non-Hispanic whites of different age cohorts.

Here we see largely the same patterns. Young whites moved in large numbers to landslide Democratic counties, and older whites moved in massive numbers into landslide Republican counties. Thus, this age gap in migratory patterns is clearly not strictly a function of the different average ages of different racial and ethnic groups. Also, we see in this figure that, although landslide Republican counties did not see an aggregate loss of young people when all demographic groups were considered, landslide Republican counties did lose large numbers of young white Americans, many of them to landslide Democratic counties. The issue of race/ethnicity and migration will receive a more thorough examination in a later chapter.

None of this definitively proves that young Americans explicitly think about politics when determining their next move. In fact, I suspect they are

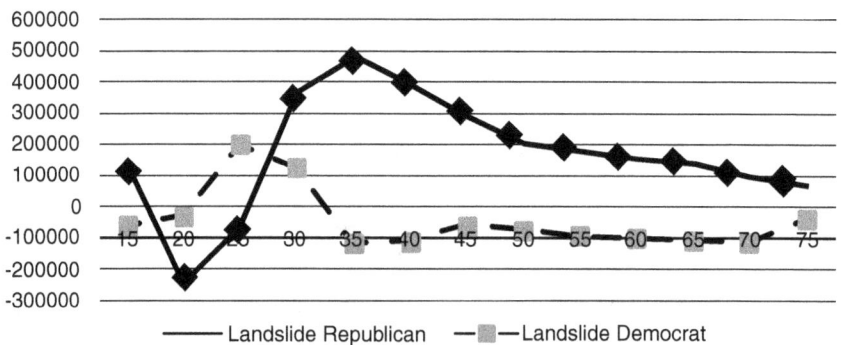

Figure 3.4 Total Net Migration by Age and County Type during the 1990s, Non-Hispanic Whites Only

less likely to do so than older Americans; the first move individuals make as adults is surely driven largely by educational or economic concerns. Nor does it demonstrate that the young Americans who moved into overwhelmingly Democratic communities were themselves Democrats—although young Americans are, on average, more Democratic than older Americans, they are nonetheless quite politically heterogeneous.

The literature on the migratory patterns of young Americans, as well as the preceding figures, suggest that young Americans are strongly attracted to the heavily Democratic urban areas of the county. It is not entirely clear why this is the case, but scholars have identified a number of possible explanations. The movement of the young and educated out of nonmetropolitan counties has been ascribed to the higher income returns on education individuals can expect in metropolitan communities (Mills and Hazarika 2001), a preference for the diversity and social tolerance considered more prevalent in metropolitan communities (Florida 2002), and a greater willingness to take on the burden of higher living expenses in exchange for more cultural amenities (Clark 2003). The fact that older Americans are not flocking to urban counties suggest that they, on average, value other community attributes.

While there are competing explanations for this finding, it is clear that the political contexts of young migrant destinations are substantially different, on average, from the political contexts of older migrant destinations. For this reason, an examination of the political determinants of young Americans' levels of community satisfaction and planned future migratory behavior is worthwhile.

It is important to note that a survey of young college students is not generalizable to all Americans; it is not even generalizable to all young Americans. Obviously, not all young Americans are college graduates or current college students. However, the migratory patterns of this group are especially important given that the number of college-educated young people in a community is an important predictor of future economic success, and communities that tend to attract many highly educated young people also have distinct political and cultural characteristics (Florida 2002). In fact, much of rural America is suffering due to its inability to attract or retain educated youth (Carr and Kefalas 2009). For this reason, even though this survey can only give us useful information about a relatively small sliver of the population, that sliver is both politically distinct and politically and economically important.

In November 2012, I conducted an online survey of 1,511 undergraduate students taking the introductory course on American and Texas government at the University of Houston. The state of Texas requires all college students to take this course, meaning there is little concern that the students who participated were more likely to be interested in or passionate about politics than other students. Most students take this course during their first two years of college. Participation in the survey was voluntary, but students were offered extra credit from their professors in exchange for their participation. The students were racially and ethnically diverse, reflecting the high levels of diversity at the University of Houston. Sixty-nine percent of the survey respondents were non-Hispanic; 31 percent identified as Hispanic. Racially, 37 percent identified as white, 22 percent identified as Asian or Pacific Islander; 15 percent identified as African American; 7 percent identified as mixed race; 1 percent identified as Native American; 17 percent identified as "other." Of those who identified as "other," the overwhelming majority subsequently identified their race as "Hispanic" or "Mexican," though several identified as Indian, Arab, or Middle Eastern.

The age of students varied from seventeen to forty-eight, but the modal age was eighteen and the mean age was twenty. An overwhelming majority of student respondents were under the age of twenty-five. As for gender, 47.09 percent of respondents were male, 52.91 percent were female. In terms of class, a plurality of students (44 percent) identified themselves as middle class; 24 percent identified as upper-middle class; 25 percent identified as lower-middle class; 2 percent identified as upper class; and 5 percent identified as lower class.

The group was diverse politically, but far more students identified as Democrat than identified as Republican; this is not surprising given the average age of respondents and the large number of racial and ethnic minorities in the sample. Of the respondents, 23.33 percent identified as Republican or leaned to the Republican Party; 55.52 identified as Democrat or leaned to the Democratic Party; the remainder declined to answer or identified as pure Independents.

Prior to asking about the partisan distribution within their neighborhood, the survey asked students their subjective opinion of their community as a place to live. Specifically, students were asked the following question: "Overall, how would you rate your community as a place to live? Excellent; Very Good; Good; Only Fair; or Poor." Most students expressed positive feelings toward their current neighborhood; 45 percent described their community as "very good" or "excellent." Only 15 percent of students described their community as "only fair" or "poor."

While the Pew Survey provided county codes that made it possible to identify the respondents' counties of residence and it was subsequently possible to determine the actual political attributes of their counties, it did not ask respondents their subjective view of the local political distribution. In this student survey, I asked students the following question: "In terms of political preferences, do you consider your community to be: Overwhelmingly Democratic; Slight Majority Democratic; Evenly Split between Republicans and Democrats; Slight Majority Republican; or Overwhelmingly Republican."

The students answered as follows: 27 percent declared that their community was evenly split between Republicans and Democrats, 36 percent said their community was either slight majority or overwhelmingly Democratic, and 37 percent said their community was slight majority or overwhelmingly Republican. Given what we will see in a later chapter about neighborhood political segregation in the Houston area, it is likely that many students overestimated the political diversity within their communities, but these subjective interpretations of their communities are nonetheless important and interesting.

When we break down levels of community satisfaction by partisan identity, we find results similar to those of the Pew Survey. More Republicans than Democrats expressed high levels of community satisfaction. In fact, 61 percent of Republicans claimed that their communities were excellent or very good places to live; only 46 percent of Democrats made such a claim. There are reasons to be careful before inferring too much from this result. It is possible that there is a racial difference driving these results. Perhaps racial minorities are more likely to both identify as Democratic and live in an unsatisfactory community. However, when looking at the distribution of respondents after restricting the sample exclusively to non-Hispanic whites, the results were virtually identical—63.03 percent of white Republicans expressed high levels of satisfaction and 49.77 percent of white Democrats expressed high levels of satisfaction.

To see if young Republicans are more likely than young Democrats to consider politics when judging their communities, it is useful to break down students according to their party identification, satisfaction rating, and subjective view of the local political context. Table 3.5 provides this breakdown.

We see in Table 3.5 that Republicans appear more sensitive to the local political context than Democrats when determining their overall levels of community satisfaction. Indeed, there appears to be a linear relationship between the probability that a Republican would describe his community as excellent and his perception of the local political climate. Of the small number (thirty) of Republicans living in what they considered overwhelmingly Democratic communities, only 3.3 percent ranked that community as excellent. Of those Republicans in overwhelmingly Republican communities, 44.4 percent ranked their community as excellent.

Interestingly, we see similar results for Democrats. Democrats were less likely than Republicans to rate their community as excellent regardless of the local political context. However, they also reported higher levels of satisfaction in more Republican communities, and were generally unsatisfied in overwhelmingly Democratic communities, so that 46.1 percent of Democrats living in overwhelmingly Democratic communities ranked their communities as fair or poor.

All of this suggests that people of all partisan persuasions are happier in heavily Republican communities—though this is surely also due to unmeasured variables, such as higher average incomes in Republican neighborhoods. However, this relationship is much stronger for Republicans.

Table 3.5 Community Satisfaction Rating by Partisanship and Subjective View of Local Political Distribution

Community Satisfaction	Republicans					Democrats				
	Strong Democrat	Majority Democrat	Mixed	Majority Republican	Strong Republican	Strong Democrat	Majority Democrat	Mixed	Majority Republican	Strong Republican
Excellent	3.3%	13.0%	16.7%	30.0%	44.4%	3.9%	8.9%	10.5%	18.2%	22.7%
Very Good	16.7%	27.8%	74.1%	44.2%	42.6%	14.7%	29.2%	41.1%	43.5%	44.3%
Good	36.7%	40.7%	66.7%	21.7%	11.1%	35.3%	39.7%	37.8%	30.0%	23.9%
Fair	33.3%	16.7%	5.6%	3.3%	0.0%	34.3%	19.5%	9.1%	6.5%	8.0%
Poor	10.0%	1.9%	0.0%	0.8%	1.9%	11.8%	2.7%	1.4%	1.8%	1.1%

This survey also asked respondents a question to better determine if politics will play any role in their future migratory decisions. Specifically, they were asked, "If you plan to move again in the next five years, which of the following statements is true: I will prefer to live in a community that is more Democratic than the community I live in now; I will prefer to live in a community that is more Republican than the community I live in now; I will prefer to live in a community that is politically similar to the community I live in now; the political views of a community do not matter to me; I do not plan to move again."

Not surprisingly, a large percentage of respondents (36 percent) stated that they do not care about a community's politics. However, sizable minorities said they would prefer to live in a community that is more Republican or Democratic than their current community (9 and 17 percent, respectively). When we break this down by partisan group, we see that large numbers of both Republicans and Democrats express a desire to move to a community that is more aligned with their own beliefs; 26.36 percent of Republicans and 25.24 Democrats say this. Virtually no Republicans or Democrats say they want to move to a community in which there are more people belonging to the opposing party. The desire to move to a community that is more congruent with respondent political beliefs was, not surprisingly, even stronger among those partisans living in a community in which the opposing party was a majority: 39.29 percent of Republicans living in communities that were majority Democrat (whether a slight or an overwhelming majority) said they wanted to move somewhere with more Republicans; 36.05 percent of Democrats in Republican communities expressed a desire to live in a community with more Democrats.

When these students make their next move, whether they graduate or not, they presumably will have some discretion in terms of where they will live. While they may have familial or economic constraints on the state or county in which they reside, they will likely have a choice of neighborhoods. These findings suggest that they will take politics into consideration when choosing their next destination and those destinations will likely be congruent with their political attitudes.

The aggregate migration data suggest that the youngest cohort of adult Americans move in huge numbers to overwhelmingly Democratic counties. These findings do not seem to suggest that they do so because they have higher rates of community satisfaction in Democratic counties. These first moves as adults are likely motivated by concerns such as finding a job, an affordable house or apartment, or going to college; a young Republican may want to ultimately live in a Republican community, but it is unlikely that he would turn down the opportunity to attend an elite university simply because it is in a liberal city. If we can trust the results of this survey, however, we can expect a large percentage of these young partisans to eventually sort themselves into the appropriate community based on their political affiliations.

3.9 CONCLUSION

Bishop and Cushing (2008) and others who argue that America is becoming increasingly geographically polarized make the case that much of this phenomenon is the result of partisan self-selection. This has been difficult to prove, however, and there were other plausible explanations for the tendencies for many communities overwhelmingly to support one party over the other. These findings bolster the argument that Americans are deliberately sorting themselves out along partisan lines.

The multilevel analysis from the Pew Survey demonstrated that Republicans' levels of community satisfaction were apparently sensitive to the local partisan climate; they were less likely to rate their community highly if they lived in a county that gave a large percentage of its vote to Democratic presidential candidates, and this was true even after controlling for a wide array of other individual and contextual variables. We further saw that the ideal state of residence for Republicans was less Democratic in the aggregate than the ideal state of residence for Democrats, and there was a linear relationship between the liberalism of a large city and Republican willingness to relocate to that area. Democrats were not apparently sensitive to the political climate when determining political satisfaction, nor was there a relationship between a city's relative liberalism and their willingness to live there. We also saw differences between Republicans and Democrats in terms of how desirable they viewed rural, urban, and suburban communities as places to live.

The examination of the student survey was congruent with these findings. Republican respondents were, on average, far more satisfied with their communities if those communities were overwhelmingly Republican. Interestingly, Democrats also appeared most satisfied in heavily Republican areas. However, when asked about their future migration plans, large percentages of both Republicans and Democrats expressed a desire to move to communities where their political party was in the local majority. The vast majority of these respondents will move again in the next five years. If their actual migratory behavior is congruent with their stated preferences, then they will further contribute to the geographic polarization of the United States.

Part II

Migration and Political Change

Migration does not have to be politically motivated to have political consequences. If migrants with different demographic and economic characteristics tend to have different migratory patterns, and those economic and demographic characteristics are associated with different political attributes, then these migratory patterns will change the political geography of the United States even if no one had politics in mind when they moved. In the next three chapters, I consider the migratory patterns of Americans of different social categories.

The next chapter will demonstrate that the rate of family formation within a community is one of the most powerful determinants of aggregate vote choice. The "marriage gap" in politics is one of the most important, and perhaps underexamined, developments in American politics. I will argue that some characteristics of a community will make it more or less attractive to individuals interested in getting married at a relatively young age. Those communities with attributes that encourage earlier marriages or draw married individuals to live within them are typically more Republican. Those communities that have later average marriages, or are otherwise unappealing to married couples, tend to be more Democratic. I will argue that the affordability of single-family homes is an important predictor of marriage rates within a community, even after controlling for many other variables.

Not all migratory patterns lead to a more geographically polarized electorate. Race and ethnicity are some of the most useful predictors of party affiliation, but the migratory patterns of certain racial and ethnic groups do not appear motivated by politics. The movements of African Americans out of states such as New York and into Southern states such as Georgia are making some Southern states more politically competitive. Similarly, the arrival of immigrants from Latin America into the American Southwest is largely responsible for the degree to which states such as Colorado have ceased to be solidly Republican. Of course, given the strong preference of minorities for the Democratic Party, eventually the movement of racial and ethnic minorities to a state will cease to make that state more competitive and turn it into an overwhelmingly Democratic state. This is what happened in California, and may eventually happen in other states that are key settlement states for immigrants and domestic minority migrants. Thus the migration of minority groups can be both a source of greater competition and the cause of landslide counties and states, depending on the baseline competitiveness.

This section will also consider how economically motivated migration can change the political geography of the United States. It is well established that income is an important predictor of vote choice. However, it increasingly appears that occupation type can be strongly correlated with party identification, even after controlling for income and other demographic characteristics. If some communities tend to draw residents working in specific fields, the aggregate political characteristics of that community may change as a result.

4 The Geography of Family Formation

4.1 INTRODUCTION

In the run-up to the 2012 election, the so-called gender gap received an enormous amount of attention from political commentators. Women were, on average, more supportive of Obama than men, who were more supportive of Romney. Indeed, Obama's strength among American women aided his victory in 2008 and 2012. Exit polls showed that 55 percent of women voted for Obama, compared to 45 percent of men (Bassett 2012). Obama's strong showing among women was largely credited to women's concerns regarding reproductive issues such as contraception and abortion, though, as this chapter will demonstrate, many scholars have attributed the gender gap in voting to other variables.

Examining the voting patterns of American women as a group masks significant political heterogeneity among women. Not all women were equally likely to support Obama in 2012. When we examine polling data of women by marital status, we see a tremendous gap between married and unmarried women (Sailer 2012). Married women actually voted for Romney over Obama by a significant margin—55.4 percent of married women claimed to support Romney. Only 31.7 percent of unmarried women supported Romney. It is possible that much of this gap can be explained by the marriage patterns of different racial and ethnic groups—African Americans and Latinos are less likely to be married (Schoen and Kluegel 1988; Lichter et al. 1992; Brien 1997; Seitz 2009) and *much* more likely to support Democratic candidates than non-Hispanic whites. However, the marriage gap is large even among non-Hispanic whites. Whereas 61.9 percent of married white women supported Romney, only 44.3 percent of unmarried women did so—a gap of more than 17 percentage points.

This chapter will provide an overview of the marriage gap in politics, describe the geography of family formation in the United States, and argue that the different migratory patterns of married and unmarried Americans are leading to greater political segregation in the United States.

4.2 THE MARRIAGE GAP

The "marriage gap" (Gershkoff 2009), that is, the tendency for married voters to be more likely to vote Republican than unmarried voters, was exceptionally large in 2012, particularly among women. This is not a new trend. The marriage gap is a well-established phenomenon in American politics, though it has spurred much debate about its scale and causes. Herbert Weisberg (1987) noted that the marriage gap first showed itself in 1972 and that married voters are about 10 to 15 percent more Republican than nonmarried voters—though he found that, when race and income were controlled for, marriage ceased to be statistically significant. Looking at 1982 Congressional elections, Martin Plissner (1983) found that nonmarried voters favored Democrats by 26 percentage points.

Though the marriage gap is well established, it can be potentially explained in a number of different ways. Edlund and Pande (2002) argued that the increasing liberalism among female voters in recent decades was directly related to declining marriage rates. They argued that because, on average, husbands are older and wealthier than their wives, marriage in the aggregate represents a transfer of wealth from men to women. They argued that this was particularly true among middle-income Americans, whose voting patterns were most likely to change as a result of marriage: "While a poor man is richer if unmarried, he is still sufficiently poor to favor redistribution; similarly, rich women, while poorer if unmarried, remain rich enough to oppose redistribution. However, among the middle-income group, marital status impacts income sufficiently to affect political preferences" (920). Because marriage, on average, tends to make women wealthier, marriage decreases their preference for economic redistribution. Considering this issue from a comparative perspective, Edlund, Haider, and Pande (2005) found that the same trend was present in Western Europe—this finding suggests that the marriage gap is largely due to a difference in preferences for redistributive policies rather than to different attitudes toward social policies such as abortion and contraception, as these social policies are much less salient and divisive in Europe than the United States. If this is the case, however, we should expect the marriage gap to narrow if the economic disparities between men and women continue to shrink (Bennett and Ellison 2010), or if the trend for men and women to choose spouses of equal social status, what Hernstein and Murray (1994) called "assortive mating," continues to reduce the income gap between husbands and wives. Given that the marriage gap in the United States seems to be growing, rather than shrinking, other potential explanations deserve consideration.

There are certainly other plausible explanations for a marriage gap in partisan politics. Marriage is traditionally associated with raising children, which should decrease an individual's tolerance of social disorder and hence lead to cultural and/or political conservatism (Plissner 1983). It is furthermore intuitive that the Republican Party's message of "family values" will be more persuasive to those voters who are currently married and raising children.[1] In a study that focused exclusively on women, Kathleen Gerson (1987) found evidence that the marriage gap among women resulted from different orders of preferences, with married women tending to be more concerned with domestic commitments, and nonmarried women being more concerned with issues such as career opportunities and gender equity.

It is also possible that the causal arrow between marriage and political attitudes points in the other direction. That is, perhaps marriage does not change attitudes, but attitudes predict the probability of getting married and, if so, at what age. Sassler and Schoen (1999) found economic independence actually increased the probability that a woman would marry; they further noted that single men and women who expressed the most positive attitudes about marriage were the most likely to marry—although, interestingly, women who claimed to support traditional gender roles were actually less likely to marry than those who did not. Clarkberg, Stolzenberg, and Waite (1995) reported that holding liberal attitudes regarding gender roles increased the probability that an individual would cohabitate rather than marry. Religiosity also appears to influence marital decisions (Thornton, Axinn, and Hill 1992), with the more religious being less likely to cohabitate and more likely to marry. Attitudes such as religiosity and views on gender roles also influence partisanship, so it may be possible that both marriage decisions and party identification are driven by some other variable, with no direct causal link between the two.

Regardless of its causes, the average age at first marriage for women is a powerful predictor of presidential vote choice at the state level. Figures 4.1 and 4.2 demonstrate the relationship between state-level median female

Figure 4.1 Support for McCain by Median Female Marriage Age
Source: United States Census Bureau, American Community Survey.

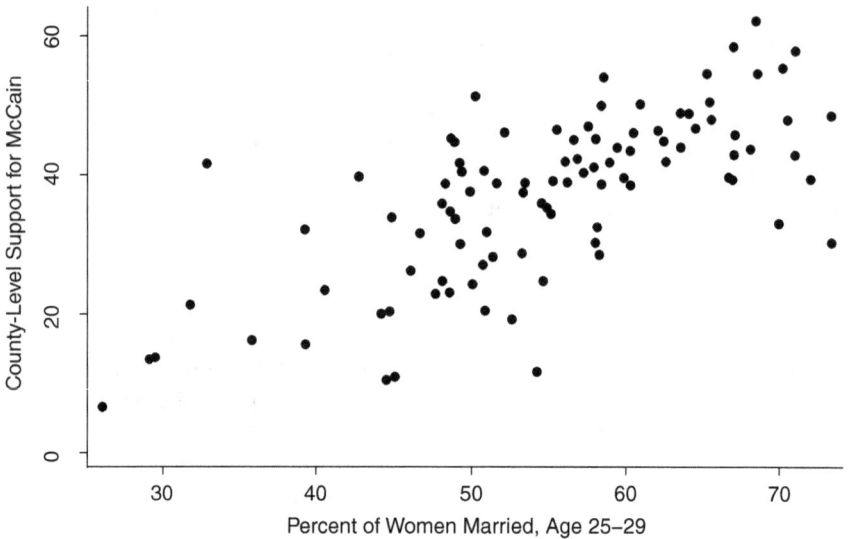

Figure 4.2   Marriage Rates of Young Women and Support for McCain in Large Counties

marriage age and the percentage of the vote that went to the Republican candidate in the 2008 presidential elections. In this election year, we saw a clear, linear relationship between the median age at first marriage for women and aggregate support for the Republican candidates. As the age of marriage went up, Republican support went down. The only observation that could plausibly be called an outlier is Hawaii in 2008, and Obama's remarkably strong showing in that state is easily explained by the fact that Hawaii was Obama's childhood state.

If we consider geographic units smaller than states we see the same patterns. Figure 4.2 was generated using the one hundred largest counties by population. Because the Census Bureau does not estimate the median age at first marriage at the county level, the Y-axis shows the percentage of women between the ages of twenty-five and twenty-nine who have ever been married. Although Republicans tend to perform poorly in large metropolitan areas, they do much better in densely populated counties with high marriage rates among young women.

This relationship between aggregate trends in family formation and aggregate trends in political preferences has been previously examined. Lesthaeghe and Neidert (2006) noted that there are dramatic differences in family formation rates in different regions of the United States, with some areas undergoing a "Second Demographic Transition" analogous to that in Western Europe—with later marriages, low fertility rates, high levels of cohabitation, and so forth—and other regions of the country where this trend is less pronounced or nonexistent. The geographic distribution followed closely the famous "Red State" and "Blue State" maps (Sandler 2012): the liberal states in the Northeast, around the Great Lakes, and on the West Coast all exhibited demographic trends analogous to those in Western Europe. The Great Plains, the South, and the Mountain States, however, continue to exhibit traditional demographic patterns and to vote in greater numbers for Republican candidates. Monson and Mertens (2011) found a strong relationship between the prevalence of postmodern family patterns— defined as absent-father families and small or delayed families—and vote choice at the state level in presidential elections. They further noted that different family patterns were helpful for explaining the "values divide" between Red States and Blue States.

Returning to the descriptive statistics from Chapter 1, we see that the different percentages of women between the ages of twenty-five and thirty who have ever been married, as of 2000, was one of the most startling differences between landslide Republican and landslide Democratic counties.[2] In the nation overall, the mean county marriage rate of this cohort was 74.52 percent. In the landslide Republican counties, however, this variable reached 80.86 percent, and in the landslide Democratic counties it was only 57.91 percent—a difference of nearly 23 percentage points. The size of this difference suggests that different patterns of marriage are a defining difference between landslide Democratic and landslide Republican counties.

The question remains, however, as to why different geographic regions within the same country would exhibit such drastically different demographic trends. Cahn and Carbone (2010) also argue that a key difference between Republican regions of the country and Democratic regions is the age of family formation. At both the aggregate and the individual level, Republicans are more likely to get married at a young age than are Democrats, even after controlling for all other relevant variables. Cahn and Carbone, however, emphasized the importance of family law, access to contraceptives and abortion, and cultural attitudes in shaping the geography of family formation trends.

Because this book argues that aggregate political change is at least partially a consequence of migration, the obvious next step is to look for what community attributes attract or repel young married Americans. In other words, if there is a large partisan "marriage gap," then perhaps at least part of the geographic sorting of the country along partisan lines is related to the degree to which some cities, counties, states, or regions are considered "family friendly."

4.3 HOME AFFORDABILITY AND FAMILY FORMATION

Measuring the degree to which a county or city is considered a hospitable place to form a family unit is inherently problematic, as this undoubtedly differs from person to person. Housing prices, however, may explain part of this phenomenon. In recent years, much of the discussion regarding home-ownership has emphasized the financial or investment aspects of buying a home. However, as Mulder (2006) correctly noted, "[T]he owner occupied home is first and foremost a place where people live, mostly with their families" (281). Assuming that most individuals prefer to live in their own home rather than a condo or apartment after forming a family unit, one indicator of a city or region's attractiveness for married couples is the cost of housing. For decades, the sociology literature has suggested that decisions regarding marriage and family formation are related to housing and other costs (Goodsell 1937; Thompson 1938).

John Hajnal (1965) argued that the rising average age of marriage in Western Europe resulted from the decreasing amount of available land for housing. Landale and Tolnay (1991), looking at the American South, also found that land availability affected the average marriage age. Felson and Solaun (1975) found evidence suggesting that renting an apartment, as opposed to owning a house, leads to lower fertility levels, which supports the hypothesis that family formation is positively influenced by homeownership. More evidence for this was provided by Mulder and Wagner (2001). Withers, Clark, and Ruiz (2008) found that families that move tend to move to communities with more affordable housing. I thus theorize that home affordability, even when controlling for variables such as urban/rural, median incomes, unemployment rates, racial/ethnic characteristics, state, and census region, may be a useful explanatory variable when considering the phenomena of geographic partisan sorting.

Beyond the likelihood of getting married and having children, there is also an apparent relationship between housing costs and the probability that a married woman will exit the labor force. Withers and Clark (2006) found that wives who moved to communities with more affordable housing were more likely to exit the labor force compared to wives who moved to communities with more expensive housing. This is important because there may be some self-selection occurring. Although most married couples may be interested in moving to communities with lower housing costs, those families in which the wife wishes to exit the labor force may be even more strongly attracted to such communities. Scholarly literature suggests a woman's desire to exit the labor force after getting married is influenced by values correlated with political affiliation. Women with fundamentalist religious beliefs are more likely to become housewives at an earlier age (Sherkat 2000; Lehrer 2004); such women are also more likely to identify as Republicans. Thus, affordable housing may not only be drawing married couples, but drawing those married couples most likely to vote Republican—couples in which the wife wishes to stay at home.

The possible relationship between home affordability and aggregate voting trends has largely been ignored by the political science literature, though the topic has been considered by the political journalist Steve Sailer (2008). Sailer hypothesized that "affordable family formation"—which he argued was closely related to housing costs—was a key difference between majority-Republican states and majority-Democratic states. Sailer went on to conclude that the relative affordability of housing accounted for the differing typical political behavior within various large cities. Sailer suggested that the relative costliness of owning a home in America's large coastal cities, such as Los Angeles, led to later family formation, which partially explained the greater support for Democratic politicians in those cities and regions. In contrast, inland American cities like Dallas and Phoenix are able to expand outward all-but indefinitely, which keeps housing costs low and makes such cities more attractive to young families. This explanation gives a major role to physical geography. A city constrained by a coastline has a more difficult time expanding outward, and therefore property values tend to skyrocket as the population becomes increasingly dense.

Because this theory regarding home values and the geographic sort draws from a wide variety of literature, and may at first seem counterintuitive, it may be useful to revisit my hypothesis and proposed causal mechanism. I argue that affordable housing is associated with greater aggregate support for Republican candidates because, as sociology literature suggests, marriage rates are associated with the relative affordability of single-family homes, and, as the political science literature demonstrates, ideology and vote choice are strongly predicted by marital status, particularly for women. In an age where people can migrate relatively easily, those who want more property and a larger house in order to get married or expand their families will move to communities where the cost of doing so is not prohibitively expensive. Those with little interest in forming a family unit, or who plan to wait until later in life to do so, are more likely to move to or remain within communities with higher housing costs.

Is there evidence suggesting that people interested in forming a family will move in order to own a home? There is. It is difficult to discern the precise causal mechanism that explains the correlation between homeownership and family formation and fertility, but research has suggested that migration can be motivated by the desire to own a home and start a family. In a study of the Netherlands, Feijten and Mulder (2002) found that many couples move into owner-occupied and single-family dwellings because they anticipate childbirth. Kulu and Vikat (2008) and Kulu and Boyle (2009) found that fertility rates increased after couples moved, which suggests that the different family patterns seen in different housing types can be explained by selective moves. Vobecká and Piguet (2011) similarly argued that selective migration can explain different family patterns in different communities. Clark and Onaka (1983) argued that life-cycle transitions such as family formation are a powerful explanation for residential mobility; specifically, growing families require more space and people will move to achieve that greater space (Clark, Deurloo, and Dieleman 1984).

If differences in family formation patterns explain the Red State/Blue State divide, and family formation patterns can at least be partially explained by differences in home prices, some relationship between home values and presidential voting should be discernible at the state level. Figure 4.3 shows the relationship between home value inflation and support for Bush in the 2004 presidential election. On the X-axis we see the degree to which home values inflated between 2000 and 2004, key years of the American housing "bubble." The Y-axis shows state-level support for President Bush in 2004. We see that states that voted strongly for Democratic presidential candidate John Kerry were also typically the states that witnessed the most dramatic explosion in home values. This relationship may be spurious, however, as plenty of variables predict both home values and aggregate vote choice.

We see similar results when we examine counties. According to census data, home values increased among all counties in the last several decades. However, the difference in the increase among the strongly Democratic counties and the strongly Republican counties was remarkable. Controlling for inflation, median home values in landslide Democratic counties (as of 2000) increased an average of approximately $24,100 between 1980 and 2000. This is more than twice the national county average increase ($10,400) and more than three times as much as the increase in median home values in landslide Republican counties ($6,600). Because this may have been primarily due to a difference in rural and urban areas, a more sophisticated statistical analysis was performed in order to provide meaningful evidence of a causal connection.

The dependent variable for the models testing my hypothesis regarding home values and vote choice was the percentage of the vote earned by President George W. Bush at the county level in the 2000 presidential

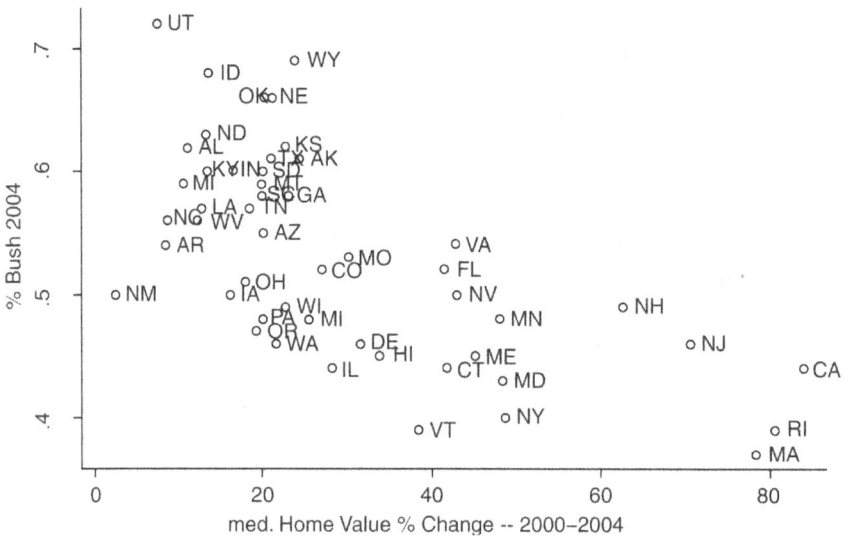

Figure 4.3   Home Value Inflation and Support for Bush

election—2000 was the ideal year to test this theory because it was a year in which there was both a decennial census and a presidential election. It also occurred before the housing bubble reached preposterous heights or subsequently "popped." My key independent variable for the models of aggregate vote choice was housing affordability at the county level, which I measured using the median value of owner-occupied housing units. Because so many variables that correlate with home values also correlate with aggregate voting patterns, it was important to include a wide variety of control variables to ensure that this is not a spurious relationship. Perhaps the most important control variable to include in this model was median income because of its high correlation with home values (Pearson's $r = 0.65$) and strong relationship with vote choice at the county level.

I also controlled for the percentage of African Americans and Hispanics within a county—a necessary control because of these demographic groups' relatively lower average socioeconomic conditions and strong preference for Democratic over Republican candidates. A variable was also included for the percentage of the population within a county that had completed a four-year college degree, which is correlated with incomes, home prices, and marriage age. I also included the percentage of the population below the poverty line, as specified by the Census Bureau, the percentage of a county classified as rural, and dummy variables for whether a county was classified as metropolitan, micropolitan, or rural (with rural serving as the base category). Because Evangelical Christians are such strong Republicans, on average, I also controlled for the percentage of the county population that belonged to an Evangelical congregation. In case there are systematic cultural, economic, or other differences between the various regions in the United States, I again included regional control variables for the nine census regions, with New England as the base category.

Using an ordinary least-squares regression model to examine these relationships is inappropriate in this case because the degree to which the values for these independent variables tend to cluster together in different regions suggests that spatial autocorrelation is potentially a serious concern. As with temporal autocorrelation, the presence of spatial autocorrelation violates the OLS assumption of independence among the observations. This will tend to lead to an underestimation of the error term.

One way to determine the scope of spatial independence is through the calculation of the Moran's I statistic (Rogerson and Yamada 2009). This statistic demonstrates the extent to which the value of a variable in one location is similar to values in neighboring locations. A matrix of spatial weights was used in order to calculate this statistic. The value of Moran's I can range from –1 (perfect dispersion) to +1 (perfect correlation). Figure 4.4 shows the Moran scatter plot for the county-level presidential vote using a first-order queen contiguity matrix. Because spatial autocorrelation is such a potentially serious problem for this analysis, some correction will be necessary to ensure accurate coefficients.

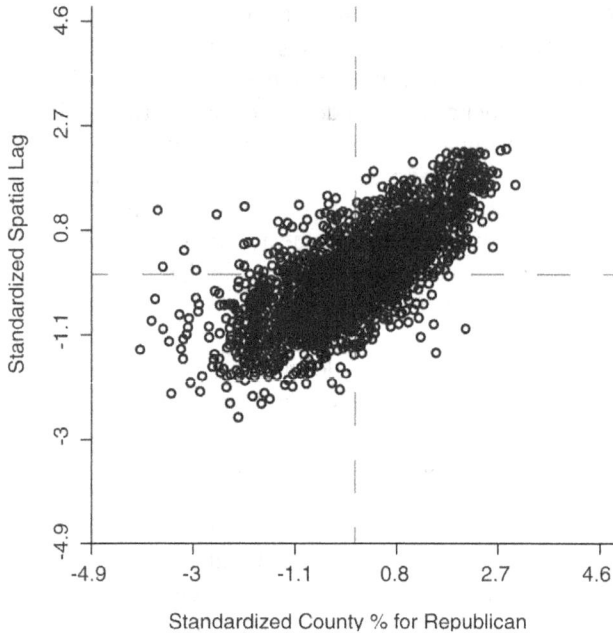

Figure 4.4 Univariate Moran Scatter Plot for Republican Vote

There are two primary models employed when conducting this sort of spatial analysis: spatial lag models and spatial error models. The spatial lag model can be written as follows:

$$y = \beta x + \rho W y + \varepsilon$$

where ρ is a spatial autoregressive coefficient and W is a connectivity matrix. The logic behind spatial lag models is similar to that of time-series models with temporally lagged dependent variables. However, estimation of ρ in a spatial model is complicated because, unlike temporal autocorrelation, spatial autocorrelation is bi-directional and two-dimensional. Therefore, ρ in a spatial model can only be estimated accurately via maximum likelihood.

Spatial error models are the other primary means of correcting for spatial autocorrelation. In these models, the spatial dependence is found in the error term rather than as an independent variable in the model. Spatial error models can be written as follows:

$$y = \beta x + \varepsilon \text{ and } \varepsilon = \lambda W e + u$$

where λ is a coefficient for spatially correlated errors and W is again a connectivity matrix. The decision to use one method or the other should be determined by whether or not the primary focus is on the spatial relationship. If spatial dependence is not the focus of the study, and the spatial correlation is instead a nuisance that must be corrected, a spatial error model is more appropriate. In this case, a spatial error model was created.[3] The results of the spatial error models can be found in Table 4.1.

We see in Model 1 that, although incomes and home costs are correlated, their coefficients are in opposing directions. Higher incomes lead to more Republican voting, but higher home values lead to less Republican voting; this is true even if you control for county population size, racial character-istics, and poverty rates—although the size of the black population and the poverty rate remained the most powerful predictors of county-level vote.

In Model 2, the variable for marriage rates among young women was introduced. We see that marriage rates are a strong predictor of aggre-gate vote choice. In terms of substantive effects, a two-standard deviation change in the rate of marriage led to a greater change in vote choice than a two-standard deviation change in income. It is also important to note that including this variable weakened the coefficient for both median income and home values, suggesting that part of the influence of home values and income on aggregate vote choice was due to the relationship between income, home values, and marriage. It is also interesting to see that, when marriage is not included in the model, the size of the population with a four-year college degree is a statistically and substantively significant deter-minant of county-level vote choice; when marriage is included, there is no apparent relationship between education and voting. It appears that any relationship between vote choice and education (at least in the aggregate) is entirely a function of the relationship between education and marriage. Higher education tends to lead to later average marriages, and later mar-riages are associated with higher rates of Democratic voting.

To better determine the relationship between community characteristics and marriage rates, in Model 3 the dependent variable was the marriage rate of young women within the county. As expected, higher home values tended to depress the rates of marriage. It is important to remember that this is true even though the model controlled for the size of the county population and whether or not it was an urban county, so this is not merely a function of cities having lower rates of marriage than rural areas.

The findings from this examination of aggregate data are congruent with the hypotheses presented here. It is important to take seriously the issue of ecological inference, however (Robinson 1950). To confidently assert that individual behavior is congruent with the aggregate findings, a model using individual-level data is necessary. Table 4.2 was generated using the 2008 Annenberg National Election Survey, conducted during the 2008 United States Presidential Election. These data have the advantage of an extraor-dinarily large N (more than 50,000 respondents) and they further provide each respondent's county of residence, making the creation of multilevel models possible. Table 4.2 shows the results of these models.

Table 4.1 Spatial Error Models for County-Level Support for Bush and Marriage Rates for Young Women

	Model 1 % Bush	Robust Std. Err.	2 Std. Dev. Δ	Model 2 % Bush w/ Marriage Mediator	Robust Std. Err.	2 Std. Dev. Δ	Model 3 Marriage Rates Women 25–29	Robust Std. Err.	2 Std. Dev. Δ
Median Income (Divided by $10,000)	2.78	(0.55)*	4.43	2.00	(0.52)*	3.19	3.21	(0.67)*	0.00
Median Home Value (Divided by $10,000)	-0.30	(0.09)*	-2.78	-0.24	(0.07)*	-2.23	-0.33	(0.14)*	0.00
% of Women Married, 25–29				0.20	(0.02)*	4.55			
% BA	-0.13	(0.03)*	-1.98	0.00	(0.03)		-0.62	(0.04)*	0.00
% Black	-0.44	(0.03)*	-12.73	-0.37	(0.03)*	-10.73	-0.36	(0.02)*	-10.40
% Hispanic	-0.12	(0.03)*	-2.91	-0.12	(0.03)*	-2.92	0.00	(0.03)	-0.01
% Evangelical Christian	0.05	(0.02)*	1.56	0.05	(0.02)*	1.55	0.03	(0.02)	0.88
% Below Poverty Line	-0.54	(0.09)*	-6.78	-0.45	(0.08)*	-5.63	-0.45	(0.09)*	-5.67
% Rural	0.02	(0.01)*	1.25	0.01	(0.01)	0.67	0.04	(0.01)*	2.72
Metropolitan	-1.25	(0.32)*		-1.04	(0.31)*		-1.03	(0.37)*	
Micropolitan	-0.22	(0.28)		-0.15	(0.27)		-0.27	(0.32)	
Log of Total Population	-0.42	(0.19)*		-0.37	(0.18)*		-0.37	(0.26)	
Pacific	3.37	(2.77)		2.90	(2.60)		5.43	(1.99)*	
Mountain	9.32	(2.61)*		8.09	(2.38)*		9.14	(1.80)*	
West-North Central	10.56	(2.64)*		9.13	(2.39)*		7.18	(1.43)*	

	Model 1		Model 2		Model 3	
East-North Central	6.94	(2.55)*	5.63	(2.29)*	4.68	(1.22)*
West-South Central	6.03	(2.95)*	4.32	(2.65)*	13.73	(1.50)*
East-South Central	7.54	(2.94)*	6.05	(2.60)*	10.68	(1.49)*
South Atlantic	9.44	(3.18)*	7.83	(2.71)*	8.37	(1.47)*
Mid-Atlantic	8.95	(2.97)*	7.95	(2.61)*	-0.63	(1.44)
Constant	58.89	(8.51)*	43.38	(8.36)*	80.14	(4.46)*
λ	0.99	(0.01)*	0.99	(0.01)*	0.67	(0.06)*
Observations	3103		3103		3103	
Lagrange Multiplier Test of λ	2394.81		2317.1		264.4	

* $p < 0.05$

Table 4.2 Multilevel Logit Model for Probability of Identifying as Republican and Being Married

Republican	Model 4 Identify as Republican	Std. Error	Odds Ratio	Std. Error	Model 5 Married	Std. Error	Odds Ratio	Std. Error
Individual Characteristics								
Constant	-0.81	(0.10)*			-1.33	(0.09)*		
Married	0.33	(0.03)*	1.40	(0.04)				
Black	-2.36	(0.07)*	0.09	(0.01)	-0.57	(0.04)*	0.57	(0.02)
Hispanic	-0.79	(0.05)*	0.46	(0.02)	0.27	(0.05)*	1.31	(0.06)
Frequently Attend Religious Services	0.75	(0.02)*	2.13	(0.05)	0.71	(0.03)*	2.03	(0.05)
Female	-0.38	(0.02)*	0.68	(0.02)	0.03	(0.02)	1.03	(0.02)
BA	0.19	(0.02)*	1.21	(0.03)	0.02	(0.03)	1.02	(0.03)
Income Quartile 2	0.30	(0.03)*	1.35	(0.04)	0.68	(0.03)*	1.98	(0.06)
Income Quartile 3	0.48	(0.04)*	1.62	(0.06)	1.51	(0.04)*	4.52	(0.17)
Income Quartile 4	0.65	(0.04)*	1.92	(0.08)	1.94	(0.05)*	6.94	(0.35)
Income Unknown	0.33	(0.04)*	1.40	(0.06)	0.72	(0.04)*	2.06	(0.08)
Age 30–44	-0.08	(0.05)	0.92	(0.04)	1.36	(0.05)*	3.90	(0.18)
Age 45–60	-0.17	(0.05)*	0.84	(0.04)	1.30	(0.04)*	3.67	(0.16)
Age 61 +	-0.10	(0.05)*	0.90	(0.04)	2.08	(0.05)*	8.04	(0.37)

Contextual Characteristics

Median Home Value (Divided by $10,000)	−0.01	(0.00)*	0.99	(0.00)	−0.01	(0.00)*	0.99	(0.00)
Median Income (Divided by $10,000)	0.10	(0.02)*	1.10	(0.02)	0.08	(0.02)*	1.08	(0.02)
% with BA	−0.01	(0.00)*	0.99	(0.00)	−0.01	(0.00)*	0.99	(0.00)
% Black	0.00	(0.00)*	1.00	(0.00)	−0.01	(0.00)*	0.99	(0.00)
% Hispanic	0.00	(0.00)	1.00	(0.00)	0.00	(0.00)*	1.00	(0.00)
Urban	−0.10	(0.06)	0.91	(0.06)	−0.31	(0.06)*	0.74	(0.04)
Suburban	0.04	(0.06)	1.04	(0.06)	−0.03	(0.06)	0.97	(0.06)
South	0.41	(0.04)*	1.51	(0.06)	0.09	(0.04)*	1.10	(0.04)
Number of Observations	42408				42408			
Number of Counties	778				778			
−2 X Log Likelihood	51077.736				44883.916			

$* p < 0.05$

We see, congruent with the aggregate models, that marriage is one of the most important predictors of party identification. Even controlling for all other variables, a married individual is 1.40 times as likely to identify as a Republican as an unmarried individual. We also see that those living in communities with higher median home values were slightly less likely to vote Republican, even after controlling for other variables such as whether the community was urban, suburban, or rural. Turning to the contextual determinants of marriage, the evidence at the individual level is not as strong as it was at the aggregate level. However, we see that those living in urban areas are only 74 percent as likely to be married as those living elsewhere, even when individual attributes are controlled for. Although the coefficient is small, we also see that higher home values were associated with a lower probability of being married.

4.4   CONCLUSION

All of the empirical findings presented in this chapter are congruent with the hypothesis that different geographic patterns of family formation are a powerful predictor of geographic political patterns. The migration literature furthermore strongly suggests that residential mobility is related to changes in marital status and other life-cycle events. However, caution should be exercised before drawing strong inferences from these models. There are other potential explanations for these findings. The different marriage patterns in Red States and Blue States might still be primarily the result of different cultural characteristics of these states. The apparent relationship between home affordability and family formation may be coincidental, though other literature suggests this is not the case.

The evidence presented here is suggestive that the causal mechanism I described is correct, but all of the models presented were based on purely cross-sectional data. A longitudinal study examining marriage patterns, migration, and voting should be conducted in the future. These findings do indicate, however, that aspects of the local community such as home prices and whether it is urban or more rural can influence the probability that someone will be married. I hypothesize that this has much to do with migration. That is, I argued that some communities are, on average, more attractive to married voters, who are more likely to weigh some community variables more heavily than are single Americans. Thus, the divergent community preferences, combined with the different average political preferences, of married and single Americans should be playing a role in the geographic partisan sort. However, I must again note that, while these findings are congruent with this hypothesis, alternative explanations are also plausible. For example, living in an urban community may not be making marriage prohibitively costly; instead, those in living in urban communities may simply have less of a desire to get married in the first place. This may be the result of some cultural attribute not measurable with these data and not captured by the included local demographic, religious, and economic attributes included in these models. Perhaps the social pressure to get married at a younger age may be stronger in some communities than others, and these social pressures may be correlated with the variables examined here, hence leading to spurious findings. This possibility deserves serious consideration. However, even if the effects can be explained by other predictors, the correlations would still be real, in the sense of representing real differences between those who get married at a comparatively young age and those who do not marry, or do so at a later age.

The strong relationship between age of first marriage and vote choice suggests the Republican Party has yet another demographic problem. Scholars and pundits have written thousands of pages noting how the growing minority population will soon guarantee the Democratic Party a permanent majority in Congress and a permanent lock on the presidency unless the GOP is able to win more votes from African Americans, Latinos, and Asian Americans. The increase in the number of unmarried Americans is similarly problematic for Republicans. While there is still a substantial racial gap in marriage rates—African Americans and Latinos are less likely to be married than non-Hispanic whites (Raley and Sweeney 2009; Lichter and Landale 1995)—and the growing minority population explains some of the decline in aggregate marriage rates, marriage rates among non-Hispanic whites are also on the decline (Murray 2012); this is especially true of lower-income whites. Given these trends, to remain competitive the Republican Party will need to find a way to increase its share of the unmarried vote or, if marriage really does cause some people to change their party identification, embrace policies that encourage earlier marriage.

Even if the federal government was determined to increase marriage rates in the United States, it is not entirely clear how it could do so. These results indicate that making homeownership more affordable is one means by which this could be achieved. However, future policy makers will surely be cautious before pursuing policies designed to nudge Americans into their own homes. The relaxed lending standards of the early 2000s that were supposed to usher in what George W. Bush called an "ownership society" surely attributed to the American housing bubble and subsequent recession.

We furthermore should not overstate the case that home affordability predicts family formation trends. Although there seems to be a relationship between housing costs and the degree to which regions of the United States appear to be undergoing a "Second Demographic Transition," there are not strong reasons to believe that a plunge in housing costs nationwide would necessarily spur an explosion in marriage and family formation. In the United States, residential mobility is relatively easy and there is tremendous heterogeneity across the nation in terms of home affordability. Thus, those who wish to get married and move into a single-family home still have the option of moving to a community where they can do so. If home affordability were to increase nationwide, we might see a more even distribution of marital patterns across the nation, but not see a major change in the overall rates.

We should keep in mind that the decline of marriage in the United States and throughout the rest of the developed world was the result of many different trends. When examining the demographic causes of the Republican defeat in the 2012 presidential election, Jonathan Last (2012), writing for the *Weekly Standard* correctly noted that many variables are responsible for this trend:

> How did we get to an America where half of the adult population isn't married and somewhere between 10 percent and 15 percent of the population don't get married for the first time until they're approaching retirement? It's a complicated story involving, among other factors, the rise of almost-universal higher education, the delay of marriage, urbanization, the invention of no-fault divorce, the legitimization of cohabitation, the increasing cost of raising children, and the creation of a government entitlement system to do for the elderly childless what grown children did for their parents through the millennia.
>
> But all of these causes are particular. Looming beneath them are two deep shifts. The first is the waning of religion in American life. As Joel Kotkin notes in a recent report titled "The Rise of Post-Familialism," one of the commonalities between all of the major world religions is that they elevate family and kinship to a central place in human existence. Secularism tends toward agnosticism about the family. This distinction has real-world consequences. Take any cohort of Americans—by race, income, education—and then sort them by religious belief. The more devout they are, the higher their rates of marriage and the more children they have.

The rise of secularism is a particularly compelling explanation for the decline in marriage rates (Kaufmann 2010). Secular Americans are less likely to get married in the first place, and it is questionable if their marriage rates would substantially increase if homes became more affordable. It furthermore is unlikely that there are any public policies that could reverse the trend toward greater secularization that would be within constitutional bounds.

Other causes of the higher average marriage age, such as the greater percentage of the population going to college and the increasing economic independence of women, are almost universally considered positive developments in American society. Although some may oppose the ease with which Americans can access contraception and abortion, and they may further believe that marriage rates would increase if these were harder to access, the Supreme Court has settled that the government does not have the constitutional authority to deny access to these methods of family planning. Last suggested that retirement benefits from the government may decrease the incentive to have children, but no politician with an interest in reelection would seriously propose major cuts to Social Security or Medicaid in order to encourage higher rates of family formation. Some governments in developed countries have experimented with pronatalist policies, such as providing more government benefits to mothers, to increase birthrates—which are correlated with marriage rates, but obviously not the same thing. There is only modest evidence that such policies are effective (Gauthier 2007).

While increasing marriage rates would presumably be good for the Republican Party, there are other reasons one might wish to encourage marriage. While one could make the case that the rise of single motherhood is due to the increasing financial independence of women, single motherhood is associated with greater poverty rates and the children of single mothers have, on average, fewer economic resources available to them (McLanahan 2004). Furthermore, if the decline of marriage is leading to a decline in fertility, this has consequences for the nation's fiscal security; low birthrates can lead to an insufficient number of workers to support a large population of retirees (Vos 2009).

The question of declining marriage rates in the United States and the rest of the developed world has puzzled demographers for decades. There is not a single explanation for this phenomenon. However, we are well aware that it has political consequences. A state or county's marriage rate is a powerful predictor of its aggregate vote choice, and the affordability of single-family homes is a predictor of marriage rates. Whether or not trends in home affordability influence the aggregate marriage rate of the nation or simply lead to a geographic sorting by marital status remains unclear. These issues deserve greater consideration from political scientists in the years ahead.

5 Race and Migration as a Source of Political Diversity and Homogeneity

5.1 INTRODUCTION

The changing racial and ethnic makeup of the United States is one of the most important determinants of political change in recent years. The Democratic Party is the main political beneficiary of the increasing minority population, as African Americans, Hispanic Americans, and Asian Americans consistently give their overwhelming support to Democratic candidates. The growth of the minority population is not uniform across the United States, however. Different racial and ethnic groups in the United States have different migratory patterns. These different patterns are playing a role in the geographic polarization of the United States. However, in some cases, these different patterns are contributing to higher levels of political polarization and in other cases they are responsible for higher levels of political competition.

A previous chapter demonstrated that the migration patterns within the United States differ by age cohort, which has political consequences because of the different voting patterns of Americans at different stages of their lives. Specifically, we saw that, during the 1990s, the youngest cohort of adult Americans moved in massive numbers to those counties that now give overwhelming victories to Democratic presidential candidates. We further saw a greater number of older Americans left those counties than moved in, and they moved in substantial numbers to counties that now give overwhelming victories to the Republican Party in presidential elections. We further saw that the family formation trends within different communities are an important predictor of aggregate political outcomes, even when controlling for a myriad of other variables. High rates of marriage, particularly among young Americans, was a strong predictor of aggregate Republican voting.

As was briefly mentioned in the preceding pages, an apparent age gap in either politics or migration may be partially explained as a racial or ethnicity gap; a much greater percentage of older Americans are non-Hispanic white, and hence, on average, more Republican. As a result of immigration and higher birthrates among minorities, a larger percentage of young Americans are minorities, and hence, on average, more Democratic. Further, while the "marriage gap" in politics is apparent within racial groups—particularly among non-Hispanic whites—the relationship between marriage patterns and aggregate vote choice is also partly a result of different marriage patterns between non-Hispanic whites and racial/ethnic minorities; marriage rates among minorities, especially African Americans, are much lower than the rates for non-Hispanic whites (Lichter et al. 1992; Wilcox and Wolfinger 2006).

This chapter will provide a brief survey of the literature on the different migratory patterns of various racial and ethnic groups, as well as how the literature suggests racial context shapes political views. It will also show the different political characteristics of the kinds of communities that tend to draw members of different groups. It will provide evidence suggesting that this geographic sorting process is largely the result of the migratory patterns of non-Hispanic white Americans. This is congruent with the earlier finding that partisan self-selection in migration occurs primarily among Republicans. This chapter will also provide evidence that the migratory patterns of minorities are making some communities more competitive, rather than less.

5.2 RACE, MIGRATION, AND POLITICAL CHANGE: WHAT THE LITERATURE SUGGESTS

Chapter 2 noted that the migration literature demonstrates that non-Hispanic whites have different migratory patterns from minority groups. The two largest minority groups—African Americans and Latinos—also differ from each other in their migratory patterns. Whereas Latinos were once heavily concentrated in a few states that have traditionally been magnets for Latin American immigrants, communities throughout the United States are now experiencing significant in-migration of Latinos, creating significant Latino populations in places not traditionally considered major immigrant destinations (Massey and Capoferro 2010). The most significant trend in African American migration has been the reversal of the Great Migration of the early twentieth century, as large numbers of blacks have returned to the South, particularly to cities such as Atlanta. There are a number of explanations for this "New Great Migration" of African Americans. New York City, which has experienced a particularly dramatic out-migration of African Americans in recent years, is now considered unaffordable to many blacks (Bilefsky 2011). There is also evidence that native-born blacks tend to leave communities that experience high levels of immigration, though the trend is more pronounced for whites (Frey 1999). We also saw evidence that all racial and ethnic groups demonstrate racial and ethnic homophily in their residential patterns (Bayer, Ferreira, and McMillan 2007).

On its face, the relationship between the migration of different racial and ethnic groups and changes in the geographic distribution of partisan support should be quite simple. Racial and ethnic minorities vote disproportionately for Democratic candidates. Therefore, a movement of minorities into a community should presumably make that community more Democratic, and the large growth of the Latino and Asian population through immigration is certainly a boon to the Democratic Party. Obama won an astonishing 96 percent of all African American votes in 2008 (Kuhn 2008), and beat McCain among Latinos by an impressive two-to-one margin (Lopez 2008). Obama's showing among all large minority groups was equally impressive in 2012.

It makes intuitive sense, then, that the rise of many landslide Democratic counties should be related to immigration. As Gimpel (2010) put it, mass immigration from Latin America represents the "demise of Republican political prospects." Gimpel further noted that the Republican Party experienced a decline of its share of the vote in 62 percent of all counties with more than 50,000 people that experienced at least a 2 percentage point increase in the immigrant population from 1980 until 2008. In counties that experienced an increase of more than 4 percent in their immigrant population, the drop was even more dramatic: 74 percent of all such counties saw a decline in the Republican share of the vote. While the African American population is not growing as a percentage of the total population, if they are migrating in large numbers to specific locations, there should be a strong correlation between the growth of the African American population in those regions and the strength of the Democratic Party. The issue of minority migration, foreign immigration, and aggregate county vote totals is more complicated than that, however, because it may not be appropriate to assume that the voting patterns of non-Hispanic whites are static and not sensitive to changes in local demographics.

In order to demonstrate that trends in immigration and the migration of racial and ethnic minorities accounts for much of the trend toward landslide counties and other geographic units in the United States, a few other assumptions must hold. It must be found that migrating racial and ethnic minorities are moving to counties that were previously closely contested (if they are moving into areas already dominated by Democrats, then their presence will play little role in the growth in the number of landslide counties). If they are moving into strong Republican territory, it must be shown that they are moving in numbers significant enough to cause a major partisan swing.

In some cases, we know that international migration has actually caused some counties to move from the landslide Republican camp into the competitive category. Orange County, California, is a prime example of such a transition. Whereas this southern California county, which was known for its affluence and overwhelmingly white demographic, was the very epitome of "Nixon Country," immigration from Asia and Latin America has drastically changed its population characteristics. Although the Republican Party remains competitive in Orange County, it is not the Republican stronghold it once was. We see the a similar trend in Fort Bend County, Texas, which contains the city of Sugar Land and was once the location of former House

Majority Leader Tom DeLay's congressional district. No Democratic presidential has won a majority of votes in Fort Bend County since 1964. The demographics of this county are changing, however, and it is becoming more competitive. The city of Sugar Land is now only 44.4 percent non-Hispanic white, and in 2008 and 2012, Barack Obama won 48.6 percent and 46.1 percent, respectively. Were it not for Latin American and Asian immigration, Orange County and Fort Bend County would surely still give massive victories to Republican candidates.

On the other hand, immigration and the internal migration of racial and ethnic minorities may change politics more dramatically than would be predicted based on their movements alone. If communities receiving large numbers of ethnic minorities subsequently also experience "White Flight," then a community's ethnic makeup, and politics, may change quite rapidly. The exit of higher-income whites from urban communities to the suburbs in the wake of desegregation has been well documented (Coleman 1975; Massey and Denton 1988, 1993; Morrill 1995). There is furthermore evidence suggesting that White Flight is also spurred by the arrival of Latin America immigrants (Frey and Liaw 1998; Gimpel 1999).

To make matters more complicated, some socioeconomic groups within the non-Hispanic white category may actually seek out racial and ethnic diversity and flock to communities possessing that attribute (Florida 2002). What is more, one could infer that this group of whites, given its preferences in community type, is also much more likely to support the Democratic Party given its reputation as the party of social tolerance. If that is the case, the combination of in-migration of racial and ethnic minorities, the out-migration of whites disturbed by their communities' demographic changes, and the in-migration of other whites who desire greater diversity, could sum up to a powerful catalyst for major political change within a geographic unit.

We must also consider the possibility that a sudden influx of new residents of a different racial or ethnic group than the majority will actually change the political preferences of native residents, though this is difficult to demonstrate using aggregate data, and even difficult with individual surveys, unless working with time-series data. To assume that there is a direct, linear relationship between minority population growth in a geographic unit and support for Democratic candidates within that unit also requires the assumption that the voting behavior of non-Hispanic white voters is unrelated to their communities' larger racial and ethnic context. This assumption is likely incorrect.

When it comes to individual-level views on politics generally, and policy matters related to race and ethnicity specifically, local demographic context matters. Political scientists have known this since V. O. Key (1949) first noted that white hostility toward African Americans was directly proportional to the relative size of the local black community. Key argued that whites viewed large black communities as a source of economic and political competition, and the size of that threat was directly related to the size of the black community. Blalock (1967) continued this line of research, largely verifying Key's intuitions. More recently, James Glaser (1994) found that the size of each racial group within an area had a strong effect on racial–political attitudes in the Deep South.

If we assume racial attitudes predict partisan preferences, and there is significant evidence suggesting that they do (Carmines and Stimson 1989), and a large minority population tends to make non-Hispanic white voters become more conservative on racial issues, then a major influx of racial and ethnic minorities may make the local white population more prone to support Republican candidates. This is not implausible, as in recent years many Southern states have had both an increase of African Americans and witnessed an increasing percentage of the white population identifying as Republican.

On the other hand, there is a competing theory regarding the relationship between local diversity and racial/ethnic views: the contact theory. The contact theory (Allport 1954; Amir 1969; Jackman and Crane 1986) suggests that as different demographic groups have increasing numbers of interactions with each other, their negative views about each other will tend to dissipate as their personal experience trumps preconceived stereotypes. Rothbart and John (1993, 42) summed up this theory as follows:

> The contact hypothesis itself has a number of variants, but the basic idea is that antagonistic groups generate unrealistically negative expectations of one another and simultaneously avoid contact. To the extent that contact occurs, the unrealistically negative perceptions of the group members are modified by experience. In other words, hostility is reduced as a result of increasingly favorable attitudes toward individual group members, which then generalize to the group as a whole.

If this is the case, an increasing number of nonwhite migrants may actually cause white residents to become less racially conservative and subsequently less likely to support Republican candidates. To be clear, contact theory does not assume that mere contact in any form is sufficient to assuage tensions between groups. Allport (1954, ch. 16) specified some conditions that must be met before contact reduces tension and prejudice. Specifically, contact is most likely to reduce prejudice if the contact is between social equals, if the parties are pursuing common goals, and if the law, customs, and the local atmosphere support contact between groups.

It is challenging to disentangle how migration, particularly foreign immigration, changes policies at the local and state level, and how those policy changes subsequently change individual attitudes and party identification. As a result of a major influx of immigrants, particularly undocumented immigrants, into a community, native-born Americans' attitudes toward immigrants may become increasingly negative (Hood and Morris 1998;

Alvarez and Butterfield 2000; Tolbert and Hero 2001). This may lead local politicians to embrace nativist policies. This is potentially problematic, however, as it may alienate the growing foreign-born population. What may be sound politics today could be disastrous in the long run.

To provide one example of the relationship between the growth of the foreign-born population, immigration policy, and electoral politics, we can consider the case of California. Discussions of historical Latino voting patterns in California tend to follow a similar pattern (Nuño 2007; Bowler, Nicholson, and Segura 2006). According to some pundits and scholars, as recently as the 1990s, Latinos in California were considered swing voters—or, if that is too strong a phrase, they were at least not monolithically Democratic. However, in 1994, Proposition 187 was placed on the ballot. This ballot initiative, which was promoted aggressively by the California Republican Party, including Governor Pete Wilson, sought to deny state services to undocumented immigrants.

Although the initiative passed by a substantial margin, it has been argued that Latino voters in California viewed the initiative as an anti-Latino policy (Pantoja and Segura 2003), and began to view the Republican Party as hostile to Latinos. This ballot initiative, as well as subsequent restrictionist initiatives such as Proposition 209, likely benefited the California Republican Party in the short term. In the long term, however, the Republican reputation for nativism ultimately drove large numbers of California Hispanics to the Democratic Party (Segura, Falcon, and Pachon, 1997) and encouraged them to vote in greater numbers (Barreto and Woods, 2000). Because Latinos are such a large percentage of the California electorate, their lopsided support for Democrats ultimately made the Republican Party uncompetitive in state-level elections. The presumed lesson of Propositions 187 and 209 is that any short-term gains Republicans enjoy as a result of an aggressive anti-immigration position will be overruled by a corresponding long-term drop in support from Latinos.

We should be careful before accepting this narrative at face value. It not entirely clear that Hispanic voters would be substantially more Republican if the Republican Party embraced less restrictionist public policies. Although George W. Bush performed comparatively well among Latino voters in 2004, and this has been largely attributed to his liberal stance on immigration, there was not a corresponding major drop in Democratic affiliation among Latinos during the Bush years (De la Garza and Cortina 2007). It is also important to remember that John McCain's comparatively liberal record on immigration did not win him a substantial share of the Latino vote; McCain only won 31 percent of the Latino vote. Although Ronald Reagan signed an amnesty bill in 1986, this did not lead to an increase in the Republican share of the Latino vote in presidential elections; George H. W. Bush earned a smaller percentage of Latinos' votes in 1988 than Reagan earned in 1984.

It is sometimes argued that because Latinos are exceptionally religious their views on social issues make them natural Republicans. The implication of this argument is that Latinos would flock to the Republican Party if it would just change its stance on immigration. While the stereotype of Latinos as being monolithically Catholic, pious, and socially conservative may persist among many Americans, this perception is not congruent with the most recent data. Although Latinos are slightly more religious by most measures than non-Hispanic whites (Putnam and Campbell 2010), church attendance has plunged among Latinos in the last twenty years (Barna Group 2011); there has also been a decline in church attendance among blacks and non-Hispanic whites, but the decline for these groups was much less dramatic. There furthermore does not seem to be a strong relationship between Latino religious traditionalism and Latino political attitudes and behavior (Kelly and Morgan 2008). Whatever the reasons for strong Latino support for Democratic candidates, it has been consistent over time and we can plausibly expect that it will continue in upcoming elections, even if the Republican Party reverses its stance on immigration.

5.3 PAST MIGRATION BY RACE INTO TODAY'S STRONG REPUBLICAN AND STRONG DEMOCRATIC COUNTIES

Using aggregate data to test whether increased diversity leads to individual political change is difficult. It is relatively straightforward, however, to examine the migratory patterns of different groups. To get an initial understanding of how the migrations of different ethnic and racial groups fit into the story of landslide counties, a useful starting point is to simply look at the migratory patterns of different racial and ethnic categories into and out of these county types. Figure 5.1 was created using the data on net migration in the United States during the 1990s (Voss et al. 2004), and shows the mean net migration of different racial and ethnic categories in landslide Democrat and landslide Republican counties. The results strongly suggest that the geographic partisan sort is largely a result of a geographic racial sort.

On average, neither county type experienced much migration of African Americans, though Democratic landslide counties experienced a mean gain of 4,689 Hispanics and Republican counties experienced a mean gain of 670 Hispanics—this seems like a big difference, but it is important to remember the different average baseline populations of these county types. The big story is in the non-Hispanic white category. Among counties that gave John McCain a landslide victory in 2008, the mean gain of non-Hispanic whites during the 1990s was 2,097. This is more remarkable when one considers that the starting population in these counties was typically rather small when compared to landslide Democratic counties. In contrast, counties that gave Barack Obama a landslide victory in 2008 lost an average of 11,944 non-Hispanic whites to migration during the 1990s.

As was the case for the examination of mean net migration by age groups, the significance of Figure 5.1 is somewhat difficult to interpret because of

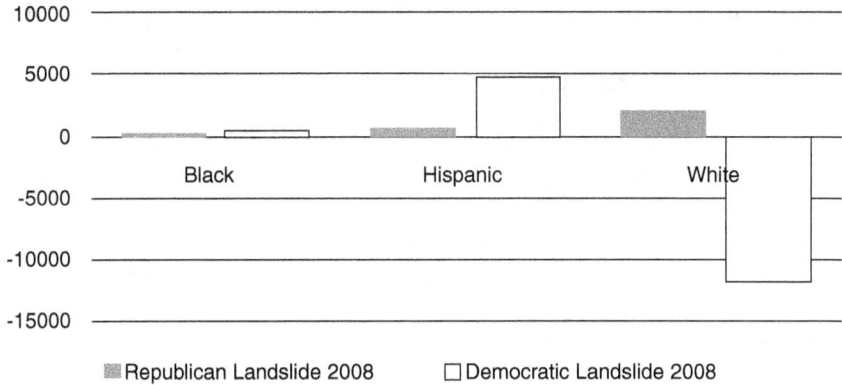

Figure 5.1   Mean Net Migration by County Type in the 1990s

the significant difference in the average population size of landslide Republican and landslide Democratic counties. Figure 5.2 provides the total net migration of these different groups in all landslide Republican and landslide Democratic counties.

Among both county types, the black population was relatively stable, neither moving into or out of landslide counties in large numbers. Similarly, both county types experienced a net gain of Hispanics, though Democratic counties experienced a greater net in-migration of this group (1,463,166 versus 933,823). Again, the big difference was among non-Hispanic whites. During the 1990s, those counties that became landslide Democratic counties lost, via migration, 3,726,624 non-Hispanic white residents, and landslide Republican counties gained 2,921,368 of them.

It is quite interesting to see that both contemporary landslide Republican and contemporary landslide Democratic counties saw an increase in both

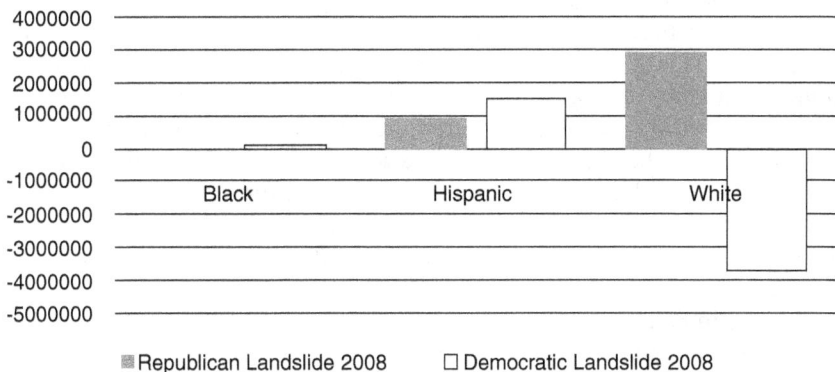

Figure 5.2   Total Net Migration by County Type in the 1990s

their black and Hispanic population due to migration during the 1990s. If white Republicans are, on average, less socially tolerant of minorities than white Democrats, and minorities prefer not to live among less tolerant whites, we might expect blacks and Hispanics to prefer Democratic communities to Republican communities. This is not what we see. In fact, when we look at black migration at the state level, we see that Republican states saw more black in-migration in the late 1990s than Democratic states. Frey (2004) estimated the numbers of African Americans in American cities and states during the last five years of the 1990s. Of those states that gave George W. Bush their electoral votes in 2000, there was a mean in-migration of 10,666.79 blacks from 1995–2000. Of those states that gave their Electoral College votes to Gore, there was, on average, an out-migration of blacks during this period—they lost an average of 15,907.09 blacks to migration during in the late 1990s. Blacks moved in especially large numbers out of New York (–165,366) and California (–63,180). While blacks may, all other things being equal, prefer to live in Democratic states, this clearly indicates that strong Democratic majorities are insufficient to keep African Americans from exiting a state; nor are strong Republican majorities a sufficient deterrent to keep blacks from moving to a state. Frey (2004) also estimated black migration in major metropolitan areas. When these data are combined with the city-level political data assembled by the Bay Area Center for Voting Research (2005), we again see that overwhelmingly Democratic cities tended to lose African Americans, but this was not the case in cities where Republicans perform comparatively well. Of the twenty largest cities in the United States, those that gave liberal presidential candidates 60 percent or more of their total votes, there was an average loss of 15,111.62 African American residents between 1995 and 2000. Of those large cities that were relatively close (the liberal majority was less than 60 percent) or where conservative presidential candidates actually won a majority of the votes, there was a mean increase of 7,774 African American residents due to migration at the end of the twentieth century.

The apparent relationship between aggregate Republican voting and black in-migration is primarily driven by the recent black migration back to the South (Hunt, Hunt, and Falk 2008). However, even within the South some of the most Democratic cities are apparently rather unattractive to African Americans. Austin, Texas, frequently tops lists of the most pleasant places to live in the United States; it is also a Democratic oasis in a strongly Republican state. However, it has failed to attract and retain large numbers of black professionals. The size of the black population in central Texas has actually declined as a percentage of the population in recent years (Copelin 2012).

We saw in Figures 5.1 and 5.2 that Hispanics were moving in large numbers to contemporary landslide Republican counties and contemporary landslide Democratic counties in large numbers during the 1990s, though they moved in slightly greater numbers to landslide Democratic counties.

The most important trend in Hispanic migration in recent years has been the dispersion of Latinos out of traditional gateway states and cities and into other regions of the country (Lichter and Johnson 2009). At present, there does not appear to be a political motivation for these migrations. Texas and California remain the states with the largest Latino populations by far, and they are, in the aggregate, on opposite ends of the partisan spectrum.

The most interesting results from Figures 5.1 and 5.2 were those for non-Hispanic whites. Although the present landslide Democratic counties have not, on average, been losing population in recent decades, they have been hemorrhaging whites, and landslide Republican counties have been gaining whites. This is not incongruent with the findings from individual data. While whites are politically heterogeneous compared to other racial and ethnic groups in the United States, whites make up the overwhelming majority of Republican voters and majorities of white voters consistently support the Republican Party. We saw in Chapter 3 that Democrats are not apparently sensitive to political context when making migratory decisions, but Republicans do seem to consider politics an important variable to consider when determining where they will live. For this reason, we should expect more white out-migration from Democratic communities and more white in-migration into Republican communities. These figures seem to confirm this. However, it is important to determine whether or not politics per se is the motivating factor for these migrations. Perhaps whites were simply leaving metropolitan areas during this time, or attempting to move away from racial and ethnic minorities who dominate inner cities.

Again, the preceding figures do not demonstrate that whites were moving for political reasons. They only show that those counties that are presently overwhelmingly Democrat lost a large number of whites in recent decades, whereas those that are presently overwhelmingly Republican experienced a major influx of whites. Were these white migrants motivated by politics? That is, did white Republicans intentionally move away from strongly Democratic communities and into strongly Republican communities, eventually turning the former into overwhelmingly Democratic communities and the latter into overwhelmingly Republican communities? One way to determine this is to look at the political context of communities at the start of the 1990s and determine if there was a relationship between county-level support for Democrats at the start of the decade and the county-level migration rates of whites throughout the rest of the decade.

Figure 5.3 shows the relationship between support for Bill Clinton in 1992 and the migration rate of non-Hispanic whites in the 1990s in large U.S. counties (more than 200,000 people). We see a meaningful negative relationship between the migration rates of whites and Democratic support. It is important to remember that the political variable here was captured near the start of the decade, meaning that counties that were already heavily Democratic tended to lose white residents. This is congruent with earlier findings regarding community satisfaction and local politics for Republicans.

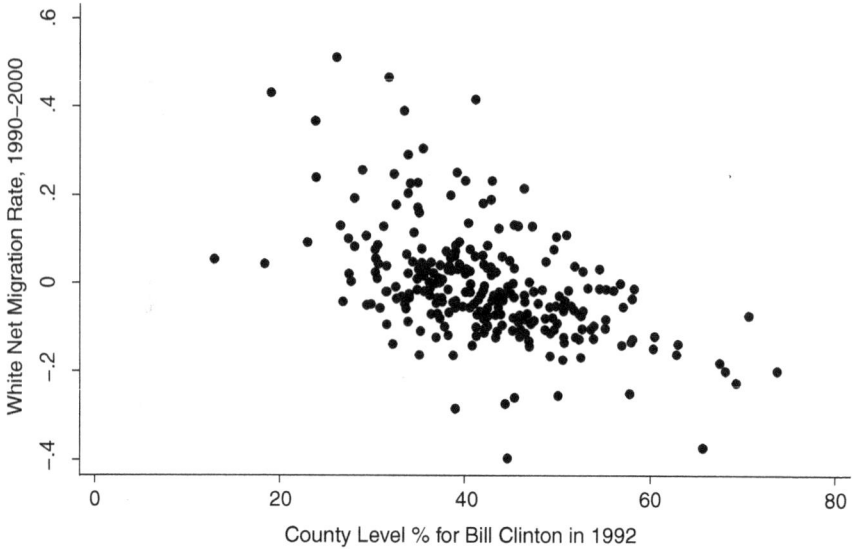

Figure 5.3   White Migration Rate by Support for Clinton in Large Counties in the 1990s

We should be careful before inferring too much from this figure, as other variables are important to consider. One of the recent important demographic trends in the United States has been the migration of Americans, particularly older Americans, into the so-called Sun Belt—states in the South and Southwest that have experienced a huge amount of in-migration from elsewhere in the country (Frey 2005). These states are considered pleasant places to live, but most of them are also known for being more Republican than the rest of the country. There may not be any direct relationship between white migration and politics at all; instead, whites may just be abandoning so-called Rust Belt cities in the North, which are traditionally Democratic, in favor of traditionally Republican cities such as Phoenix and Dallas. It is therefore important to note that the relationship between white migration rates in populous counties and support for Clinton in those counties was consistent throughout the different regions of the United States. Across the entire nation, the correlation between support for Clinton in counties with more than 200,000 persons and white migration rates was –0.45. In those states considered part of the Sun Belt, the correlation was –0.43. In all states not in this region, the correlation was –0.50. Indeed, in all regions of the country, there was a negative and statistically significant correlation between support for Clinton in 1992 and white migration rates in the 1990s. It is worth noting that there was also a negative correlation between the percentage of the electorate supporting Bill Clinton and the migration rate of blacks and Latinos in large counties. However, this relationship was *much* weaker—for blacks the Pearson's R was –0.27 and for Latinos it was –0.22.

There might nonetheless be some other explanation for these findings. To further demonstrate a relationship between white migration and politics, I created a model for the migration rate of whites in the three hundred largest counties in the United States. The dependent variable was the net migration rate of non-Hispanic whites at the county level during the 1990s.[1] The percentage of the county vote won by Democratic candidate Bill Clinton in 1992 was the key independent variable in this model.

As we saw from the descriptive statistics in the opening chapter of this book, a large number of variables are correlated with aggregate vote choice at the county level, and they must be controlled for in order to be confident that any relationship between net migration rates and vote choice is not spurious. Because there is such an extensive literature on "white flight"—the movement of whites away from communities with a large minority population—it was especially important to control for the size of the African American and Hispanic populations. Home values and median incomes were once again included in this model, as were the poverty rate and unemployment rate in 1990. This model also controlled for economic variables such as the percentage of the population employed in manufacturing, the percentage employed in public administration, and the percentage employed in agriculture. To ensure that significant results were not exclusively due to a flight of white Americans from large cities during these years, the model also included the log of the total county population in 1990.

Results for this analysis can be found in Table 5.1. In these largest counties, we see a relationship between migration rates of non-Hispanic whites during the 1990s and support for Clinton in 1992. Those large counties where Bill Clinton's support was weakest saw higher levels of white in-migration. Again, while ecological inference remains an important concern, this is congruent with the individual-level findings. If white Democrats, who are smaller in number than white Republicans, do not consider politics when moving, but the migrations of white Republicans are motivated by politics, then we should see more whites moving into Republican communities than into Democratic communities.

Interpreting coefficients for migration rates is somewhat challenging, which is why it is important to remember what this variable actually measures. The net migration rate is calculated as the total net migration of that cohort divided by the expected population not attributable to migration. Thus making sense of the total numbers in question requires knowledge of the starting population. Model 1 shows that a 1-percent increase in the support that a county provided Clinton in 1992 was associated with a 0.002 decrease in the migration rate of non-Hispanic whites. To put that in real numbers, if a county's expected population for that cohort was 500,000 people, the model predicts that each percentage point increase in support for Clinton resulted in an additional 400 non-Hispanic white out-migrants, and

Table 5.1 Determinants of White Migration Rate in the Three Hundred Largest Counties in the United States during the 1990s

	Model 1	Std. Err.	2 Std. Dev. Δ
% Democratic, 1992	−0.002	(0.00)*	−0.048
Median Income (Divided by $10,000)	0.015	(0.02)	0.028
Median Home Value (Divided by $10,000)	−0.001	(0.00)	−0.023
Metropolitan County	−0.130	(0.13)	−0.021
Unemployment Rate	0.005	(0.01)	0.022
% Black	−0.004	(0.00)*	−0.119
% Hispanic	−0.002	(0.00)*	−0.061
% BA	0.000	(0.00)	−0.007
% Employed in Manufacturing	−0.005	(0.00)*	−0.070
% Employed in Public Administration	−0.004	(0.00)	−0.025
% Employed in Agriculture	−0.004	(0.00)	−0.020
Crime Rate	0.000	(0.00)	−0.022
Travel Time to Work	0.001	(0.00)	0.008
Sun Belt	0.080	(0.02)*	
Constant	0.343	(0.17)*	
Observations	300		
Adjusted R-Squared	0.39		

* $p < 0.05$

a two-standard deviation increase in support for Bill Clinton was associated with a loss of 24,000 whites.

The next important question to ask is whether or not these migrations lead to a subsequent change in voting patterns in these communities that draw large numbers of whites. During the 1990s, the median net migration rate of non-Hispanic whites was 0.014. The median change in support for Democratic presidential candidates from 1992 to 2000 (calculated as support for Gore in 2000 minus support for Clinton in 1992) was −0.05, though that number is not weighted by county population size. If we only look at those three hundred largest counties, the median change in support was a positive 6.98—the difference between those two numbers indicates that densely populated counties became more Democratic over the 1990s and sparsely populated counties became more Republican. Among all counties where the net migration rates of whites was less than the median value for all counties, the median change in support for Democrats was 0.14. That is, there was virtually no change, though Democrats did see a slight improvement. Of those counties with a net migration rate of whites higher than the median value, the support for Democrats dropped; in these counties, the median drop was 1.29 percentage points.

Drawing strong inferences from this is challenging because of the large number of sparsely populated counties. For this reason, it will be useful to again just look at the largest counties in the United States. In the three hundred largest counties, the migration rate of whites during the 1990s was −0.017; that is, more whites moved out than moved in. However, those counties that lost more whites to migration became more Democratic. Of those largest counties with white migration rates lower than the median for those counties, Democrats increased their share of the vote between the two elections by 8.05 percentage points.

These findings suggest that whites tended to move away from counties where Democrats performed well. As a result of these migrations, the Democratic Party's share of the vote increased further. It appears that white migration patterns are exacerbating the trend toward geographic sorting, and there is increasing evidence that at least some of these migrations are politically motivated. However, blacks and Latinos have different migration patterns, and they apparently exhibit political homophily when determining where they will live.

Hispanic migration patterns seem to be largely driven by economic considerations. Hispanics, particularly low-income immigrants, are probably not moving to places like the rural Midwest because they like Midwestern politics. Rather, they are apparently drawn to plentiful jobs in industries such a meatpacking (Flores et al. 2011). Similarly, blacks are not leaving New York for Georgia because they would prefer Saxby Chambliss to Charles Schumer. However, although probably not politically motivated, these migrations have political consequences. Although Georgia gave its electoral votes to Republican candidates in 2008 and 2012, the Republican victory in that state would surely have been much more decisive had it not seen its African American population grow by 579,335 persons between 2000 and 2010 and its Latino population grow by 418,462 persons. The large number of black and Latino migrants into North Carolina was a key contributor to Obama's victory in that state in 2008, though that state also experienced an in-flux of white Northern Democrats in recent years (Hood and McKee 2010).

The changing partisan complexion of the American Southwest is also due to the migratory patterns of Latino migrants, both from abroad and within the United States. Although John McCain won a strong majority among non-Hispanic white voters in New Mexico (56 percent), Barack Obama carried the state with relative ease because of his overwhelming support from that state's large Latino population (Obama won 69 percent of the Latino vote) (Lopez 2008). If only non-Hispanic whites had voted in Arizona in 2008, John McCain would have won his home state by a lopsided 59 percent. However, the quickly growing Latino population gave Barack Obama

56 percent of its votes in 2008, causing the state to be much more competitive. Colorado's transition from strong Republican state, to swing state, to what is apparently now a strong Democratic state, can best be explained by its growing Latino population and white Democratic migrants from states such as California.

Although we do not see evidence that the two largest minority groups in the United States (African Americans and Latinos) are moving for political reasons, that may change. We might particularly expect this in the case of Latinos. While they may not do so for *partisan* reasons, the political climate of a state may influence policies—particularly immigration policies—that attract or repel Latino migrants. Arizona is a prime example of this. In 2010, Governor Jan Brewer signed into law the Support Our Law Enforcement and Safe Neighborhoods Act (Arizona SB 1070). At the time this was one of the strictest state laws against illegal immigration in the country. This law required all immigrants to carry registration documents demonstrating that they were in the country legally. It furthermore required police to determine an individual's immigration status during any detention or arrest. Other states, such as Alabama, Georgia, and South Carolina, subsequently passed similar laws. Many were concerned that laws of this kind amounted to racial profiling and there were complaints that the law would violate the civil rights of both immigrants and native-born Latinos. Before SB 1070 took effect, many of its most controversial provisions were struck down by the U.S. Supreme Court.

This relates to the issue of migration because there is some evidence that this law did influence the migration patterns of Latinos. According to Russell Pierce (2012), the author of SB 1070, the undocumented immigrant population in Arizona declined by 23 percent following the passage of the bill, despite the fact that judges struck down many of the law's provisions.

Not all states that attempt to deal with immigration policy themselves pass restrictionist policies, however. In 2012, Maryland passed a law providing college tuition reductions for undocumented immigrants in the state. In that same year, California passed a bill allowing some undocumented immigrants to obtain drivers' licenses. If Latinos, particularly foreign-born Latinos, are more likely to migrate to states with liberal immigration policies and eschew states with restrictionist immigration policies, and if state-level immigration policies are correlated with the strength of the Republican Party within a state, we may see a stronger correlation between state-level politics and Latino migration in the future.

5.4 CONCLUSION

In recent decades, we have witnessed an exodus of non-Hispanic whites out of the most Democratic communities in the United States. As a result of their migrations, the communities they left behind became, on average, even more strongly Democratic. Although aggregate data cannot definitively demonstrate that these white migrants who left Democratic communities were themselves Republicans, we can plausibly hypothesize that they were given the evidence from individual-level data indicating that Republicans prefer to live among the politically like-minded.

If the entire electorate was non-Hispanic white, or if minorities were equally likely to exhibit political homophily when making migratory decisions, we might expect even higher levels of geographic partisan sorting in the United States than we see today. However, at present there is no evidence indicating that African Americans and Latinos move for political reasons. We also have little reason to believe that white Democrats seriously consider politics when moving.

6 Income and Occupation as a Source of Political Diversity and Homogeneity

6.1 INTRODUCTION

This chapter examines the relationship between economics and the geographic partisan sort, considering whether the clustering of Americans by class and occupation is a major cause of the clustering by party identification. There is evidence of economic clustering, especially among the wealthiest Americans. The number of households in the one hundred wealthiest zip codes in the United States grew by 7.4 percent between 2000 and 2011 (Wong 2011), suggesting that the wealthy are relocating to live among people of similar income levels. If these wealthy Americans share a common party affiliation, then their increasing propensity to move to the same communities is surely playing a role in the rise of uncompetitive counties.

On the other hand, it may be less useful to view economics and occupations as a *cause* of geographic partisan sorting than as a *constraint* on the phenomenon. That is, if all possible jobs were available in all possible locations, then the sorting phenomenon might be *much* more pronounced than it already is. In such a world, finding a community with like-minded neighbors can be a paramount concern. In reality, earning a living surely takes precedence over most other considerations. While some individuals may believe the residents of Casper, Wyoming, or Burlington, Vermont are, on average, the most similar to themselves culturally, ethnically, religiously, and politically, they will likely not move to Casper or Burlington unless they have job offers in those communities, or at least the plausible expectation of gainful employment. Especially in times of economic distress, people may move in large numbers to economically strong communities they might otherwise never consider. To take a recent example, there is at present a population surge in North Dakota, which for years was a state suffering some of the nation's worst rates of out-migration. It was not a change in the political or demographic landscape that served as a catalyst for this new growth. An oil boom in the western part of the state, combined with a well-managed economy, made North Dakota one of the few states to avoid the high unemployment rates and crippling budget deficits plaguing the rest of the nation in recent years. While many people may be wary of the chilly winters in

Bismarck, and completely ignorant of the culture and politics of that community, many are clearly happy to move there in order to find work.

In order to infer that geographic polarization is being driven by the different migratory patterns of Americans in different occupations, two things must be demonstrated: (1) where people live is at least partially determined by what they do for a living; and (2) what people do for a living can help predict how they vote. Previous literature can help answer this question. Before moving onto a discussion of occupation, migration, and vote choice, however, it may be useful to begin with a subject that has long interested political scientists: the relationship between income and party identification.

6.2 INCOME AND VOTE CHOICE

The precise relationship between income, class, and vote choice has long been a Gordian knot in political science. The challenge arises from the fact that the individual data does not agree with the aggregate data. Many of the nation's poorest states, such as Mississippi and Kansas, regularly provide Republican candidates with overwhelming victories. In fact, with the exception of North Carolina, John McCain beat Obama in all of the ten poorest states.[1] In 2012, Mitt Romney won all of the ten poorest states in the nation. On the other hand, rich states such as Connecticut and New Hampshire voted for Obama by significant margins in both elections. Of the top ten wealthiest states, only Alaska and Utah gave their electoral votes to McCain.

Using the knowledge that wealthier states tend to vote Democratic in the aggregate, we could subsequently infer that the Democrats are the party of the rich, and Republicans the party of the poor. This is precisely the argument made by liberal columnist Thomas Frank (2004), who argued that Republicans convince poor rural voters to vote against their economic interests by appealing to social issues such as abortion and gay marriage. The typical critique from the conservative pundits is that the Democratic Party has become the party of rich, "Limousine Liberals." On the other hand, data from individual surveys tell a different story.

When we look at the relationship between household income and personal vote choice, we see that wealthier individuals are more likely to vote Republican (Bartels 2008; McCarty, Poole, and Rosenthal 2006). Gelman et al. (2008) argued that the poor in the United States are actually rather supportive of the Democratic Party across the nation. The real difference is seen in the behavior of the rich in different states. In rich states, wealthy voters are much less Republican than wealthy voters in comparatively poorer states. They argue that this is because rich voters in wealthy states are considerably more liberal on social issues than rich voters in poor states, and are therefore more prone to vote against their presumed economic interests because they disagree with Republican social policies—though they note that, even in the wealthiest states, the rich are more likely to be Republican than the poor.

The descriptive statistics from Chapter 1 demonstrated that the aggregate characteristics of U.S. counties are similar to those of the states. Among landslide Democratic counties, the mean county median household income in 2008 was $45,817, which is slightly higher than the national county median income ($44,006), which was higher than the mean county median income of landslide Republican counties ($42,239). The interesting thing to note, however, is that these differences are relatively small, and the Pearson's R correlation coefficient between household income and county type was extraordinarily small. These basic descriptive statistics furthermore mask the true relationship between income and aggregate partisanship—Table 4.1 in Chapter 4 demonstrated that, controlling for all other relevant variables, increases in county median household incomes were associated, on average, with greater support for Bush in 2000 at the county level.

Perhaps the mean is not the only descriptive variable of interest. Learning about how these variables are distributed may also provide insights into the nature of the relationship between aggregate income and county type. Figure 6.1 provides a Kernel density plot of county median incomes for both landslide Republican and landslide Democratic counties. For Republican landslide counties, the median income is distributed approximately normally, with a mean near the overall national mean. The distribution of Democratic counties is decidedly different. The distribution of median incomes in landslide Democratic counties has two peaks, one considerably lower than the national median income, and another considerably higher, with a substantial dip right in the center. Thus we can safely infer that landslide Democratic

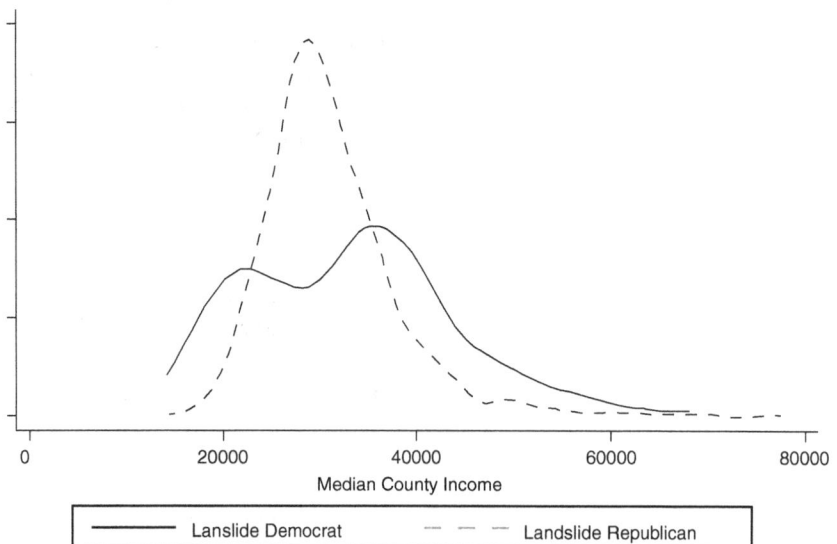

Figure 6.1   Distribution of County Median Incomes by County Type

counties tend to be either extraordinarily rich or extraordinarily poor in the aggregate. Again noting issues of ecological inference, this grants some plausibility to conservative columnist Sam Francis's (1997) argument that the Democratic Party is a coalition of the wealthy and the destitute, but not of the middle class, and suggests that David Callahan's (2010) argument that the rich are moving steadily to the political left is not off base. It also further underscores the degree to which landslide Democratic counties are more heterogeneous in terms of their average social class than are Republican counties.

Interestingly, recent remarks by political analysts suggest that the Democratic Party is increasingly willing to explicitly embrace its reputation as the party of the upper class, particularly successful professionals, as well as the party of poorer ethnic and racial minorities, and increasingly comfortable with the exodus of working- and middle-class non-Hispanic whites from the Democratic coalition. Writing in the *New York Times*, political journalist Thomas B. Edsall (2011) made the following remark about the Democratic Party the year prior to the 2012 presidential election:

> All pretense of trying to win a majority of the white working class has been effectively jettisoned in favor of cementing a center-left coalition made up, on the one hand, of voters who have gotten ahead on the basis of educational attainment—professors, artists, designers, editors, human resources managers, lawyers, librarians, social workers, teachers and therapists—and a second, substantial constituency of lower-income voters who are disproportionately African-American and Hispanic.

In spite of Edsall's comments about the Democratic Party's willingness to abandon the white working class, 2012 did not suggest that the white working class had abandoned the Democrats. Outside of the South, working-class whites were relatively supportive of Obama (Weigel 2012). Obama also performed relatively well among middle-class voters, though how well depends on how one defines middle class (Noah 2012).

That being said, the aggregate data do suggest that Democrats perform best in the wealthiest communities and the poorest communities, but the most solidly Republican communities tend to be in the middle. Whether or not such a coalition is sustainable for the Democratic Party given the potential diverging economic interests of these community types remains to be seen. Nor is it clear whether such a conglomeration of voters can provide the Democrats a long-term minimum-winning coalition. However, if working- and middle-class whites ultimately become a solid Republican voting bloc, then the migrations of such people will shape the electoral landscapes of the communities they enter and exit.

At this point, the usefulness of income alone as a predictor of vote choice at either the individual or the aggregate level is probably exhausted. Far more useful and important for the purposes of this study is the question of how people make their money. Do certain industries tend to cluster together geographically? Do people move based on their industries? And is there a strong relationship between occupation type and partisan identification?

6.3 DO AMERICAN INDUSTRIES CLUSTER GEOGRAPHICALLY?

In many cases, the relationship between occupation and geographic location is obvious. Some occupational clustering is determined by geography. You will only drill for oil if you can reasonably expect to find some. A farmer who wishes to remain a farmer will not move to Manhattan. A software engineer will almost certainly not move to rural Kentucky or the Aleutian Islands. On the other hand, many occupations can be performed in any number of locations. A lawyer can move to virtually any city and continue to be a lawyer. A waiter can live anywhere there are restaurants.

The notion of economic clustering is not new, Alfred Marshall discussed the subject in 1890, and it has many possible definitions (Martin and Sunley 2003), but one of the most useful definitions was offered by Michael Porter (1998): "Clusters are geographic concentrations of interconnected companies and institutions in a particular field. Clusters encompass an array of linked industries and other entities important to competition" (78).

Beyond those industries that tend to cluster geographically because of natural resource constraints, we also know that industries heavily reliant on innovative technology tend to cluster together (Feldman 1999; Feser and Sweeney 2000). Firms within these clusters tend to be more competitive. Much of this has been attributed to "knowledge spillovers" between firms; workers, even if they are in different firms, are nonetheless working on similar things and benefit from each other's research (Griliches 1992). It has also been suggested that clustering leads to physical spillovers—the presence of a firm in one area will lower transportation costs to other firms in the area (Krugman 1991). The explosive growth of the high tech industry in Silicon Valley and biotechnology in the Boston area are two of the best-known examples of this.

Industries that rely on the most advanced technologies are not the only industries that tend to cluster together. The well-known case of automobile manufacturing in Detroit is one of the most famous examples of an industry clustering within a geographic area. There is considerable variation between industries with regard to the degree of geographic concentration, however; some industries exhibit high levels of coagglomeration and others exhibit virtually no coagglomeration (Ellison and Glaeser 1997).

If different professions such as higher education, advertising, and technology tend to be clustered together, we should be able to find some evidence for this in the aggregate data. To better understand whether there are certain types of occupations that tend to cluster in counties, and to reduce the number of potential occupation variables from several dozen down to a more manageable number, I calculated the percent of each county's workforce employed in different occupations in 2005 using the 2000–2007 ICPSR County Characteristics file, which was compiled using census data.[2] This file provided both the total number of employed persons in a county, as well as the total number of persons employed in each profession type. By dividing the latter by the former it was straightforward to determine the percentage of each county employed in specific fields of work. These percentages were then used to conduct a factor analysis, which created four factors that had both an eigenvalue greater than one and multiple variables with a factor loading greater than 0.5.[3] Based on this factor analysis, scales were created by combining different occupation types, attempting to create scales with the highest scale reliability coefficient. Table 6.1 provides these scales, their scale reliability, as well as the variables used in their creation.

The first thing worth noting is that there is a scale with a reasonably high reliability coefficient that tracks very closely with the occupational groups identified by Judis and Teixeira (2002) as "professionals," who tend to vote disproportionately for Democrats—though managers, also included in that scale, were not among the groups listed by Judis and Teixeira as being strong Democrats, on average.[4] This group will be discussed in greater detail in the pages ahead. Another interesting find is that, although Florida (2002) listed artists as being in the same class as knowledge workers, this analysis

Table 6.1   Occupation Scales

S1: Professionals	S2: Arts and Accommodations
Information	Real Estate, Rental, and Leasing
Finance and Administration	Arts, Entertainment, and Recreation
Management	Accommodation and Food Services
Professional and Technical Services	(reliability = 0.68)
Administrative and Waste Services	
Education	
Health Care	
(reliability = 0.65)	
S3: Construction, Retail, and Other Services	**S4: Federal Employees**
Construction	Federal Employee, Civilian
Retail Trade	Federal Employee, Military
Other Services, Except Public Administration	(reliability = 0.41)
(reliability = 0.61)	

All reliabilities are Cronbach's Alpha

does not show that the two groups load on the same scale. Other than the professional scale, the other scales are less obviously political—although artists and real-estate agents apparently work in proximity to each other, it is not immediately obvious that they will vote together. Similarly, civilian and military government employees may live in the same county, but probably do not exhibit comparable voting patterns.

Although different industries exhibit different degrees of geographic clustering, an individual's location has a strong influence on the probability of working in a specific industry. This leads to an additional question: do people move based on their line of work?

6.4 RESIDENTIAL MOBILITY AND OCCUPATION TYPE

Different occupations are associated with different probabilities of moving, as well as the distance of the move. Larry Long (1973) found that different occupation types were associated with different migratory patterns. Blue-collar workers were more likely to make short-distance moves, but white-collar workers and professional or technical workers were more likely to make long-distance moves. However, education level was actually a better predictor of migratory behavior than occupation type. Goss (1985) argued that a powerful determinant of a worker's future geographic mobility was her ratio of general to specific skills—those with many general skills are more likely to move for employment reasons.

Again, it is obvious that many people's migratory decisions were at least partially motivated by their type of work, at least if they prefer to work in certain industries. All the software engineers in Silicon Valley did not grow up there. Many migrated to the region across a great distance because it was the best place for them to find employment in their field. The aerospace engineers working at Boeing were not drawn exclusively from Everett, Washington. That being said, it is less plausible to imagine an individual moving a great distance to clean equipment and maintain backroom storage at the Pepsi Bottling Venture in Nampa, Idaho. Many people will take the jobs available in their local area. Even people with highly specialized skills may have developed those skills specifically because they are in demand within their local area, rather than because they have a passion for a particular line of work.

High levels of specialization are associated with higher migration rates. The finding that workers with highly specialized skills will move to regions where those skills are in demand is not new (Sjaastad 1962), and long-distance migrants tend to be more skilled than short-distance migrants (Kleiner 1982; Hunt 2004). Zimmer (1973) found that moving was associated with an upward occupational change. However, even among the highly skilled and highly specialized, there are important variations between industries.

Those professions that require state occupational licensing, such as attorneys who will have to retake the bar exam if they cross state boundaries, are less likely to move great distances (Pashigian 1977). Even within industries, workers differ in their likelihood of migration according to their demographic characteristics; unmarried information-intensive workers are more likely than married workers to move from one metropolitan area to another, and women in these industries are less likely to move than men (Bagchi-Sen 2003).

The Pew Mobility Survey asked respondents to name their major and minor reasons for their most recent move; 45.16 percent named "job or business opportunities" as a major reason and an additional 17.1 percent named it as a minor reason. So although people now move for a wide variety of reasons, work remains an important determinant of the migratory patterns of a majority of Americans. Unfortunately, this survey did not ask respondents to name their type of employment, so it is of limited use for considering this question.

However, the 2008 National Annenberg Election Study (NAES) did ask respondents what they do for a living. It also asks how long it has been since their last move. These data can therefore be used to determine if some occupations are associated with a greater probability of migration. Respondents were given a number of occupations to choose from when identifying themselves: professional workers (e.g., lawyer, doctor, scientist, teacher, engineer, registered nurse, accountant, programmer, musician), skilled tradespersons (e.g., printer, baker, tailor, electrician, machinist, linesperson, plumber, carpenter, mechanic), clerical or office workers (e.g., typist, secretary, postal clerk, telephone operator, computer operator, bank clerk), service workers (e.g., police officer, fire fighter, waiter or waitress, maid, nurse's aide, attendant, hairstylist), laborers (e.g., plumber's helper, construction worker, longshoreperson, garbage collector, other physical work), managers (e.g., store manager, sales manager, office manager), semi-skilled workers (e.g., machine operator, assembly line worker, truck driver, taxi driver, bus driver), salesperson, business owner, and other.

Overall, 34.57 percent of all respondents said they moved within the last five years. However, respondents employed in different fields had different migration rates. Laborers were the most mobile group, as 43.08 percent of all laborers moved within the previous five years, followed by service workers (42.47). The occupations with the least mobile members were business owners (34.06 percent) and office workers (36.97 percent). Unfortunately, this survey did not ask respondents for the reason for their most recent move, so we cannot know with any certainty whether or not people in different industries are more likely to move for work-related reasons. However, it is important to note that there was not a tremendous amount of variation between the different occupation types and the propensity to change addresses over a five-year period.

Given that the economics literature demonstrates that many industries tend to cluster together, and a large portion of American workers move for occupational reasons (though the NAES survey does not indicate that there is a strong relationship between occupation type and mobility), it is important to determine whether or not there is a relationship between occupation type and vote choice.

6.5 OCCUPATION TYPE AND VOTE CHOICE

On the subject of occupation type and vote choice, there is already useful literature to guide us. Even after controlling for income, there is apparently a relationship between how a person makes a living and how she votes. This is not a new finding (MacRae 1955). Unskilled workers are more likely to be Democratic than skilled workers, though this trend declined during the 1980s (Brooks and Manza 1997). Even controlling for income, belonging to a union increases the likelihood of Democratic voting, though union membership has been on the decline (Sousa 1993).

Some specific industries are associated with vote choice for one party or the other. Government employees vote in greater numbers than those employed in the private sector (Bennett and Orzechowski 1983; Corey and Garand 2002) and are more likely to support Democratic candidates (Garand, Parkhurst, and Seoud 1991). One group that is of particular interest, however, is a category of workers that tends to support Democratic candidates despite relatively high levels of affluence.

In *The Emerging Democratic Majority,* Judis and Teixeira (2002) argued that there are two main social groups that regularly provide predominant support for Democrats: minorities (whom we have already discussed) and "professionals" whose ranks include "architects, engineers, scientists, computer analysts, lawyers, physicians, registered nurses, teachers, social workers, therapists, designers, interior decorators, graphic artists, and actors" (29). According to Judis and Teixeira, this group represented approximately 21 percent of all voters in the 2000 election and was continuing to rise. This group votes heavily for Democratic candidates and largely corresponds to Florida's "Creative Class" (2002), which includes "people in science and engineering, architecture and design, arts, music, and entertainment, whose economic function is to create new ideas, new technology and/or creative content" (8). While Florida discussed the partisan preferences of this class only briefly, he noted that social tolerance was one of their hallmarks. This group also roughly corresponds to the class once referred to as "yuppies" ("Young Urban Professionals") (Hammond 1986) or the "New Class" (Dekker and Ester 1990; Brint 1984), and has long been known to vote more frequently for Democratic candidates than their socioeconomic status would suggest.

Callahan (2010) speculated on why members of the group he dubbed the "new-economy rich" tend to vote for Democrats and support liberal public policies in spite of their relative affluence:

> Many of the new-economy rich are trending Democrat, while the old-economy rich are more likely to be Republican. There are a number of reasons for this.
>
> For starters, these two groups have different views of wealth creation. If you work in the knowledge economy, you may tend to see wealth creation as a collective enterprise, not as stemming from Ayn Randian individual heroics. The success of your business will depend on your hiring highly educated employees, and you'll rely on public schools and universities to turn out such people. If you own a factory or chain store, you can get by with high school grads. Not so if you're running a litigation firm or software company.
>
> Likewise, you'll be attuned to how government investments in scientific research can play a key role in propelling your industry. If you own one of Austin's many biotech firms, you'll applaud every time that the National Institutes of Health ups its research budget and every time a state promises to put money into stem cell research, because some of the breakthroughs from this work may eventually lead to new products and profits at your firm. At a broader level, you will worry about the physical and technological infrastructure that allows goods and services to move around. You will understand the centrality of capital markets in ensuring that you have the money to invest in growth. You will sense the importance of a stable global order in which peace prevails, talented immigrants can move across borders, and open trade is the norm. (22)

While there is certainly variation in regard to the kinds of employment people tend to have in different counties, that does not necessarily mean that different types of occupations tend to cluster together in counties in a systematic way throughout the nation. Although lawyers, teachers, and artists may tend to vote for Democrats, that fact is of greater significance to the question of geographic sorting if these different groups tend to live in the same communities. Judis and Teixeira (2002) suggest that they tend to cluster together in communities they call "ideopolises," which they describe as follows:

> Some of these metro areas specialize in producing . . . soft technology—entertainment, media, fashion, design, and advertising—and in providing databases, legal counsel, and other business services. New York and Los Angeles are both premier postindustrial metropolises that specialize in soft technology. Most of these postindustrial metropolises also include a major university or several major universities, which funnel ideas and, more important, people into the hard or soft technology industries.

Boston's Route 128 feeds off Harvard and MIT. Silicon Valley is closely linked to Stanford and the University of California at Berkeley. Dane County's biomedical research is tied to the University of Wisconsin at Madison. And all of them have a flourishing service sector, including computer learning centers, ethnic and vegetarian restaurants, multi-media shopping malls, children's museums, bookstore-coffee shops, and health clubs. (72–73)

If different professions really do exhibit dramatically different voting patterns, and professionals are a key component of the Democratic Party's electoral coalition, some evidence of this should be apparent in survey data. As noted previously, the NAES provides the occupation of its working respondents, as well as their party identification. Once again, those who leaned toward one party or the other were classified as partisans: 48.18 percent of NAES respondents in 2008 identified as Democrats or leaned toward the Democratic Party; 40.14 percent of respondents identified as Republican. The next question is whether or not occupation type was a meaningful predictor of party identification.

There does seem to be significant variation between occupation types and the probability of identifying as a Democrat, but in some cases the difference is not as great as the literature might imply. Among those identified as professional workers, 50.36 percent identified as Democrats and 39.84 identified as Republicans—a gap of 10.52 percentage points. This is substantial, but insufficient to demonstrate that professionals are overwhelmingly Democratic. There is a larger gap within clerical workers—51.1 percent identify as Democrats and 38.85 identify as Republican—and within service workers—49.49 percent of these workers identify as Democrats and 38.02 identify as Republicans. Managers are about evenly split. The only groups that are were far more Republican than Democrat in 2008 were salespersons (49.18 identified as Republican or leaned Republican) and business owners (51.02 identified as Republican or leaned Republican).

It is worth noting that there were some changes in the propensity for people in different occupations to identify as Republican or Democrat in 2004 and 2008. When examining the 2004 NAES, there was only a 5 percentage point gap between the parties among professionals, suggesting that this group became more Democratic, on average, over the course of this four-year period. The gap also grew within the clerical group. The gap shrunk, however, for business owners and salespersons. This is not surprising as virtually all groups became, on average, more Democratic between 2004 and 2008.

None of this can tell us definitively that occupation per se predicts party identification. What you do is obviously correlated with how much money you make and how educated you are. For this reason, a more sophisticated statistical analysis is needed in order to control for other variables. I created a logit model in which identification with the Democratic Party was the dependent variable. Occupations were broken into nine dummy variables based on the categories provided by NAES. Managers were excluded as the base category, because this was the most evenly split group.

Control variables included race, ethnicity, gender, education, marital status, income, religious commitment (coded as 1 for those respondents who attended religious services at least once a week), and age. In Model 1, which is in Table 6.2, we see that, even controlling for all other variables,

Table 6.2   Occupation Type and Democratic Identification

	Model 1	Std. Error	Odds Ratio	Std. Error
Professional	0.30	(0.10)*	1.35	(0.14)
Skilled Trade	0.03	(0.11)	1.03	(0.11)
Clerical	0.13	(0.11)	1.14	(0.12)
Service	0.03	(0.11)	1.03	(0.11)
Labor	0.04	(0.11)	1.04	(0.12)
Manager	0.00	(0.11)	1.00	(0.11)
Semi-Skilled	0.10	(0.12)	1.11	(0.13)
Sales	−0.14	(0.11)	0.87	(0.10)
Business	−0.17	(0.12)	0.84	(0.10)
Black	2.05	(0.06)*	7.75	(0.44)
Hispanic	0.70	(0.05)*	2.01	(0.09)
Frequently Attend Religious Services	−0.81	(0.03)*	0.44	(0.01)
Female	0.50	(0.03)*	1.65	(0.04)
Married	−0.40	(0.03)*	0.67	(0.02)
BA	−0.08	(0.03)*	0.92	(0.02)
Income Quartile 2	−0.05	(0.04)	0.95	(0.04)
Income Quartile 3	−0.12	(0.04)*	0.88	(0.04)
Income Quartile 4	−0.23	(0.05)*	0.80	(0.04)
Income Unknown	−0.40	(0.05)*	0.67	(0.03)
Age 30–44	0.06	(0.05)	1.06	(0.05)
Age 45–60	0.18	(0.04)*	1.19	(0.05)
Age 61 +	0.13	(0.05)	1.14	(0.06)
Constant	−0.07	(0.11)		
Observations	32657			
−2 X Log Likelihood	41191.44			

*$p < 0.05$

there are differences based in occupation type. Specifically, we see that, compared to managers, those in professional occupations were 1.35 times as likely to identify as Democrats. No other profession was a statistically significant predictor of Democratic affiliation after controlling for all other variables. This seems to confirm the previously established finding that professionals, for whatever reason, are an important element of the Democratic coalition.

It is worth considering whether being in a professional occupation nudges people into the Democratic Party, or whether people with different political attributes are drawn to different fields. This is difficult to prove either way, but one way to consider this question is to look at the political identities and academic majors of college students. Do students in different majors have, on average, different political beliefs? Previous literature suggests that they do. Porter and Umbach (2006) found that liberal students were less likely to choose science majors.

The student survey conducted at the University of Houston may provide some answers to this question. In this survey students were asked their college major or, if they had yet to declare a major, what they intended to be their college major. Between types of majors there was some political variation. The majors could be broken into three general categories: liberal arts (including degrees such as education, art, history, sociology, etc.), science, technology, and engineering (biology, electrical engineering, computer science, etc.), and business (business degrees, finance, hotel management, accounting, etc.). Among those earning a degree in one of the liberal arts, 58.05 percent identified as Democrats or leaned toward the Democratic Party; 55.07 percent of those earning a degree in science, technology, or engineering identified were so classified, as were 51.28 percent of all business majors. These differences are not particularly substantial, but they do suggest that the people with degrees more closely associated with Florida's Creative Class (artists and engineers) are also more likely to be Democrats than those with business-oriented degrees.

It is possible that these differences between major types are again really the result of racial differences—perhaps racial minorities are more drawn to certain majors, and this is what accounts for the apparent political difference. However, we see similar patterns when the sample is restricted exclusively to non-Hispanic whites, though in all major categories the percentage of Democrats was lower when there was such a restriction: 42 percent of whites earning a liberal arts degree identified as Democrats, compared to 37 percent of those earning a business degree.

This indicates that at least some of the political difference between different occupation types may be due to self-selection by different partisan groups. Some fields that require a college degree tend to draw Republicans, and others tend to draw Democrats. However, it is important to again note that the difference is relatively small.

6.6 OCCUPATION TYPES AND AGGREGATE VOTE CHOICE: EVIDENCE FROM U.S. COUNTIES

If different occupations tend to cluster in certain communities, people tend to move to communities where they can perform their occupations, and people within different occupations tend to have different party identifications, there should be a discernible relationship in the aggregate data between the types of work performed and support for candidates of a particular party in presidential voting. To examine this issue, county data are again a useful source of information.

Table 6.3 provides the results of a spatial error model of vote choice in the 2004 presidential election, in which support for President George W. Bush was determined by the percentage of the population working in the different occupation scales created from the factor analysis described earlier in this chapter. The model also includes a variable for the percentage of the population employed in agriculture, although this variable was not part of any of the employment scales. The spatial model does not provide strong evidence that the types of industries in which people work is a meaningful predictor of how the county will vote after controlling for all other variables.

We see, for example, that the percentage of the population working as professionals was not a statistically or substantively significant predictor of aggregate vote choice, although the coefficient was signed in the expected direction. The construction scale was statistically significant, and showed that counties in which a greater percentage of the population worked in one of these industries gave a greater share of their votes to Bush, though the effect was small. We further see that counties in which a large share of the population works in agriculture gave a greater share of their votes to Bush. The effect of occupation type, however, was dwarfed by variables such as income, marriage rates, racial and ethnic characteristics, and poverty rates.

In spite of these apparent null results, the possibility that a relationship exists between the size of the professional class and aggregate vote choice should not be dismissed, given the previous literature that suggests that the voting patterns of this group are an important development in American politics. Perhaps we could hypothesize that the second peak in the income distribution of the landslide Democratic counties shown in Figure 6.1 is primarily occupied by those counties dominated by this professional class. To see whether this was the case, I looked at both the median incomes and the vote totals for those counties with a disproportionately large percentage of the population employed in one of the occupations I identified as professional. Among all counties, the mean percentage of the population in a professional occupation was 15.8 percent. Among all landslide Democratic counties, however, that number was 21.6 percent.

Given what we saw in Figure 6.1, however, it may make more sense to divide landslide Democratic counties further, into those wealthier than the

Table 6.3   County-Level Support for Bush in 2004 by Occupation Scales

	Model 2	Std. Error	2 Std. Dev. Δ
Professional Scale	−0.01	(0.02)	−0.15
Arts and Accommodation Scale	−0.01	(0.03)	−0.15
Construction Scale	0.06	(0.02)*	0.78
Government Scale	0.03	(0.03)	0.25
Agriculture	0.16	(0.03)*	2.62
Median Income (Divided by $10,000)	3.32	(0.49)*	5.29
Median Home Value (Divided by $10,000)	−0.24	(0.08)*	−2.17
% of Women Married, 25–29	0.21	(0.02)*	4.80
% Evangelical Christian	0.08	(0.01)*	2.32
% Below Poverty Line	−0.49	(0.07)*	−6.20
% BA	−0.21	(0.03)*	−3.31
% Rural	−0.02	(0.01)*	−1.02
Metropolitan	−0.77	(0.31)*	−0.74
Micropolitan	0.38	(0.28)	0.31
% Black	−0.36	(0.02)*	−10.38
% Hispanic	−0.12	(0.03)*	−2.81
Log of County Population	−0.19	(0.20)	
Pacific	2.90	(3.21)	
Mountain	7.54	(2.52)*	
West-North Central	8.52	(2.49)*	
East-North Central	5.81	(2.33)*	
West-South Central	4.65	(2.76)	
East-South Central	5.88	(2.65)*	
South Atlantic	6.59	(2.78)*	
Mid-Atlantic	7.49	(2.66)*	
Constant	41.38	(9.63)*	
λ	0.99	(0.01)*	
Observations	3103		
−2 X Log Likelihood	19323.99		

*$p < 0.05$

national county mean, and those poorer than the national county mean. Among those landslide Democratic counties with an above-average median household income, the mean percentage of the population classified as professional was a comparatively high 28.7 percent. In landslide Republican counties, only 13 percent of the population was employed in a career in the professional sector. It should be further noted that, of the fifty counties with the highest percentages of professionals, Barack Obama won forty-six of them, and twenty-six gave Obama a landslide victory in 2008, a strikingly high number when one considers that landslide Democratic counties were only about 10 percent of all counties in that election year. The relationship between professionals and aggregate vote choice is not simple and linear, however. It is important not to neglect the large number of landslide Democratic counties that are much poorer than the national average. Among those landslide Democratic counties with a median income below the mean county median income in 2008, the mean percentage of the population employed in professional jobs was only 14.4 percent, less than the national county mean, and barely above that of Republican counties. Perhaps we should not think about professional workers in regard to all counties, but look just at how they influence the aggregate voting trends of middle-class and wealthy counties.

Figure 6.2 shows the relationship between aggregate vote choice and the percentage of the population employed in professional careers in two types of counties: those where the median household income was below $40,000 in 2008 and those where the median household income was above $50,000. We see that the relationship between professionals and aggregate vote choice is only immediately apparent in wealthier counties, and in those counties the relationship is strong. This perhaps helps explain why finding a clear, linear

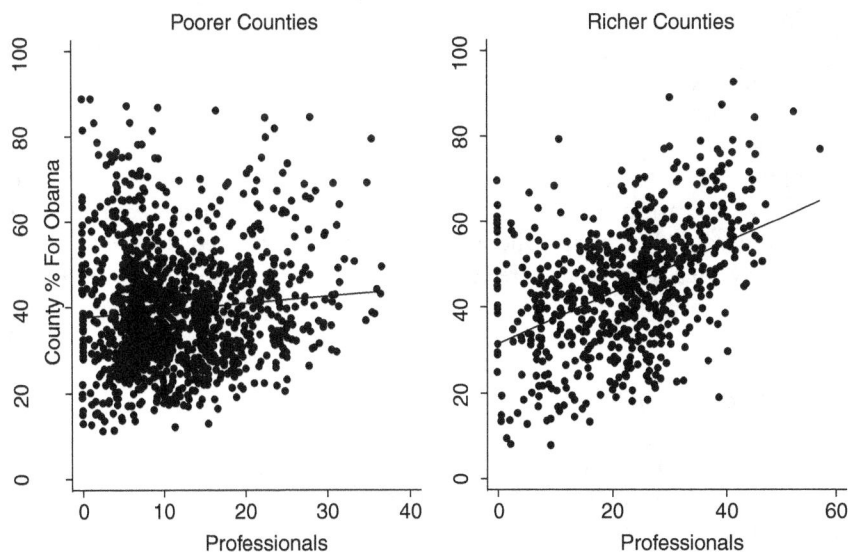

Figure 6.2 Professional Workers and Vote Choice by County Wealth

relationship at the aggregate level between income and politics is so difficult. Yes, poor counties are typically more Democratic than middle-class and rich counties, but to know how a middle-class or wealthy county is going to vote, you also need to know how its residents make their money. If a large percentage of a wealthy county's population is employed as knowledge workers, educators, managers, or health-care professionals, these findings suggest that it is a good bet that such a county will also support Democratic candidates, at least at the aggregate level. Wealthy counties where most of the population works in other professions, however, are more likely to support Republicans.

6.7 EDUCATIONAL ATTAINMENT

Educational attainment is also tied to the questions of income, employment type, and voting. Education is a tricky subject, as it is positively correlated with higher income, which suggests that it should make individuals more Republican, but when socioeconomic attainment is controlled for, higher education is actually negatively correlated with conservatism and Republican voting (Greeley and Spaeth 1970; Lottes and Kuriloff 1994; Weiner and Eckland 1979). The analysis presented in Chapter 4, however, was congruent with this finding only in models that fail to control for female marriage rates. Once we control for the fact that higher education pushes up the average age at first marriage, the negative relationship between education and aggregate vote choice disappeared. The models presented in this chapter revealed different results.

One might hypothesize that the relationship between education and vote choice is also a function of employment type. That is, given that professional class workers are surely more likely to be college educated and to vote for Democrats, the inclusion of the professional class as a covariate should presumably have an influence on the coefficient for education. What is so interesting to see here is that, after controlling for occupation types in a county, education once again had a statistically significant influence on aggregate vote choice, and the effect was in the expected direction: more residents with a four-year degree or higher were associated with lower levels of Republican voting.

6.8 CONCLUSION

Economics clearly is playing a role in the geographic partisan sort, as economic considerations are critical to migratory decisions. It is nonetheless important to note that, even if this analysis provided conclusive evidence that the clustering of occupations is related to the clustering of co-partisans, this would not definitively prove that migration is playing a role. We can, however, hypothesize that many people first choose a profession and subsequently will move to a location where they can practice that profession. The high rates of work-related migration in the United States certainly suggest this happens quite often.

We should not discount the fact that where you grew up will often play an important role in both where you live and what you do for a living. Someone who graduated from high school in Silicon Valley is surely more likely to be an engineer than a farmer, though the reverse is surely true of someone who grew up in rural Nebraska. It is important to remember, however, that college-educated Americans in particular are quite mobile, as demonstrated by the fact that college-educated young people from rural communities have a tendency to move to a major metropolitan area rather than return to their hometowns.

Previous research suggests that occupation type also appears to play a role in the geographic sort. In recent years the percentage of Americans employed as engineers, lawyers, scientists, and educators has risen dramatically, and despite their high average wealth, this group tends to support Democrats. However, when examined statistically, the cross-sectional model of aggregate vote choice and the size of the professional class does not appear to influence support for one political party or the other. A meaningful relationship between the size of the professional class and aggregate vote choice is only apparent in wealthier counties.

In spite of all of these findings, it remains likely that economics is more of a constraint on geographic polarization than a cause of it. Even among the professions that tend to give the most lopsided support to one party or the other, there are large minorities that identify with the opposing party. None of the major profession categories is monolithically Republican or Democratic. Furthermore, while some occupation types tend to cluster in very small geographic regions, others are dispersed throughout the nation. We know that a large percentage of long-distance moves are motivated for work-related or financial reasons, and we can plausibly hypothesize that the relative importance of economic considerations overwhelms political considerations.

Part III

A Case Study

Scholars studying the issue of geographic polarization in the United States have relied heavily on data from states, congressional districts, and counties. These geographic units of analysis can be quite useful for examining general trends and testing theories. Counties can be particularly useful because of the substantial amount of available data for counties, their comparatively small size, and their fixed boundaries. There are limits to what we can learn from counties. Using counties to measure political segregation may lead to an overestimation of the degree to which Americans live in politically diverse communities.

Although counties are small in geographic size compared to states and most congressional districts, they are not necessarily small in population. Most counties contain many different communities, and those communities contain many different neighborhoods. The politics of these different communities and neighborhoods can vary drastically. If a county contained two municipalities of approximately equal size, and each of those municipalities provides an overwhelming victory to different candidates, the aggregate data would erroneously suggest that the residents of that county experience high levels of political diversity.

The previous chapter discussed how occupation and economic considerations can be both a cause of geographic polarization and a constraint on this trend. That is, some occupations may tend to draw people with certain characteristics, and those occupations may cluster in certain areas of the country. On the other hand, the correlation between occupation and party identification is not strong compared to other economic and demographic variables. Furthermore, although an individual may ultimately prefer to live in a city that is dominated by co-partisans, it seems unlikely that this person would turn down her dream job because it is in a city in which the "wrong" party consistently wins a majority of the votes. Thus, we can plausibly predict that economics will be a more important predictor than politics when it comes to determining which county a person will ultimately live in.

When we look at geographic units smaller than cities we might expect to find that politics matters much more in terms of where people settle. A person may have to live in a specific city or county because she works nearby.

Within that city or county, however, she will likely have a great deal of discretion regarding where she will settle. Will she choose the neighborhood with the trendiest restaurants and bars, or the community with a church of her denomination? Does she want her home to be near the best public schools, or does she want to be able to walk to work? Does she want neighbors who attend Tea Party rallies or neighbors who support the Occupy Wall Street movement? Does she want to live in an ethnically diverse neighborhood? Of course, where people live in a city or county will also be constrained by economic considerations—the wealthiest neighborhoods are not affordable for most who might wish to live there. Nonetheless, except for the very poorest residents, people can have a great deal of choice regarding their neighbors. For this reason, we can expect to find higher levels of political segregation in smaller geographic units than in larger ones.

Therefore, a closer examination of a large and, in the aggregate, competitive county will be a useful addition to this study. Specifically, the forthcoming chapter will take a closer look at Harris County, Texas, the third-largest county in the United States, and by far the largest competitive county in the nation. The chapter will provide a qualitative overview of the county and its largest city, Houston. It will also discuss migration patterns into and out of the county, and show how migration is changing its politics. This chapter will demonstrate that, at the neighborhood level, this county exhibits extraordinarily high levels of political segregation.

7 Harris County, Texas
Political Segregation in the Nation's Largest Swing County

7.1 INTRODUCTION

An important critique one could make against Bishop and Cushing's (2008) argument that the electorate is geographically sorting along partisan lines is that they relied on a relatively crude geographic unit: counties. When examining the geographic distribution of counties that gave consistent landslide victories to one party or the other in recent elections, we see that a huge increase in the number of overwhelmingly Republican counties can be found in the sparsely populated rural counties in the center of the country. From these maps, one who knew nothing about the distribution of the U.S. population might incorrectly infer that the Republican Party is the dominant political power in the United States.

The tremendous range in the county population sizes makes counties a difficult unit of analysis. Loving County in rural west Texas had only eighty-two residents as of the 2010 census. Los Angeles County had a population of more than 9.8 million. Many of the nation's largest counties contain multiple U.S. congressional districts within them. Performing statistical analyses of aggregate data that treat all counties equally is therefore problematic. We might also be concerned that county characteristics have greater or lesser salience in different contexts. In rural counties, the office of county commissioner may be the most important local political office. In urban counties, the county may be a far less salient geographic unit than the city—the mayor of Chicago is considered by most locals a more important position than the president of the Cook County Board of Commissioners. That being said, within political science there is a long tradition of using counties when examining contextual effects on political attitudes and political behavior. Counties are also the smallest geographic unit for which there are readily available data for presidential results in all states. Counties furthermore benefit from fixed boundaries across time, and a huge variety of different economic, political, demographic, and cultural variables are available at the county level.

Nonetheless, counties may be a problematic unit of analysis for examining geographic political segregation because they may significantly underestimate the total level of segregation. As noted earlier, just because a county is competitive in the aggregate does not mean that smaller communities within that county are politically competitive. Strongly Democratic towns and neighborhoods may be directly beside strongly Republican towns and neighborhoods within that same county.

This chapter will demonstrate the remarkable political segregation within the nation's largest "swing county"—Harris County, Texas. Although this county has given a majority of its presidential votes to candidates from both political parties in recent years, this aggregate heterogeneity masks the enormous level of political segregation within the various cities and neighborhoods within its borders.

The results of this analysis suggest that political segregation is actually much more dramatic in the United States than one might infer from a study based solely on counties. This is not the first study to show that geographic partisan polarization is exceptionally high within metropolitan areas; Kinsella (2011) demonstrated that Cincinnati was highly geographically polarized, and that the clustering of co-partisans within that community has increased over time.

7.2 HARRIS COUNTY

Harris County, Texas, has the third-largest population of any county in the United States; only Cook County, Illinois, and Los Angeles County, California, have more people. The county is dominated by the City of Houston, the largest city in Texas by population and the fourth-largest city in the United States after New York, Los Angeles, and Chicago. The metro area's population has doubled over the past three decades, primarily through migration. According to the 2010 United States Census, the City of Houston had 2.1 million residents; Harris County had a population of 4.1 million at that time. Harris County is also racially and ethnically diverse: 33 percent of the county is non-Hispanic white, 18.9 percent is African American, 6.2 percent of the population is Asian American, and 32.93 percent of the population is Hispanic of any race. Furthermore, 25 percent of Harris County's population was born outside the United States.

The economy of Harris County is largely based on the energy industry, particularly oil. The aerospace industry and biomedical research are also important sectors of the local economy, as are banking and financial services. The Texas Medical Center in Houston is the largest medical center in the world. The county contains four public universities: the University of Houston, University of Houston–Downtown, University of Houston–Clear Lake, and Texas Southern University. It also contains four private universities: Rice University, North American College, Houston Baptist University, and University of St. Thomas.

A comparatively large percentage of Harris County's adult population has earned bachelor's degrees or higher (27.9 percent), and the median household income is about $52,000 a year. Approximately 17 percent of the population lives below the poverty level. Compared to some of the other most populous counties in the United States, single-family homes in Harris County are relatively affordable. The median value for owner-occupied homes is approximately $130,000. The median value of homes in Cook County, Illinois, is almost twice that much, and the median value in Los Angeles is more than three times higher.

Houston is a major port city, and the Port of Houston is one of the busiest ports in the United States in terms of tonnage. However, unlike other port cities such as San Francisco and Seattle, Houston's growth has not been hindered by its proximity to a major body of water. Houston is about 50 miles from the Gulf of Mexico, which means it has long had plenty of room to grow in all directions. Harris County is also quite flat. The Houston area has therefore had few geographic constraints on growth, which has further held down the costs of single-family homes.

Houston exhibits high levels of economic inequality and high levels of economic segregation. The Pew Research Center calculated the Residential Income Segregation Index (RISI) for all of America's largest cities, and, although economic segregation is present in most major metropolitan areas, it found that Houston is the most economically segregated city in the nation (Fry and Taylor 2012). The RISI score is calculated by determining the percentage of low-income households living in low-income tracts and high-income households living in high-income tracts. In Houston, the RISI score was 61, as of 2010, up from 32 in 1980. Thus Houston has both the highest overall score in the nation and has experienced the greatest increase in economic segregation in the past thirty years.

Although rising RISI scores may be troubling to those who wish to see greater economic diversity within neighborhoods, economic segregation tends to grow faster in cities experiencing high levels of in-migration. In recent decades, Houston has experienced large population growth from two sources. Many of the new Houstonians are poor immigrants, many undocumented, who tend to cluster together. Houston has also experienced an influx of highly skilled, highly paid workers and wealthy retirees. The different settlement patterns of these new arrivals are partially responsible for this increase in income segregation. We see similar patterns in other quickly growing metro areas such as San Antonio, Phoenix, and Miami.

Related to economic segregation, the City of Houston and Harris County also exhibit high levels of racial and ethnic segregation. However, Houston is not one of the top-ten most racially segregated metropolitan areas in the United States (Denvir 2011). One way to measure racial and ethnic segregation is through the use of a dissimilarity index. This index measures the degree to which groups can be found in equal portions in all neighborhoods. One can interpret the index as the percentage of individuals from a given group who would have to change neighborhoods in order to reach a state of perfect integration. According to this measure, Houston is the least racially segregated large city in America (Glaeser and Vigdor 2012).

Houstonians generally have a positive view of their city compared to other cities. According to the Houston Area Survey (Urban Research Center of Houston 2009), when asked to compare their city to other metropolitan areas, 41 percent said Houston was a "slightly better" place to live, and 44 percent said it was a "much better" place to live.

Harris County also has relatively high marriage rates compared to other densely populated counties. According to the American Community Survey conducted by the United States Census Bureau, 47.5 percent of all Harris County residents over the age of fifteen are married, compared to 43 percent in Los Angeles County and 42.1 percent in Cook County. Of the ten most populous counties in the United States, only Maricopa County, Arizona, and Orange County, California, have higher rates of marriage. One of the reasons densely populated counties have comparatively low marriage rates compared to other regions of the country is their large minority populations—Latinos and African Americans tend to have lower marriage rates and live in populous counties. For this reason, it may be useful to compare the marriage rates of non-Hispanic whites in Harris County to their marriage rates elsewhere. Among non-Hispanic white residents, the marriage rate in Harris County is quite high (53.1 percent) compared to other densely populated counties. Of the twenty most populous counties, only Tarrant County, Texas, has a higher marriage rate for non-Hispanic whites. This finding is not surprising given my argument that comparatively affordable homes are associated with higher rates of marriage. Given its strong economic performance and affordable housing (at least compared to the other largest cities in the United States), Houston is a desirable city to raise a family. For this reason, we should also expect the Houston area to exhibit higher rates of Republican voting than other metropolitan areas of comparable size.

7.3 ZONING LAWS IN HARRIS COUNTY

Houston is an unusual large city because of its lack of a zoning ordinance. Specifically, there are no land-use regulations within the City of Houston or in the very large unincorporated areas within Harris County. Houstonians, and most Harris County residents, may buy land and use it for whatever purpose they wish with very few exceptions (liquor stores and strip clubs must be a certain distance from schools, for example). If a Houstonian buys a tract of land, she can use it for a mansion, a convenience store, a manufacturing plant, or a high rise. However, within the City of Houston there are a number of independent municipalities such as West University Place and Bellaire that do have zoning laws. Besides the City of Houston, there is a total of thirty-three municipalities either entirely or partly within the county's borders, and most of these municipalities have zoning laws. However, the percentage of Harris County residents living within these municipalities is relatively small. According to the most recent census, only 437,716 Harris County residents live in a municipality other than Houston.

Houston has allowed its residents to determine the issue of zoning laws, and in each referendum—the most recent occurred in 1993—the city's voters rejected the establishment of zoning. Houston is the only city in the United States with a population of more than 100,000 residents that allowed its residents to determine whether or not it would have a zoning ordinance.

There are a number of justifications offered for zoning laws. Zoning is said to enhance or at least protect property values, particularly the value of single-family homes (Ohls, Weisberg, and White 1974). Specifically, zoning is said to protect property from negative externalities. For example, the use of land for industrial purposes may lower the value of neighboring land used for residential purposes. Critics of zoning have argued that it is unfair to some property owners who may wish to use their property for nonresidential purposes. Others have argued that it is exclusionary, and is deliberately designed to keep certain people, particularly minorities and the poor, from moving into specific neighborhoods (Kosman 1993).

Houston may not permanently retain its status as a city without a zoning ordinance. Because of the city's explosive growth, a large number of voices have called for new restrictions. In recent years there has been tremendous controversy over the so-called Ashby High Rise—an apartment complex more than twenty stories tall that is being planned in a residential neighborhood near Rice University that is presently dominated by single-family homes. Residents in this neighborhood are concerned that the new building will lead to major traffic congestion on their narrow roads and a cause a decline in property values. In spite of local concerns, the City of Houston does not possess any legal means to stop the construction of the building. Concerns such as this have led to an increasing interest in zoning ordinances in Houston.

Whether or not zoning is a good thing for a community is a question beyond the scope of this book. However, its lack of zoning increases the usefulness of Houston for this particular study because we know that residential patterns within Houston and most of the surrounding communities are not being manipulated by municipal ordinances. The people living in a certain area do so because they want to and can afford to live there.

7.4 MIGRATION TO HARRIS COUNTY

Harris County has experienced significant growth in recent decades primarily due to migration, both domestic migration and immigration from abroad. The Houston metropolitan area is somewhat unusual in this regard. Although most of the largest cities in the United States are not losing population, the growth of many of them is largely sustained by foreign immigration, and among domestic migrants, they are actually losing more than they gain.

In recent years Houston has experienced high levels of foreign immigration and domestic in-migration.

Houston leads all other Southern cities in terms of population growth. From April 2010 to July 2011, the city added 45,716 residents (Pulsinelli 2012). Much of this growth is due to the growing Latino population. Latinos have not always been such a large percentage of the Houston and Harris County population. As of 1960, 73.9 percent of the Harris County population was non-Hispanic white, and the local black population was actually twice the size of the local Latino population. Starting in the 1960s, Harris County experienced a population boom, driven primarily by Anglos. During the 1960s, the non-Hispanic white population in Harris County grew by 31 percent; it grew by an additional 25 percent during the 1970s (Klineberg 2008).

The population began to change dramatically in the 1980s. In the early 1980s, declining consumption led to a decrease in oil prices and a decline in U.S. domestic oil exploration. Although declining oil prices were good for the overall U.S. economy, the oil collapse spurred a severe local recession in Houston. Concurrently with this local recession, the non-Hispanic white population in Harris County stopped growing and actually declined. The cessation of Anglo in-migration during this period did not stop Harris County's growth. Instead, the growing population of the Houston area became overwhelmingly driven by immigration and the children born to immigrants. During the 1990s, the Latino population in Harris County grew by 74 percent.

Given the dramatic growth of the Latino population in the United States, particularly in border states, Harris County is not unique in having a large and growing foreign-born Latino population. Houston also has a large population of African immigrants. The Houston area has the largest number of Nigerian immigrants in the nation. African immigrants are one of the most highly educated demographic groups in Houston; almost 35 percent of African immigrants in Houston have college degrees, which is a far higher percentage than among native-born African Americans and even higher than native-born non-Hispanic whites (Romero 2003). Harris County has also experienced a dramatic growth in its Asian population and Houston has one of the largest Vietnamese American populations in the country. Asians are still a much smaller percentage of the population than blacks and Latinos, however.

Beyond economically motivated migration, Houston also recently experienced a major demographic event due to a natural disaster. After Hurricane Katrina devastated the city of New Orleans, refugees from that city—predominantly African Americans—dispersed across the nation. Because of its close proximity to the Louisiana border, Houston had more Katrina refugees than any other city. It is estimated that Houston experienced an influx of as many as 250,000 refugees, and as many as 150,000 chose to remain long-term in Houston (Hamilton 2010). There has been some tension between Katrina refugees and native Houstonians. By 2008, 70 percent of Houstonians expressed the opinion that the Katrina refugees have been "a bad thing" for Houston (Urban Research Center 2009).

7.5 MAJOR NEIGHBORHOODS IN HARRIS COUNTY

Harris County has many different communities within its borders that differ dramatically from each other in terms of demographics, economics, and culture. This is important because it means migrants to Houston have many options when it comes to neighborhood attributes. Virtually any migrant who exhibits homophilous tendencies in community selection can find an area dominated by people sharing her major characteristics.

Within America's major metropolitan areas, there is a common pattern: poor minority neighborhoods are clustered near the city center and they are surrounded by wealthier and whiter suburbs and exurbs. This general pattern is true in Harris County, but there are also prominent exceptions. There are a number of exceptionally wealthy neighborhoods in Houston that are minutes away from the downtown area; there are also quite poor suburbs far from the center of Houston.

River Oaks, located near the geographic center of Houston, is the most affluent neighborhood in the city and one of the most affluent neighborhoods in the United States. A much greater percentage of its population (85.7 percent) is non-Hispanic white compared to most areas within Houston. The median home value of this neighborhood is more than 1 million dollars. Other wealthy areas within Houston city limits include West University Place (which has its own municipal government despite being entirely surrounded by the City of Houston), and the Memorial area.

On the other end of the economic spectrum, Houston's poorest neighborhoods are predominantly African American or Hispanic. Houston's Second Ward in the eastern part of the city was one of Houston's first Mexican American barrios and it remains overwhelmingly Hispanic. Several wards are traditionally African American, including the Fourth and Fifth Wards. The community of Alief is more than 20 percent Asian.

Houston neighborhoods are not only distinguished from each other in terms of wealth and race, so knowing a neighborhood's racial and economic characteristics is not always a great predictor of its aggregate political behavior. The neighborhood of Montrose, for example, is predominantly white and relatively affluent. It is also home to a large gay community and overwhelmingly votes for Democrats.

Outside city limits, Houston's many suburbs differ from each other racially, economically, and politically. The Woodlands, a master planned community in both Harris County and neighboring Montgomery County, is more than 90 percent white, wealthy, and Republican. The same is true of the city of Friendswood, which is in both Harris County and Galveston County. The city of Pasadena, the second-largest city in Harris County, is trending Hispanic and a majority of its residents in the northern half of the municipality supported Barack Obama. Jacinto City is also overwhelmingly Hispanic and predominantly Democratic.

There are many other large communities considered part of the Houston metropolitan area, such as the city of Sugar Land, which is where former

House Majority Leader Tom Delay's congressional district was located. Sugar Land is outside of Harris County, however, and thus not included in this analysis.

7.6 GENTRIFICATION IN HOUSTON

Like many growing metropolitan areas in the United States, Houston is experiencing substantial gentrification in its poorest areas. That is, middle-class migrants are settling in areas once completely dominated by the urban poor. The causes and consequences of gentrification have long been hotly debated by researchers. Some scholars posit cultural explanations for the increasing gentrification of America's metropolitan areas; a case can be made that professional, middle-class people have adopted different lifestyles compared to earlier periods of American history. As a result of these lifestyle changes, such Americans are no longer drawn in large numbers to the suburbs (Lipton 1977). There are also economic explanations for this trend. As gas prices rise, someone employed in a city center may be less inclined to live in a distant suburb. This is an especially salient concern in Harris County. Although the Woodlands neighborhood may be an attractive place to live, it is also 30 miles from Houston, and in traffic the commute may take well over an hour. Even if a gentrifying urban neighborhood may not be an individual's ideal location, it may be the best available option when commuting times and gas prices are considered.

While early scholars of gentrification were typically highly critical of the gentrification process because it displaced cities' poorest residents and could potentially destroy communities, in recent years scholars and journalists have embraced, on average, more positive views on gentrification (Slater 2006). The newcomers into a gentrifying neighborhood bring with them a greater tax base and more economic opportunities for all residents, including low-income residents (Byrne 2003). One could also argue that gentrification is leading to a decrease in racial and economic segregation within urban areas, and perhaps we should be encouraged that non-Hispanic whites and the relatively affluent are increasingly willing to live in neighborhoods that remain predominantly poor and African American. This is not to say gentrification no longer has critics. Many scholars continue to emphasize the darker side of gentrification (Wacquant 2008), and working-class groups continue to fight the process when it begins in their neighborhoods (Hackworth 2007).

Because of their proximity to the Houston downtown area, many traditionally African American and poor neighborhoods are drawing large numbers of Anglo and relatively affluent migrants. As is the case in other metropolitan areas, gentrification in Houston is not welcomed by everyone. The arrival of new and relatively affluent migrants to places such as Houston's Third Ward has led to higher property values, and there is concern that low-income African Americans will be priced out of the community.

This ward is considered particularly attractive because of its proximity to downtown, the Texas Medical Center, and the museum district. Texas State Representative Garnet Coleman, who represents Houston's Third Ward, has expressed his determination to halt the gentrification process.

In other traditionally black regions of Houston there has been even greater gentrification. The city's Fourth Ward, which was once called Freeman's Town because it was home to freed slaves who settled there following the Civil War, has changed substantially in recent decades. The resident African American population has declined while non-Hispanic white growth has surged.

Given that African Americans overwhelmingly vote for Democratic candidates, an influx of people from any other race into a formerly all-black community will almost assuredly make it more Republican. However, the types of non-Hispanic whites who tend to be the vanguard of gentrification may differ politically from other whites. Thus, a trend toward gentrification does not necessarily imply a neighborhood's partisan distribution will change quickly or dramatically, as the forthcoming analysis will demonstrate.

7.7 POLITICS OF HARRIS COUNTY

Within living memory, the partisan distribution of Harris County has swung dramatically. In 1964, Lyndon Johnson won Harris County with 59.9 percent of the vote. However, like much of the South, non-Hispanic white Harris County voters subsequently realigned and the county became heavily Republican. Republican presidential candidates carried the county in each election for the next four decades. Richard Nixon won an impressive 62.6 percent of the vote in Harris County in 1972. As recently as 2004, President George W. Bush won the county with 54.6 percent of the vote. The City of Houston was not so strongly dominated by Republicans during this period. City elections in Houston are nonpartisan, but since the 1960s the partisan identity of incumbents has been clear. Houston has not had a Republican mayor since Mayor Jim McConn lost his reelection bid to Democrat Kathryn Whitmire in 1981. Anise Parker is presently the Democratic mayor of Houston. She is the second female mayor of the city and one of the first lesbian mayors of a large U.S. city.

Houston has a reputation as a city with a laissez faire attitude toward economics, a reputation that is well deserved when the city is compared to other metropolitan areas of comparable size. According to Robert Fisher (1989):

The ideological thrust in Houston in the twentieth century has remained anti-government, anti-regulation, anti-union, anti-public planning, anti-taxes, anti-anything which seemed to represent in fact or fantasy the implementation of limits on the economic prerogative and activity of the city's business community. For example, Houston is the only major city in the nation without a zoning ordinance. Planning has always been done, until very recently, by the private, not the public, sector, or done by the public sector, at the request and under the guidance of private sector leadership. There are no state or city income taxes . . . As one historian put it, according to "this version of capitalism . . . the private sector is the driving force in the city. In this atmosphere, the government provides a minimum of basic services and assists business growth. Citizens who want more than the minimum of public services go to the private sector to obtain support." (146)

Harris County has become more Democratic in recent years. Barack Obama won 50.5 percent of the county's vote in 2008. The Republican Party regained some ground in the county in 2012, but Obama nonetheless narrowly defeated Mitt Romney by less than 1,000 votes—Mitt Romney won 584,866 and Barack Obama won 585,451. This is therefore one of the nation's most closely divided large counties. Harris County's turn toward the political left can be largely ascribed to migration and the county's demographic changes. The growth of the Latino population in particular has been a boon to the Democratic Party in Harris County. Although Harris County remains exceptionally close in the aggregate, and the county was slightly more Republican in 2012 than 2008, all of the demographic trends suggest the county will continue to become more Democratic. By the end of the decade, Harris County may join Travis County (which includes Austin) as one of the few reliably Democratic counties in Texas that is not contiguous with the Mexican border.

However, although these demographic changes have been critical to the political changes in Harris County, the growth of the Latino population in the county has not changed the political distribution as dramatically as one might expect. It is important to remember that a significant percentage of Harris County's immigrant population is in the country illegally and thus not eligible to vote. As many as 400,000 of the immigrants in the greater Houston area are undocumented (Hegstrom 2005). This huge population of undocumented immigrants has important economic and cultural consequences for the Houston area, but the political consequences of these newcomers are muted. Legal immigrants and the children of all immigrants that are born in the United States are eligible to vote, but it is important to note that Latinos exhibit far lower levels of voter turnout than other demographic groups (Highton and Burris 2002; Barreto 2005). For all of these reasons, native-born, non-Hispanic white Americans continue to have more political clout in Harris County than one might expect given their percentage of the overall population.

Seven U.S. congressional districts are located within Harris County. The political diversity of these representatives reflects the diversity of the county.

Four of these districts are represented by Republicans and three by Democrats. There is also a huge ideological distance between Harris County's most conservative and most liberal members. By examining roll call votes, the American Conservative Union ranks each member of Congress each year to determine the degree to which a member is liberal or conservative—a score of 100 indicates a member was as conservative as a member could possibly be in terms of policy; a score of zero indicates a member has only ever voted for liberal policies. Harris County's most conservative member of congress, John Culberson, has a lifetime conservative score of 96.42. Harris County's most liberal member, Sheila Jackson-Lee, has a lifetime conservative score of 5.76.

7.8 POLITICAL SEGREGATION IN HARRIS COUNTY

A look at the aggregate political characteristics provides a useful starting point, but smaller units of analysis can provide a much stronger indication of the degree to which Harris County exhibits political segregation. The best units of analysis for examining this question are Voter Tabulation Districts (VTDs). VTDs are the geographic units the Census Bureau relies on for reapportionment and redistricting purposes.

VTDs are especially useful because they are quite small in size. As of 2010, Harris County had 885 VTDs, with an average population of 4,624. I argue that, when you look closer at a competitive county like Harris County you will actually find relatively few competitive neighborhoods. We do see that the vast majority of VTDs within Harris County provide hugely lopsided victories to candidates of one party or the other. In 2008, the average gap between the percentage earned by John McCain and the percentage earned by Barack Obama was an astonishing 41.17 percentage points. Of the 885 VTDs in Harris County, there were only 57 in which the gap between the two candidates was fewer than 5 percentage points.

Bishop and Cushing (2008) expressed concern that nearly half the U.S. population lived in counties in which one party could expect to consistently win more than 60 percent of the vote. The analysis of this particular "swing" county suggests that residential segregation may actually be much more dramatic than Bishop and Cushing suggested. Of the more than 1 million Harris County residents who cast a vote in 2008, 72 percent lived in VTDs that gave one candidate more than 60 percent of the vote, and 45 percent lived in VTDs in which more than *70 percent* of the vote went to one candidate. Thus Bishop and Cushing's use of counties as the primary unit of analysis appears to underestimate the degree to which partisans are segregated from each other.

Figure 7.1 shows the geographic locations of landslide Republican and landslide Democratic VTDs in Harris County in terms of vote choice in the 2008 presidential election. The remarkable thing to note about this figure

VTDs in which Obama won 60 percent or more

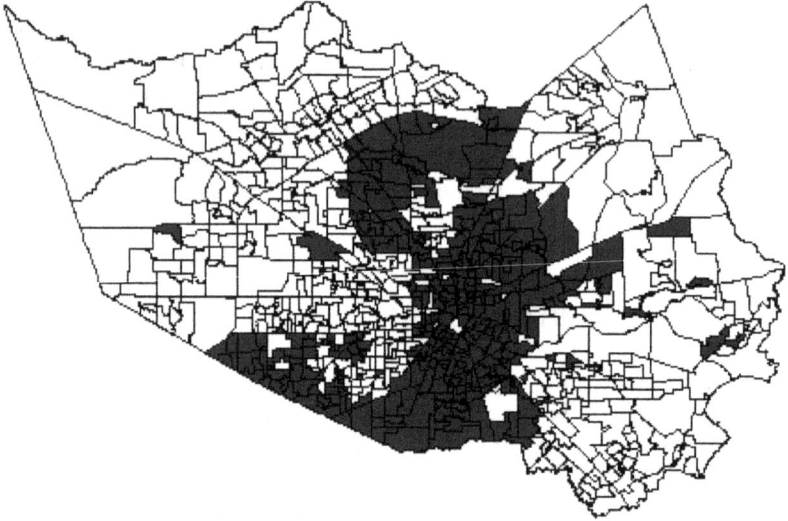

VTDs in which McCain won 60 percent or more

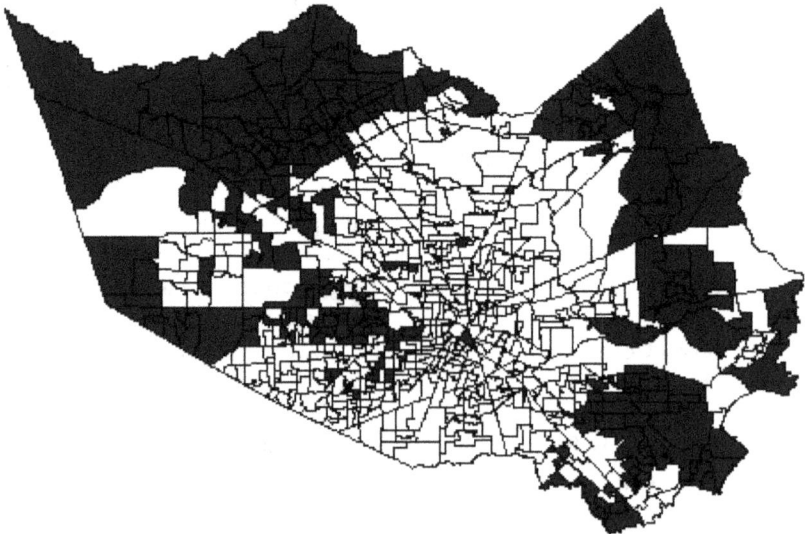

Figure 7.1 Landslide Republican and Landslide Democratic VTDs in Harris County for 2008 Presidential Election

is that the overwhelming majority of Harris County VTDs are either solidly Republican or solidly Democratic. In the aggregate, the county appears competitive. When we look closer, we see that if you are a Republican living in Harris County, your neighbors are probably also Republicans. The same is true for Harris County Democrats.

It is also worth noting that, while there is a general pattern of strong Democratic neighborhoods in the center of the county and within Houston city limits, and strong Republican neighborhoods in the outlying suburbs, there are plenty of exceptions to this pattern. As noted previously, there are a number of exceptionally wealthy neighborhoods within Houston city limits. These neighborhoods correspond to the small number of Republican landslide VTDs in the center of the county. There are also a number of extraordinarily strong Democratic communities far beyond the city center. These also generally correspond to neighborhoods that are increasingly dominated by minorities.

Although there are examples of strong Republican VTDs surrounded by strong Democratic VTDs, and strong Democratic VTDs ensconced within otherwise overwhelmingly Republican suburbs, there is clear evidence of spatial clustering within Harris County. Recall that in Chapter 4 the Moran's I measure of spatial autocorrelation was calculated for county-level presidential results. The Moran's I at the county level for this variable was an impressive 0.57, indicating a high level of spatial clustering. Within Harris County, the level of spatial clustering was substantially higher. The queens-weighted Moran's I for the percentage of the vote cast for President Obama in Harris County VTDs is 0.72. That is, within Harris County, a presumably competitive and politically diverse county, the measure of spatial autocorrelation is even higher than the measure of spatial autocorrelation at the county level when considering the entire United States.

7.9 POPULATION CHANGE AND POLITICAL CHANGE IN HARRIS COUNTY

Given both the explosive growth of Harris County in recent decades and the extraordinary level of political segregation within the city, it is clear that Democratic migrants to Harris County tend to move to Democratic neighborhoods and Republican migrants tend to move to Republican neighborhoods. Of course, much of this is surely driven by racial segregation patterns; if Anglos move to Anglo neighborhoods, blacks move to black neighborhoods, and Latinos move to Latino neighborhoods, there will be political segregation even though politics per se was not the motivating factor.

To develop a better understanding of how migration influences voting patterns within Harris County, an examination of population changes and political changes within Harris County voting precincts will be useful.

Unfortunately, an examination of political and demographic change at the precinct level over time is quite difficult, as these boundaries change as a result of redistricting. Following the 2010 Census there was a necessary redrawing of voter precinct lines because the previously existing precincts no longer contained substantially equal populations. However, in spite of redistricting it is possible to reconstruct a majority of old precinct lines using contemporary data in order to use consistent boundaries. The forthcoming analysis relies on the 740 voting precincts in Harris County that had voters within their boundaries and for which there was reliable political data for every election year from 2000 to 2012 and reliable demographic data for 2000 and 2010.[1]

Although studies of geographic sorting often focus on presidential voting for practical reasons (the same candidates are on all ballots nationwide and it is relatively easy to collect presidential voting data for all U.S. counties), it may be useful to consider other offices when examining this question. Presidential votes may not always be a strong indicator of party identification for some groups. For example, although a relatively high percentage of U.S. Latinos cast votes for President George W. Bush in 2004, this did not indicate that Latinos became more Republican overall (De la Garza and Cortina 2007). Therefore, in this case the ideal political variable at the precinct level was the average partisan breakdown of down-ballot partisan votes, for offices such as judges. The use of down-ballot votes provides the further benefit of increasing the number of years for which there were data. Several decades ago this would have been quite problematic, particularly in the South, as many white Southerners continued to strongly support Democratic candidates at the state and local level, but support Republican candidates for president. This is no longer the case; the correlation between partisan voting for president and partisan voting for down-ballot elections is now extraordinarily high—this was particularly true in 2012.

Not surprisingly, just as the county has become more Democratic over the past decade in the aggregate, most individual precincts have also become more Democratic since 2000. Of all precincts for which there are reliable and available data for this period of time, the mean increase in the percentage of the vote going to Democratic candidates from 2000 to 2012 was 5.24 percent and the median was 4.4 percent. This growth in Democratic strength has not been linear over time.

Although there was a general upward trend for the Democratic Party in most voter precincts after 2000, there was nonetheless considerable fluctuation from year to year, and these fluctuations seem to correspond to developments in national politics. Down-ballot Democrats had only the slightest advantage at the start of the decade during the first years of the Bush administration. Democrats saw a large jump in support in 2006, which corresponded to the Republican Party's disastrous showing in the mid-term congressional elections of that year. Democratic support remained strong in 2008. The Republican Party's down-ballot candidates had an impressive

resurgence in 2010, which also corresponded with that party's strong showing in congressional elections. The Democratic Party returned to its previous
levels of strong support in 2012.

We should keep in mind that the use of the overall mean as a unit of
analysis might lead to an incorrect inference that most of these precincts
were relatively competitive—after all, the mean never rose above 60 percent for either party in any election. In truth, most precincts were highly
uncompetitive in every election year. In 2000, less than one-quarter of all
voter precincts were won by fewer than 20 percentage points. Even fewer of
these precincts (22.43 percent) were within 20 percentage points in 2012.
In total in 2012, 216 of these voting precincts gave Democratic candidates
fewer than 40 percentage points and 358 gave Democratic candidates more
than 60 percentage points.

It is also worth noting that few precincts stay competitive for long. Only
13.1 percent of all voter precincts were competitive in both 2000 and 2012.
Most of those that were competitive in 2000 but became landslide precincts
by 2012 transitioned into the landslide Democratic category—79 precincts
in total made such a transition. Despite the overall trend toward Democrats,
some districts transitioned from competitive to being landslide Republican
districts from 2000 to 2012—a total of 8 districts were so classified.

It is important to remember that this growth in Democratic support has
not been uniform throughout all precincts, and many of these changes can be
explained by changing demographics driven by migration. Figure 7.2 shows
the relationship between the change in the non-Hispanic white voting-age
population from 2000 to 2010 and the change in the support for down-
ballot Democratic candidates from 2000 to 2012. On average, we see that
every percentage point decrease in the voting-age Anglo population was
associated with a 0.48 percentage point increase in the support for Democratic candidates.

While this relationship is strong and linear, it is important to note that
there is not a one-to-one relationship between percentage changes in the

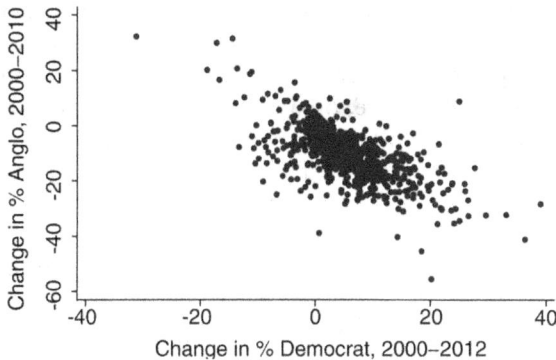

Figure 7.2 Change in Percent Democrat by Change in Percent Anglo

voting-age Anglo population and percentage changes in support for Democrats. In a perfectly racialized political system, in which all nonwhites voted for Democrats and all whites voted for Republicans, we would see a stronger relationship here. In fact, we see that some places became less white and more Republican over this period. Of the 143 voting precincts that were more Republican in 2012 than 2000, 89 of them were less non-Hispanic white, in terms of the voting-age population, than they were in 2000. The increase in the Republican share within these districts was almost certainly not because the increasing minority population was more Republican than the Anglos who previously lived in the district.

Part of the reason why an increase in the nonwhite population does not immediately translate into an increase in Democratic voting is that many newcomers are undocumented immigrants and thus not eligible to vote. We should also keep in mind that Latinos tend to vote at lower rates than non-Hispanic whites. That being said, it is still difficult to explain why many districts became both less white and more Republican. One possible explanation for this finding is that many Anglos actually become more likely to vote Republican as the local nonwhite population increases, or that this demographic trend encourages Anglo Republicans to turn out in greater numbers. It is also important to note that many of the precincts in which non-Hispanic whites are declining as a percentage of the population are experiencing significant growth in the Asian population. Although Asians nationwide vote, on average, heavily for Democrats, in many Harris County suburbs the voting patterns of Asians and Anglos are very similar.

There are other reasons why Harris County defies the parsimonious expectation that changes in demographic composition lead to easily predictable changes in voting patterns. In ninety-two of the voting precincts considered here, Anglos were a greater percentage of the voting-age population in 2010 than they were in 2000. Not all of these precincts became more Republican. A sizable minority (38 percent) of precincts that witnessed an increase in their Anglo share of the voting-age population during this decade also became more Democratic. Why might this be? It may be that in communities undergoing gentrification the long-term residents (who will tend to be overwhelmingly Democratic) may vote in greater numbers in response to this perceived threat. It is also important to remember that, while non-Hispanic whites are, on average, far more likely to be Republicans than any other racial or ethnic group, they are not all equally likely to vote Republican. The whites who tend to be on the frontlines of gentrification are particularly unlikely to be Republican.

The stereotypical gentrifier is a childless, well-educated individual who is single or has a spouse who works outside the home (Zukin 1987; Lees, Slater, and Wyly 2008). Although such a person is white and probably rather affluent, she is not the kind of white person who can be expected to consistently pull the lever for Republicans. Representative Coleman, who was mentioned previously as one of the opponents of gentrification in Houston, represents the 147th House District in Texas. His district contains nineteen voter precincts that became more non-Hispanic white from 2000 to 2010. While he may be justifiably concerned that these new arrivals are displacing many of his district's poorer African American residents, there is little danger that they will displace him from his seat. In 2012, Coleman again secured his reelection with more than 90 percent of the vote, and Democratic candidates in his district secured a greater share of the mean precinct down-ballot vote in 2012 than in 2000.

Another state legislative district in Harris County with the most precincts that experienced a substantial increase in their white population was the 142nd district—a district in which African Americans are the plurality—represented by Harold Dutton Jr. Although twenty voting precincts within Representative Dutton's district increased in their share of the Anglo population from 2000 to 2010, and Anglos reached 25.5 percent of the voting-age population in his district in 2010, this has not led to a corresponding increase in the share of the vote for Republican candidates. Representative Dutton has run unopposed in his last five elections. Looking at down-ballot elections in that district, those precincts that became more Anglo from 2000 to 2010 experienced virtually no political change; these districts were only 0.16 percentage points less Democratic in 2012 than they had been in 2000.

It is worth noting that, just as Harris County appears politically diverse in the aggregate but politically segregated when we examine smaller units, so too does it appear demographically diverse in the aggregate but racially and ethnically segregated when we look at individual precincts. Although no racial or ethnic group represents a majority of the population in Harris County, only 20 percent of the precincts considered in this analysis do not have a racial or ethnic group within their boundaries that is a clear majority. If we consider a geographic unit truly diverse if no racial or ethnic group even has a plurality greater than 40 percent, only 7.3 percent of all precincts reach that standard. This racial segregation explains a great deal of the partisan segregation, though not all of it. Of those precincts analyzed in 2012, there were fourteen voting precincts in which Republican down-ballot candidates won more than 60 percent of the vote despite the fact that non-Hispanic whites were less than a majority of the voting-age population. Similarly, there were at eleven voting precincts in which Democrats won 60 percent or more of the vote despite the fact that Anglos represented a majority of the voting-age population.

As we would predict based on findings from the analysis of county-level data, overwhelmingly Democratic areas are exceptionally stable politically, but landslide Republican communities are typically less stable. Of the 280 precincts that gave down-ballot Democrats overwhelming victories in 2000, only 10 had moved into the comparatively competitive category in 2012. In contrast, of the 271 precincts that gave down-ballot Republicans an overwhelming victory in 2000, 58 had transitioned into the competitive category by 2012. Because competitive precincts do not apparently remain competitive for long, we can plausibly predict that many of these newly competitive, but formerly strong Republican, precincts will move into the strong Democratic category within another decade.

It may be objected that the main reason landslide Republican voting precincts appear less stable than landslide Democratic precincts is simply that the whole county became more Democratic over this period, so we should expect more precincts to have transitioned out of the landslide Republican category. To respond to this, we can compare results from the 2000 election to results of the 2010 election. Because of the exceptionally strong showing of down-ballot GOP candidates in 2010, the mean support for Democrats at the voting-precinct level was actually lower in that year than it had been in 2000. In spite of this, the percentage of landslide Democratic precincts in 2000 that were still landslide Democratic precincts in 2010 was slightly higher than the percentage of landslide Republican precincts that remained landslide Republican precincts.

While there are advantages to using voter precincts as units of analysis for this kind of study, it may be useful to thoroughly consider geographic units that correspond to meaningful political units. There were twenty-five Texas House districts in Harris County in the first decade of the twenty-first century, and they vary dramatically in terms of political, economic, and demographic characteristics. Of these twenty-five districts, twelve were represented by Democrats following the 2010 election and thirteen were represented by Republicans. State legislative districts are of course determined by partisan gerrymanders, so it should not be surprising that most of these districts are exceptionally uncompetitive and many representatives run unopposed. A closer look at these districts can shed light on the differences between Republican and Democratic areas within Harris County.

The American Community Survey (ACS) conducted by the Census Bureau provides detailed estimates for current Texas legislative districts by aggregating surveys conducted between 2007 and 2011. From these data, we see that most legislative districts within Harris County have experienced substantial migration, somewhat higher than the state average. The mean percentage of Texans who reported moving within the previous year according to these census data was 17.6 percent. In all Harris County legislative districts that percentage was 18.1 percent. A slightly greater percentage of residents (18.97) in Democratic districts reported a recent move than residents in Republican districts (17.15). Republican and Democratic districts differ in more interesting and important ways on other variables.

In Texas House districts within Harris County, the mean Anglo percentage of the population was 37.6 percent. In Republican districts, the mean Anglo percentage was 58.15. In Democratic districts the mean Anglo percentage was 18.69 percent. Even within these districts with different partisan complexion there was considerable variation. In the 138th District, represented by Republican Dwayne Bohac, Anglos were less than 40 percent of the population and Latinos were a plurality in 2010. Nonetheless, Bohac has won all of his recent reelection efforts by comfortable margins. This demonstrates that Republican candidates can remain competitive far longer than one might anticipate given demographic changes.

7.10 CONCLUSION

The lessons we can draw from a closer examination of a single county are of course rather limited. The chapter indicates the degree to which the use of counties as units of analysis may seriously underestimate the phenomenon of geographic polarization. When looking at VTDs in Houston in recent elections, the measure of spatial clustering was stronger than it was when we examined spatial clustering at the county level nationwide. This is despite the fact that, in the aggregate, Harris County elections are often extraordinarily close. Very few Harris County precincts are remotely competitive, and those that are competitive do not typically remain competitive for long. Only a small fraction of all voter precincts considered here were within 20 percentage points in both 2000 and 2012.

That being said, when looking at the smallest geographic units it is difficult to make the case that politically motivated migration is the main driver of this phenomenon. The political sorting of Harris County is clearly driven strongly by the racial sorting of the county. The overwhelmingly black and Latino precincts are typically also overwhelmingly Democratic. Still, it is not always possible to predict a community's political composition by looking at its racial composition. There are precincts in which whites are substantially outnumbered by minority groups and Republicans nonetheless remain competitive. There are also majority white precincts that give the Democratic Party an overwhelming majority. Furthermore, an influx of Anglo residents into what were once overwhelmingly minority precincts does not apparently translate into an increase in the Republican share of the vote.

Further, there is evidence that uncompetitive Democratic areas are more politically stable than uncompetitive Republican areas. This is consistent with the finding in individual data that Republicans prefer not to move to heavily Democratic areas, but a community's local partisan distribution does not seem, on average, to influence Democrats' overall levels of community satisfaction.

There is another important lesson from Harris County that can be applied to other communities. While changing demographics obviously pose a serious challenge to the Republican Party, the GOP can remain competitive and even dominant in many areas even as the non-Hispanic white population shrinks dramatically as a percentage of the total population. Although the Republican share of the vote tends to decrease as Anglos shrink as a percentage of the overall population, it does not always shrink as dramatically as one might anticipate and in some cases the Republican Party actually strengthens. If white voters become more Republican, on average, in the years ahead, the GOP will remain a strong party much longer than many pundits anticipate.

8   Conclusion

This book attempted to provide a useful overview of contemporary trends in migration and voting patterns in the United States and make the case that political scientists should pay close attention to demographic trends. It argued that migration patterns are leading to a more geographically polarized electorate, but noted that some migration trends are making certain communities and states more politically competitive, rather than less. This book also examined individual-level survey data in order to better determine whether or not Bishop and Cushing's (2008) hypothesis that Americans are deliberately "sorting" into politically homogenous neighborhoods was congruent with Americans' migratory behavior and their levels of community satisfaction. The findings presented here largely confirm Bishop and Cushing's intuitions— though it appears that partisan self-selection in migration is a predominantly Republican phenomenon. This book also considered the question of whether or not Republicans and Democrats systematically differ in their migration patterns for reasons not directly related to partisan politics. This was also largely confirmed by the findings presented in the preceding pages.

Rich Karlgaard, whose quote (2004) about the exodus of people out of San Francisco opened this book, is a Republican. It is interesting to contrast Karlgaard's statements with those made by Richard Florida (2002), who regularly notes that San Francisco is a top destination for people of a certain demographic—those he calls "the Creative Class." Florida is a political progressive. Both writers were correct in their analysis. Unless you are looking at total numbers (in the case of San Francisco, the total population has changed relatively little in recent decades), whether a city appears to be hemorrhaging population or experiencing a boom largely depends on the demographic groups you are considering. In Karlgaard's case, he focused on older, family-oriented individuals seeking a lower cost of living and perhaps a slower pace of life—people more like himself. Florida, on the other hand, was more focused on young college grads seeking job opportunities and the cultural amenities associated with a major urban center. To someone whose social circle predominantly includes people in the former category, the degree to which many metropolitan areas have lost people "like them" must surely be a salient demographic trend. In contrast, those who fit in

Florida's Creative Class category are less likely to even notice that their communities are losing such people.

While politics per se is not the main focus of either writer's research on migration, the groups they considered differed, on average, politically. The chapters in the second section of this book demonstrated that different demographic groups, which also exhibit different average political characteristics, exhibited fundamentally different migration patterns. The youngest migrants, who are more Democratic, tended to move out of rural areas, whereas the oldest migrants were more likely to move to such areas. Married couples, who are more likely to vote Republican, tended to congregate in communities with lower housing costs. We also saw evidence confirming the hypothesis that "professionals" tend to be more Democratic than other types of workers and that they tend to cluster together geographically.

Although the exploding minority population in the United States is one of the most important demographic trends in the country, the findings regarding the migration patterns of different racial and ethnic groups suggested that non-Hispanic whites are the main catalyst of political segregation in the United States. We saw that a key difference between landslide Republican counties and landslide Democratic counties was that Republican counties gained large numbers of whites entirely through migration, and landslide Democratic counties actually lost millions of whites in recent decades because of migration. Aggregate data cannot definitively tell us that these migrants were themselves Republicans. However, the individual data suggests that Republicans (the vast majority of whom are white) are particularly sensitive to political context when determining their levels of community satisfaction and willingness to relocate to a particular city. Racial and ethnic minorities, who are overwhelmingly Democratic, do not seem to be similarly sensitive to a community's aggregate political characteristics when determining whether or not they will live in a city, county, or state. Both landslide Republican and landslide Democratic counties gained substantial numbers of minorities in recent decades. The recent migration of African Americans back to the South seems to further confirm that the presence of large numbers of Republicans does not dissuade African Americans from moving to a state.

It may seem odd that, given that the explosive growth of the Hispanic population in recent years, non-Hispanic whites appear to be the primary catalyst for some of the most dramatic changes in the geographic–political landscape. It is true that the growing Latino population is one of the most important sociological trends in the United States. The political consequences of this trend, however, lag far behind other social changes precipitated by this major demographic development. To begin with, a large number of the Hispanics residing in the United States are not citizens and thus are not eligible to vote. Further, Hispanic citizens vote at lower rates than non-Hispanic white and African American citizens (Camarota 2010).

We should also remember that Hispanic Americans are disproportionately below the voting age. Also, although Democrats virtually always win a majority of Hispanic votes, their victories among this politically important minority group are not as lopsided as is the case for African Americans. For these reasons, many rural counties with a large number of Hispanics have remained dominated by the Republican Party, and this will likely remain the case for many election cycles to come. It is also important to note that many urban immigrant destinations, such as Chicago and New York City, would likely have voted overwhelmingly for Democrats in national elections even without the new arrivals.

Although the political impact of the growing Hispanic population is lagging behind other social impacts, that impact will surely arrive. Undocumented immigrants are not eligible to vote, but any children they have in the United States are citizens and therefore will be eligible to vote when they turn eighteen. Many agricultural communities that rely heavily on undocumented immigrant labor, which at present are some of the most reliably Republican areas of the country, may become increasingly competitive if the children of undocumented immigrants remain in the communities in which they were born. Immigration may eventually turn much of that giant swath of red in the center of the country purple or even blue.

Not all sparsely populated rural counties are major immigration destinations. Many counties experiencing population loss are likely to remain in the landslide camp—particularly the staunch Republican rural counties in the Great Plains and Mountain states and those dark blue rural counties that are majority minority. If these counties continue to empty out, their political clout will wane further and an ever-smaller share of the total U.S. population will live in such communities. At present, the exodus from rural America continues (Carr and Kefalas 2009). A scenario in which the vast majority of the U.S. population lives clustered around a relatively small number of metropolises and their suburbs and exurbs, with vast empty spaces in between, is not inconceivable.

The finding that, for at least some partisans, politics directly motivates migration patterns is important because it suggests that the phenomenon Bishop and Cushing called "The Big Sort" is here to stay. It was conceivable that this sorting process was the result of some ephemeral economic trends. That is, perhaps the degree to which certain industries (with workers tending to share political characteristics) were clustering in different communities was responsible for the changing political geography of the United States. If that was the case, perhaps changes in the American economy could "undo" the geographic partisan sort. However, if people are choosing their destinations with politics explicitly in mind, then we should expect these trends to continue until the day when Republicans and Democrats no longer prefer to have co-partisans as neighbors. Further, if members of the younger generations living in these uncompetitive contexts are themselves more likely to be socialized into being strong partisans and ideologues, they may also be more likely to eschew migrating into communities dominated by the opposing party or even into competitive counties.

To a certain extent, making demographic forecasts is easier than other kinds of forecasting in political science. Unlike any particular election cycle, which can swing wildly from initial predictions as a result of any number of stochastic elements, demography changes at a glacier's pace and predictability. We can make strong inferences about how the electorate will look in twenty years based on what the electorate looks like today. However, it is a mistake to assume that any demographic trend will continue indefinitely. The tide from the country to the cities has reversed in the past and may do so again. It is easy to imagine a scenario in which the lower cost of living in rural America makes rural communities increasingly attractive, and "rural gentrification" (Nelson, Oberg, and Nelson 2010) increases in much of the country. If we see such a reversal, then the political characteristics of these new migrants will largely determine the future political characteristics of rural America.

Humility is in order when attempting to forecast any nation's demographic future. Prognosticators confidently assert the date at which non-Hispanic whites will cease to be a majority of the population in the United States. Estimating this date should presumably be relatively simple, given that the nation has already reached the point where non-Hispanic whites represent a minority of total births. That being said, demographic predictions by erudite and celebrated scholars have been laughably wrong in the past. The developed world escaped the cycle of growth, starvation, and population decline that Thomas Malthus (1798) suggested was inescapable. During the Great Migration of Southern blacks to industrial cities in the North at the start of the twentieth century, few would have predicted that before the century was over this migration pattern would reverse and blacks would abandon New York in favor of Atlanta. The "population bomb" that Ehrlich and Ehrlich (1971) insisted would lead to mass starvation never went off. Outside of Sub-Saharan Africa, the world instead faces problems associated with dangerously low fertility and an aging population. Given this poor track record, it would be a mistake to simply assume that present migration and fertility patterns will continue indefinitely.

We should also note that American policy makers have a record of being ridiculously incorrect when predicting the demographic consequences of new policies relating to migration. No policy change had a more profound impact on American demography than the Immigration and Nationality Act of 1965. This policy opened America's doors to immigrants from Asia, Africa, and Latin America. In retrospect, the consequences of this policy change should have been obvious. However, this was apparently not obvious at the time. Edward Kennedy, who supported the law, confidently declared, "Out of deference to the critics, I want to comment on . . . what the bill will not do. First, our cities will not be flooded with a million immigrants annually. Under the proposed bill, the present level of immigration remains substantially the same . . . Secondly, the ethnic mix of this country will not be upset . . . Contrary to the charges in some quarters, S.500 will not inundate America with immigrants from any one country or area, or the most populated and economically deprived nations of Africa and Asia. In the final analysis, the ethnic pattern of immigration under the proposed measure is not expected to change as sharply as the critics seem to think."

This was not the last time a migration-related policy had unforeseen consequences. The Immigration Reform and Control Act of 1986, which provided amnesty to a portion of the undocumented population in the United States, was supposed to permanently solve the issue of undocumented immigration. This was presumably going to restrict the ability of employers to hire undocumented workers and ultimately lead to a smaller undocumented population. The enforcement provisions never came into being. Instead of solving the problem, the undocumented immigrant population in the United States rose even higher after the law was implemented.

Stronger border enforcement was supposed to lead to a decrease the number of illegal crossings into the United States. Indeed, it is difficult to imagine any other outcome. However, Douglas Massey (2007) has argued that increased border security has actually *increased* the undocumented population in the United States. Massey noted that tighter border controls near San Diego encouraged Mexican migrants to cross the border in Arizona, in places where they were actually less likely to be caught. Further, by making illegal border crossings more treacherous, strict border controls decrease the probability that an illegal immigrant will return home; an undocumented immigrant from Mexico might actually prefer to spend most of the year in Mexico, and only reside in the United States while performing seasonal work. If entering the United States requires a dangerous trek through the desert, however, he may just decide to stay in the United States permanently rather than repeat the trip multiple times.

Might current estimates about America's demographic future be similarly off base? Many projections about the future demographic profile of the United States assume that present birthrate and migration trends will persist. This might be an implausible assumption. The number of immigrants to the United States appears quite sensitive to the success of the U.S. economy. Following the recession that began in late 2007, immigration flows from Mexico declined substantially (Camarota and Jensenius 2009; Papademetriou et al. 2010). It is widely assumed that migration from Latin America and elsewhere will return to its previously high level when the economy begins to grow again, but this may not be the case. Some of the migration to the United States from Mexico and elsewhere can potentially be explained by the excess population in those immigrant-sending countries and the lack of economic opportunities within them. However, the fertility rate within Mexico has experienced a serious long-term decline. Thus the size of the population in the prime migration years (those between fifteen and thirty-nine) is a much smaller share of the population in Mexico than it was in recent decades.

There is also an argument that the birthrates of immigrants and other minority groups have been exaggerated. Emilio Parrado (2011) argued that measures used to estimate the fertility rates of immigrant women introduce serious bias into the results. When this bias is corrected, it appears immigrant women do not have a fertility rate substantially greater than that of native-born women in the United States. Furthermore, although the recent recession led to a declining birthrate for all demographic groups in the United States, it had a much stronger impact on the Latino population; from 2007 to 2010, the birthrate of all foreign-born women dropped by 14 percent and the birthrate for Mexican-born women in the United States dropped a remarkable 23 percent (Livingston and Cohn 2012). While the non-Hispanic white population will surely continue to shrink as a percentage of the overall U.S. population in the decades ahead, it may not shrink as quickly or as dramatically as many have predicted.

Just as caution should be exercised when predicting future migration and fertility patterns of demographic groups in the United States, scholars should exhibit similar restraint when predicting the voting patterns of different demographic groups. The demise of whites as an important voting bloc has probably been overstated. Although non-Hispanic whites are already a minority in some states, and they will likely be a minority nationwide within a few decades, they will remain a majority of the *electorate* for far longer. What is more, it seems as though many of those making predictions about future election cycles assume that the voting patterns of each major demographic group within the United States will remain fixed. This may also be an implausible assumption.

Although non-Hispanic whites remain the most politically heterogeneous racial/ethnic group in the United States, we cannot take it for granted that this will remain the case forever. As America becomes increasingly diverse, will non-Hispanic whites remain such an evenly split voting bloc? We can imagine a scenario in which white voters, made increasingly uneasy by the demographic changes occurring in the United States, solidify into a firm Republican coalition as they already have in many Southern states that have always been racially diverse. Such a trend would pose an important challenge to American democracy, as elections would become little more than racial head counts. This is already how the electorate behaves in states such as Alabama and Mississippi, where race is almost a perfect predictor of vote choice. On the other hand, we have the case of California, where minorities vote overwhelmingly for Democrats, but non-Hispanic whites have not made a corresponding move into the Republican camp. If younger non-Hispanic whites are at ease with the ongoing demographic changes in the United States, the Republican Party will also have to make peace with these changes if it wishes to remain a viable national party.

A look at current trends among young people might provide insights into questions about future electoral patterns. On the one hand, young voters, as a group, have been quite supportive of the Democratic Party in recent election cycles. However, it cannot necessarily be taken for granted that young Americans will remain strong Democrats indefinitely.

It is true that Obama won by a large margin among voters under the age of thirty in the 2008 presidential election. However, it is possible that the strong Democratic showing among younger voters was a short-term phenomenon related the particular circumstances surrounding that particular election. In that year there was a tremendous amount of enthusiasm among young voters for the charismatic Obama who offered an inspiring vision of change at a time of economic hardship and military quagmires in Iraq and Afghanistan—all of those circumstances were furthermore attributed to the incumbent Republican president. With such a strong showing among young voters of all racial and ethnic groups, the future for the Democratic Party at the national level seemed bright. However, that Democratic momentum appears to have stalled, as the inspiring message of the 2008 failed to translate into strong economic growth or long-term solutions to America's many seemingly interminable foreign entanglements.

As noted previously, however, some of the Democratic Party's advantage among young voters is due to racial and ethnic differences across age categories, and these advantages are not likely going to go away any time soon. Minorities are a greater share of the young population than the older population. It may therefore be interesting to look exclusively at the voting patterns of young whites. Within this demographic category, there has been a substantial swing in recent years. In 2008, Obama won a sizable victory among every racial and ethnic group, including non-Hispanic whites, under the age of thirty (Keeter, Horowitz, and Tyson 2008). Because of this, the Democratic Party's future as the majority party seemed secure. In 2012, Obama again won a majority of young voters, but his support from young whites eroded substantially. In 2008, Obama won 54 percent of the under-thirty white vote. In 2012, Obama only won 44 percent of the votes of young whites (Pew Research Center 2012)—a drop of 11 percentage points in only four years. The drop was especially substantial among white men—Obama won this demographic group in 2008, but Romney carried this group easily in 2012. The decline in Democratic support from 2008 to 2012 was most dramatic among non-Hispanic whites with lower levels of education. Obama earned a majority of votes from young whites without a college education in 2008, but in 2012 he only received 38 percent of their votes. Mitt Romney, co-founder of Bain Capital, was probably not the ideal Republican candidate for wooing young, working-class whites; however, one can imagine a GOP presidential candidate more capable of capitalizing on the waning support lesser-educated whites give to Democrats. Again, there is no way to confidently assert how different groups will vote in the future. The dream that race would become a less important issue in American politics after the election of Barack Obama has not materialized. Since 2008, the racial gap in politics appears to be growing, even among the youngest voters. If whites, particularly working-class whites, become increasingly Republican, then several large states that were once overwhelmingly Democratic will perhaps be in play. This will be true even if the Democratic Party maintains its lopsided advantage among nonwhites. Immigration may cost the

Republican Party the Southwest, but a more racially polarized electorate could cost the Democrats some Upper Midwest states such as Wisconsin, Michigan, and Minnesota.

The relationship between home values, marriage rates, and aggregate voting patterns also suggests that changes in the housing market will shape future political landscapes. The bursting of the U.S. housing bubble was the catalyst for a major economic crisis, and that crisis remains the salient economic impact of that particular market correction. It remains to be seen how the housing market will change when robust economic growth returns, though it is unlikely that home values will return to their former stratospheric heights. The degree to which housing was prohibitively expensive in many markets may have been a short-term phenomenon. If homes in many urban markets remain affordable, will we still see young, Republican-leaning married couples move out to the suburbs and exurbs when they decide they want to buy a home? If not, we can imagine a scenario in which many former Democratic strongholds become increasingly attractive to Republicans. Again, we should be cautious about assuming how economic changes will influence migratory patterns given that politics seems to directly play a role in such decisions; even if liberal metropolises become more affordable, Republicans may avoid such communities simply because of their reputation for liberalism.

It should again be reiterated how problematic it is to make confident predictions about America's electoral future. It was not long ago that some respected pundits were confident that America was on the verge of establishing a "permanent Republican majority" (Hewitt 2006). The GOP appeared down for the count after its disastrous performances in 2006 and 2008, but experienced an historic resurgence in 2010—though it was unable to maintain that momentum in 2012.

There are a number of groups that received relatively little attention in this book, but whose migrations and voting behaviors could potentially have important electoral consequences. The movements of gay Americans deserve further attention from scholars. Richard Florida (2002) has written extensively about how the presence of a large number of gay Americans predicts a large number of cultural, economic, and political attributes. Gay households were not examined here because of a dearth of reliable data. According to the most recent estimates from the United States Census Bureau (2010), there were 440,989 same-sex unmarried couples in the United States in 2010, which is a very small number in comparison to the entire U.S. population. What is more, these numbers tell us nothing about the migration patterns of such couples, which is the focus of this research. These numbers only provide estimates of gay households, and provide little reliable information about the total number of homosexuals living in a community—for understandable reasons, the census does not ask respondents to provide their sexual orientation. Nonetheless, it is easy to imagine how the movements of gay Americans may be changing the political landscape in important ways. For example, if a community develops a reputation for social tolerance (which also tends to correspond with political liberalism and Democratic voting), it may become a major destination for gay Americans. As a result of these migrations, a community may develop a reputation as a "gay neighborhood," which will assuredly attract some residents but repel others. Even if, in the aggregate, only a relatively small minority in a community identifies as gay, that reputation may shape the immigration and emigration patterns of other groups in that community. Should more reliable migration data for gay Americans become available, this possibility should be examined more thoroughly.

Asian Americans are another demographic group that received little attention in this book but deserve greater study from political scientists in the future. Asian Americans are a smaller percentage of the electorate than African Americans and Latinos, but they are a potentially important voting bloc because the group is growing quickly and overwhelmingly supported the Democratic Party in 2012 (May 2012). That being said, Asian Americans tend to be clustered in a handful of states, and those states tend to be uncompetitive. Three-quarters of the Asian American population lives in ten states. Of the five states with the largest percentage of the population that identifies as Asian (California, Hawaii, New Jersey, New York, and Washington), all were uncompetitive Democratic states in 2012. Of the ten states with the largest Asian population as a percentage of the state population, only Nevada and Virginia can be appropriately described as swing states. That being said, the Asian population has been growing quickly, and its voting patterns will be important in the years ahead. The size of this population in a number of states has been growing tremendously in recent decades, though the baseline population was relatively small. From 2000 to 2010, the Asian population grew by 71 percent in Florida and 62 percent in Pennsylvania (Hoeffel et al. 2010).

Beyond the way migration is influencing the outcomes of partisan elections, can we say anything definitive about the normative consequences of a rise in the number of uncompetitive geographic units? That depends on the weight you give to different variables. If you consider competitive elections per se a good thing, then this trend is obviously problematic. On the other hand, if it is a positive development when more Americans are represented by the people they actually voted for, then geographic polarization should be welcomed. Whether or not the political or cultural changes associated with this geographic sort represent a "good thing" is beyond the scope of this book. However, it appears that some of this spatial clustering is due to the certain elements of the American electorate considering politics directly when determining where to live. Furthermore, many of those Americans who end up in neighborhoods where the local political attitudes are congruent with their own seem to be happier with their communities. While this may be leading to a slightly more polarized electorate, it is unclear what, if anything, can or should be done about this trend. If individual Americans are genuinely happier as a result of their moves, perhaps their happiness should trump concerns about nebulous problems such as polarization.

Notes

NOTES TO CHAPTER 1

1. It is important to note that not all political scientists believe the number of swing states in the United States is low by historical standards (Glaeser and Ward 2006).
2. The Glenmary data are not without problems. Some smaller congregations did not respond to the survey. Therefore some of the county-level data may underestimate the total number of religiously observant residents. Also, some congregations clearly overestimated their membership, as some smaller counties show that more than 100 percent of all residents belong to a religious congregation. In spite of these potential problems, the Glenmary data are the best source for aggregate religious affiliation data for the first decade of the twenty-first century.
3. In Chinni and Gimpel's (2010) categorization, these counties are called "Evangelical Epicenters," "Mormon Outposts," and "Tractor Country." They, on average, gave John McCain 66 percent, 72 percent, and 64 percent of their votes, respectively.
4. It is important to distinguish between all voters and all residents because, in some rural counties, there is a large nonvoting Hispanic population. However, much of that population is undocumented or under the age of eighteen and therefore not eligible to vote.

NOTE TO CHAPTER 2

1. By this, Ravenstein meant that the migrants into urban areas typically came from the countryside immediately surrounding those urban areas, and migrants into the rural areas outside urban areas migrated from more distant rural areas.

NOTES TO CHAPTER 3

1. Other models were created but not provided in this chapter. I initially thought an ordered logit, in which all categories were retained, would be an appropriate model. However, diagnostic tests of this model demonstrated that it violated the parallel regression assumption. A multinomial logit model was also created, and it provided results similar to the logit model. I ultimately decided to provide only the logit model because of its greater simplicity.

2. This report did not provide vote totals for Seattle, Washington, so I collected those data by using vote totals for King County, which includes the entire city of Seattle and its surrounding suburbs.
3. I found similar results when comparing the 2000 election to the 2008 election. I chose to compare the 1996 and the 2008 election in the above analysis because the Democratic candidate won by a significant margin in both elections.
4. A line for the migration patterns in competitive "purple" counties was not included in order to make it easier to interpret Figures 3.2, 3.3, and 3.4. However, had the trend line for competitive counties been included it would have fallen in between the other two lines for all age cohorts.

NOTES TO CHAPTER 4

1. Interestingly, though there is a strong marriage gap in partisan politics, there does not seem to be such a readily apparent relationship between parenthood and partisan preferences (Elder and Greene 2007). For this reason, I will focus primarily on marriage for the rest of this section.
2. Specifically, this variable was created using the 2000 United States Census and includes all those women currently married, those separated, those widowed, and those divorced.
3. Although only the spatial error models are presented in this book, I also tested all of these hypotheses using spatial lag models. The results were substantively identical in all cases.

NOTE TO CHAPTER 5

1. The migration rate, rather than net migration, was the dependent variable for these models because the total net migration was heavily skewed by a relatively small number of counties that experienced massive net changes. Taking the natural log of this variable was not an option because the net migration was very often zero or negative. The county migration rate in these data is simply the net migration during the 1990s divided by the 2000 population not attributable to migration. Although they are problematic, models were also created in which net migration was the dependent variable, with similar results.

NOTES TO CHAPTER 6

1. Based on median income.
2. Specifically, the data file provided the following occupation categories: farm employment, forestry/fishing/related, mining, utilities, construction, manufacturing, wholesale trade, retail trade, transportation/warehousing, information, finance and insurance, real estate/rental/leasing, professional/technical services, management of companies/enterprises, administrative and waste services, educational services, health care and social assistance, arts/entertainment/recreation, accommodation/food services, other services except public administration, civilian federal employment, military federal employment, state and local government employment.

3. To be sure, 0.5 is obviously a rather low factor loading—in the social sciences, you rarely see a loading of less than 0.7 used when generating scales. This is a weakness in this analysis, and may account for the null results presented in the forthcoming pages.
4. It is, however, congruent with James Burnham's (1941) argument that managers at large corporations were actually the opposite of a bulwark of capitalism, and instead would be leaders in America's move toward a more socialistic society.

NOTE TO CHAPTER 7

1. I thank Dr. Richard Murray of the University of Houston for sharing these data with me.

Works Cited

Abramowitz, Alan I. 2010. "Transformation and Polarization: The 2008 Presidential Election and the New American Electorate." *Electoral Studies* 29 (4): 594–603.
———, and Kyle L. Saunders. 2008. "Is Polarization a Myth?" *Journal of Politics* 70 (2): 542–55.
Abramson, Paul R., John H. Aldrich, and David W. Rohde. 2010. *Change and Continuity in the 2008 Elections*. Washington, DC: CQ Press.
Agrawal, David. 2006. *New England Migration Trends*. No. 06–1. Federal Reserve Bank of Boston.
Aistrup, Joseph A. 1996. *The Southern Strategy Revisited: Republican Top-Down Advancement in the South*. Lexington: University Press of Kentucky.
Allard, Scott W., and Sheldon Danziger. 2000. "Welfare Magnets: Myth or Reality?" *Journal of Politics* 62 (2): 350–68.
Allport, Gordon W. 1954. *The Nature of Prejudice*. New York: Doubleday.
Alvarez, R. Michael, and Tara L. Butterfield. 2000. "The Resurgence of Nativism in California: The Case of Proposition 187 and Illegal Immigration." *Social Science Quarterly* 81: 167–79.
Amir, Hehuda. 1969. "Contact Hypothesis in Ethnic Relations." *Psychological Bulletin*. 71 (5): 319–342.
Artz, Georgeanne. 2003. "Rural Brain Drain: Is It a Reality?" *Choices*, 18 (4): 11–15.
Bach, Robert L., and Joel Smith. 1977. "Community Satisfaction, Expectations of Moving, and Migration." *Demography* 14 (2): 147–67.
Bagchi-Sen, Sharmistha. 2003. "An Empirical Analysis of Migration in Information-Intensive Work in the United States." *Service Industries Journal* 23 (1): 136–66.
Bajari, Patrick, and Matthew Khan. 2005. "Estimating Housing Demand with an Application to Explaining Racial Segregation in the Cities." *American Statistical Association Journal of Business & Economic Statistics* 23 (1): 20–33.
Barff, R. A.1989. "Migration and the Labor Supply in New England." *Geoforum* 20: 293–301.
———. 1990. "The Migration Response to the Economic Turnaround in New England." *Environment and Planning*. 22 (11): 1497–1516.
Barna Group. 2011. *Major Faith Shifts Evident among Whites, Blacks, and Hispanicssince1991*.http://www.barna.org/faith-spirituality/510-major-faith-shifts-evident-among-whites-blacks-and-hispanics-since-1991. Accessed November 30, 2012.
Barreto, Matt A. 2005. "Latino Immigrants at the Polls: Foreign-Born Voter Turnout in the 2002 Election." *Political Research Quarterly* 58 (1): 79–86.
———, and Nathan D. Woods. 2000. *Voting Patterns and the Dramatic Growth of the Latino Electorate in Los Angeles County, 1994–1998*. Claremont, CA: Tomas Rivera Policy Institute.

Bartels, Larry. 2000. "Partisanship and Voting Behavior, 1952–1996." *American Journal of Political Science* 44 (1): 35–50.

———. 2002. "Beyond the Running Tally: Partisan Bias in Political Perceptions." *Political Behavior* 24 (2): 117–50.

———. 2008. *Unequal Democracy: The Political Economy of the New Gilded Age.* New York: Russell Sage Foundation.

Bassett, Laura. 2012, November 7. "Gender Gap in 2012 Election Aided Obama Win." *Huffington Post.* http://www.huffingtonpost.com/2012/11/07/gender-gap-2012-election-obama_n_2086004.html. Accessed November 22, 2012.

Bay Area Center for Voting Research. 2005. *The Most Conservative and Liberal Cities in the United States.* San Francisco, CA: Bay Area Center for Voting Research.

Baybeck, Brady, and Robert Huckfeldt. 2002a. "Spatially Dispersed Ties among Citizens: Connecting Individuals and Aggregates." *Political Analysis* 10: 261–75.

———. 2002b. "Urban Contexts, Spatially Dispersed Networks, and the Diffusion of Political Information." *Political Geography* 21: 195–220.

Bayer, Patrick, Fernando Ferreira, and Robert McMillan. 2007. "A Unified Framework for Measuring Preferences for Schools and Neighborhoods." *Journal of Political Economy* 115 (4): 588–638.

Beatty, Kathleen Murphy, and B. Oliver Walter. 1988. "Fundamentalists, Evangelicals and Politics." *American Politics Research* 16: 43–59.

Bennett, James T., and William P. Orzechowski. 1983. "The Voting Behavior of Bureaucrats: Some Empirical Evidence." *Public Choice* 41 (2): 271–83.

Bennett, Jessica, and Jesse Ellison. 2010, July 6. "Women Will Rule the World: Men Were the Main Victims of the Recession. The Recovery Will Be Female." *Newsweek.* http://www.thedailybeast.com/newsweek/2010/07/06/women-will-rule-the-world.html. Accessed November 22, 2012.

Berelson, Bernard R., Paul F. Lazarsfeld, and William N. McPhee. 1954. *Voting: A Study of Opinion Formation in a Presidential Campaign.* Chicago: University of Chicago Press.

Bickford, Susan. 2000. "Constructing Inequality: City Spaces and the Architecture of Citizenship." *Political Theory.* 28 (3): 355–376.

Bilefsky, Dan. 2011, June 21. "For New Life, Blacks in City Head to South." *New York Times.* http://www.nytimes.com/2011/06/22/nyregion/many-black-new-yorkers-are-moving-to-the-south.html?pagewanted=1&_r=2&emc=eta1. Accessed December 2, 2012.

Bishop, Bill, and Robert Cushing. 2008. *The Big Sort: Why the Clustering of Like-Minded America Is Tearing Us Apart.* New York: Mariner Books.

Blais, Andre. 2000. *To Vote or Not to Vote?* Pittsburgh, PA: University of Pittsburgh Press.

Blalock, H.M. 1967. *Towards a Theory of Minority Group Relations.* New York: Wiley.

Blanchard, Olivier Jean, and Lawrence F. Katz. 1992. "Regional Evolutions." *Brookings Papers on Economic Activity* 1: 1–37.

Bogue, Donald J., Gregory Liegel, and Michael Kozloski. 2009. *Immigration, Internal Migration, and Local Mobility in the U.S.* Cheltenham, UK: Edward Elgar.

Books, John, and Charles Prysby. 1991. *Political Behavior and the Local Context.* New York: Praeger.

Borjas, George. 1999. "Immigration and Welfare Magnets." *Journal of Labor Economics* 17 (4): 607–37.

Bowler, Shaun, Stephen P. Nicholson, and Gary M. Segura. 2006. "Earthquakes and Aftershocks: Race, Direct Democracy, and Partisan Change." *American Journal of Political Science* 50 (1): 146–59.

Brandon, Emily. 2008, October 8. "10 Great Retirement Spots for Democrats and Republicans." *U.S. News & World Report.* http://money.usnews.com/money/personal-finance/best-places-to-retire/articles/2008/10/08/10-great-places-to-retire-for-democrats-and-republicans. Accessed November, 25, 2012.

Brien, Michael J. 1997. "Racial Differences in Marriage and the Role of Marriage Markets." *Journal of Human Resources* 32 (4): 741–78.

Brimicombe, Alan J. 2007. "Ethnicity, Religion, and Residential Segregation in London: Evidence from a Computational Typology of Minority Communities." *Environment and Planning B: Planning and Design* 34 (5): 884–904.

Brint, Steven. 1984. " 'New-Class' and Cumulative Trend Explanations of the Liberal Political Attitudes of Professionals." *American Journal of Sociology* 90: 30–71.

Brooks, Clem. 2002. "Religious Influence and the Politics of Family Decline Concern: Trends, Sources, and U.S. Political Behavior." *American Sociological Review* 67 (2): 191–211.

———, and Jeff Manza. 1997. "Class Politics and Political Change in the United States, 1952–1992." *Social Forces* 76 (2): 379–408.

———, and Jeff Manza. 2004. "A Great Divide? Religion and Political Change in U.S. National Elections, 1972–2000." *Sociological Quarterly* 45 (3): 421–50.

Brown, Clifford W., Lynda W. Powell, and Clyde Wilcox. 1995. *Serious Money: Fundraising and Contributing in Presidential Nomination Campaigns.* Cambridge, UK: Cambridge University Press.

Brown, David L., Benjamin C. Bolender, Laszlo J. Kulcsar, Nina Glasgow, and Scott Sanders. 2011. "Inter-County Variability of Net Migration at Older Ages as a Path Dependent Process." *Rural Sociology* 76 (1): 44–73.

Brown, Lawrence A., and Eric G. Moore. 1971. "The Intra-Urban Migration Process: A Spatial Perspective." In *Internal Structure of the City: Readings on Space and Environment,* edited by L. S. Bourne, 200–209. New York: Oxford University Press.

Brown, Thad. 1988. *Migration and Politics.* Chapel Hill: University of North Carolina Press.

Brunell, Thomas L. 2006a. "Rethinking Redistricting: How Drawing Uncompetitive Districts Eliminates Gerrymanders, Enhances Representation, and Improves Attitudes toward Congress." *PS: Political Science & Politics* 39 (1): 77–85.

———. 2006b. *Redistricting and Representation: Why Competitive Elections Are Bad for America.* New York: Routledge.

Bullock, Charles S., Donna R. Hoffman, and Ronald Keith Gaddie. 2005. "The Consolidation of the White Southern Congressional Vote." *Political Research Quarterly* 58 (2): 231–43.

Burnham, James. 1941. *The Managerial Revolution: What is Happening in the World.* New York: John Day.

Byrne, J. Peter. 2003. "Two Cheers for Gentrification." *Howard Law Journal* 46 (3): 405–32.

Cadwallader, Martin. 1992. *Migration and Residential Mobility: Macro and Micro Approaches.* Madison: University of Wisconsin Press.

Cahn, Naomi, and June Carbone. 2010. *Red Families v. Blue Families: Legal Polarization and the Creation of Culture.* New York: Oxford University Press.

Cairncross, Frances. 1997. *The Death of Distance: How the Communications Revolution Will Change Our Lives.* Boston: Harvard Business School Press.

Callahan, David. 2010. *Fortunes of Change: The Rise of the Liberal Rich and the Remaking of America.* Hoboken, NJ: John Wiley and Sons.

Camarota, Steven. 2010, October. "The Hispanic Vote in the Upcoming 2010 Elections." *Backgrounder.* Washington, DC: Center for Immigration Studies.

————, and Karen Jensenius. 2009. *A Shifting Tide: Recent Trends in the Illegal Immigrant Population.* Washington, DC: Center for Immigration Studies.

Campbell, Angus, Philip E. Converse, Warren E. Miller, and Donald E. Stokes. 1960. *The American Voter.* New York: Wiley and Sons.

Carmines, Edward G., and James A. Stimson. 1989. *Issue Evolution: Race and the Transformation of American Politics.* Princeton, NJ: Princeton University Press.

Carr, Patrick J., and Maria J. Kefalas. 2009. *Hollowing out the Middle: The Rural Brain Drain and What It Means for America.* Boston: Beacon Press.

Cassese, Erin. 2007. "Culture Wars as Identity Politics." PhD diss., Stony Brook University.

Cesca, Bob. 2009, August 5. "Keep Your Goddamn Government Hands off My Medicare!" *Huffington Post.* http://www.huffingtonpost.com/bob-cesca/get-your-goddamn-governme_b_252326.html. Accessed November 20, 2012.

Charles, Camille Zubrinsky. 2003. "The Dynamics of Racial Residential Segregation." *Annual Review of Sociology* 29: 167–207.

Chinni, Dante, and James Gimpel. 2010. *Our Patchwork Nation: The Surprising Truth about the "Real" America.* New York: Gotham Books.

Cho, Wendy K. Cam, and James Gimpel. 2007. "Prospecting for (Campaign) Gold." *American Journal of Political Science* 51 (2): 255–68.

Cho, Wendy K., James G. Gimpel, and Iris Hui. 2009. "Regional Migration Flows and the Partisan Sorting of the American Electorate." Presented at the American Politics Workshop, University at Buffalo, The State University of New York.

Choldin, Harvey M. 1973. "Kinship Networks in the Migration Process." *International Migration Review* 7 (2): 163–75.

Clark, Rebecca. 1992. *Does Welfare Affect Migration?* Washington, DC: Urban Institute.

Clark, Terry Nichols. 2003. "Urban Amenities: Lakes, Opera, and Juice Bars: Do They Drive Development?" In *The City as an Entertainment Machine*, ed. Terry Nichols Clark, 103–176. Oxford: JAI/Elsevier.

Clark, William A. V., and Jun L. Onaka. 1983. "Life Cycle and Housing Adjustment as Explanations of Residential Mobility." *Urban Studies* 20 (1): 47–57.

Clark, William A. V., M. C. Deurloo, and F. M. Dieleman. 1984. "Housing Consumption and Residential Mobility." *Annals of the Association of American Geographers* 74 (1): 29–43.

Clarkberg, Marin, Ross M. Stolzenberg, and Linda J. Waite. 1995. "Attitudes, Values, and Entrance into Cohabitational versus Marital Union." *Social Forces* 74 (2): 609–32.

Cohn, D'Vera, and Rich Morin. 2008. *Who Moves? Who Stays Put? Where's Home?* Pew Research Center. http://pewsocialtrends.org/2008/12/17/who-moves-who-stays-put-wheres-home/. Accessed February 23, 2011.

Coleman, James S. 1975. "Recent Trends in School Integration." *Educational Researcher* 4 (7): 3–12.

Converse, Philip. 1964. "The Nature of Belief Systems in Mass Publics." In *Ideology and Discontent*, ed. David Apter, 206–261. New York: Free Press.

————. 1966. "The Concept of the Normal Vote." In *Elections and the Political Order*, eds. Campbell Angus, Philip E. Converse, Warren E. Miller and Donald E. Stokes, 9–39. New York: Wiley.

————. 1976. *The Dynamics of Party Support: Cohort-Analyzing Party Identification.* Beverley Hills, CA: Sage Press.

Copelin, Laylan. 2012, October 27. "Austin Struggling to Recruit, Retain Black Professionals." *Austin American-Statesman.* http://www.statesman.com/news/news/local/austin-struggling-to-recruit-retain-black-professi/nSpjg/. Accessed November 29, 2012.

Corey, Elizabeth C., and James C. Garand. 2002. "Are Government Employees More Likely to Vote?: An Analysis of Turnout in the 1996 U.S. National Election." *Public Choice* 111 (3/4): 259–83.

DaVanzo, Julie. 1978. "Does Unemployment Affect Migration? Evidence from Micro Data." *Review of Economics and Statistics* 60 (4): 504–14.

De la Garza, Rodolfo O., and Jeronimo Cortina. 2007. "Are Latinos Republican but Just Don't Know It?" *American Politics Research* 35 (2): 202–23.

Dekker, Paul, and Peter Ester. 1990. "The Political Distinctiveness of Young Professionals: 'Yuppies' or 'New Class'?" *Political Psychology* 11 (2): 309–30.

Denvir, Daniel. 2011, March 29. "The 10 Most Segregated Urban Areas in America." *Salon.* http://www.salon.com/2011/03/29/most_segregated_cities/. Accessed December 10, 2012.

DiMaggio, Paul, John Evans, and Bethany Bryson. 1996. "Have Americans' Social Attitudes Become More Polarized?" *American Journal of Sociology* 102 (3): 690–755.

Dyck, Joshua D., Brian D. Gaines, and Daron R. Shaw. 2009. "The Effect of Local Political Context on How Americans Vote." *American Politics Research* 37 (6): 1088–1115.

Easterlin, Richard A. 1980. *Birth and Fortune: The Impact of Numbers on Personal Welfare.* New York: Basic Books.

———. 2000. "Twentieth-Century American Population Growth." In *The Cambridge Economic History of the United States.* Vol. 3, eds. Stanley L. Engleman and Robert E. Gallman. Cambridge, UK: Cambridge University Press, 505–548.

Edlund, Lena, and Rohini Pande. 2002. "Why Have Women Become Left-Wing? The Political Gender Gap and the Decline of Marriage." *Quarterly Journal of Economics* 117: 917–62.

Edlund, Lena, Laila Haider, and Rohini Pande. 2005. "Unmarried Parenthood and Redistributive Politics." *Journal of the European Economic Association* 3 (1): 95–119.

Edsall, Thomas B. 2011, November 27. "The Future of the Obama Coalition." *Campaign Stops: Strong Opinions on the 2012 Election.* http://campaignstops.blogs.nytimes.com/2011/11/27/the-future-of-the-obama-coalition/. Accessed December 6, 2011.

Ehrlich, Paul R., and Anne Ehrlich. 1971. *The Population Bomb.* New York: Buccaneer Books.

Elder, Laurel, and Steven Greene. 2007. "The Myth of 'Security Moms' and 'NASCAR Dads': Parenthood, Political Stereotypes, and the 2004 Election." *Social Science Quarterly* 88 (1): 1–19.

Ellison, Glenn, and Edward L. Glaeser. 1997. "Geographic Concentration in U.S. Manufacturing Industries: A Dartboard Approach." *Journal of Political Economy* 105 (5): 889–927.

Erikson, Robert, and Kent Tedin. 2005. *American Public Opinion.* 7th ed. New York: Pearson-Longman.

Evans, John. 2003. "Have Americans' Attitudes Become More Polarized? An Update." *Social Science Quarterly* 84 (1): 71–90.

Farley, Reynolds, Charlotte Steeh, Maria Krysan, Tara Jackson, and Keith Reeves. 1994. "Stereotypes and Segregation: Neighborhoods in the Detroit Area." *American Journal of Sociology* 100 (3): 750–80.

Feijten, Peteke, and Clara H. Mulder. 2002. "The Timing of Household Events and Housing Events in the Netherlands: A Longitudinal Perspective." *Housing Studies* 17 (5): 773–92.

Feldman, Maryann P. 1999. "The New Economics of Innovation, Spillovers, and Agglomeration: A Review of Empirical Studies." *Economics of Innovation and New Technology* 8 (1–2): 5–25.

Felson, Marcus, and Mauricio Solaun. 1975. "The Fertility-Inhibiting Effect of Crowded
Apartment Living in a Tight Housing Market." *The American Journal of Sociology.* 80 (6): 1410–27.

Feser, Edward J., and Stuart H. Sweeney. 2000. "A Test for the Coincident Economic and Spatial Clustering of Business Enterprises." *Journal of Geographic Systems* 2: 349–73.

Finifter, Ada W. 1974. "The Friendship Group as a Protective Environment for Political Deviants." *American Political Science Review.* 66 (2): 607–25.

Fiorina, Morris. 1981. *Retrospective Voting in American Elections.* New Haven: Yale University Press.

Fiorina, Morris, Samuel J. Abrams, and Jeremy C. Pope. 2005. *Culture War? The Myth of a Polarized America.* New York: Pearson Longman.

Fiorina, Morris and Samuel J. Abrams. 2008. "Political Polarization in the American Public." *Annual Review of Political Science.* 11: 563–588.

Fisher, Patrick. 2010. "The Age Gap in the 2008 Presidential Election." *Society* 47: 295–300.

Fisher, Robert. 1989. "Urban Policy in Houston, TX." *Urban Studies* 26: 144–54.

Flores, Lisa Y., Monique M. Mendoza, Lizette Ojeda, Yuhong He, Rocio Rosales Meza, Veronica Medina, Julie Wagner Ladehoff, and Shiloh Jordan. 2011. "A Qualitative Inquiry of Latino Immigrants' Work Experiences in the Midwest." *Journal of Counseling Psychology* 58 (4): 522–36.

Florida, Richard. 2002. *The Rise of the Creative Class.* New York: Basic Books.

———. 2008. *Who's Your City? How the Creative Economy Is Making Where to Live the Most Important Decision of Your Life.* New York: Basic Books.

Francis, Sam. 1997. *Revolution from the Middle.* Raleigh, NC: Middle America Press.

Frank, Thomas. 2004. *What's the Matter with Kansas: How Conservatives Won the Heart of America.* New York: Metropolitan Books.

Freeman, Richard B. 1979. "The Effect of Demographic Factors on Age-Earnings Profiles." *Journal of Human Resources* 14: 289–318.

Frey, William. 1999. "New Black Migration Patterns in the United States: Are They Affected by Recent Migration?" In *Immigration and Opportunity: Race, Ethnicity, and Employment in the United States,* eds. Frank D. Bean and Stephanie Bell-Rose. New York: Russell Sage Foundation, 311–344.

———. 2004. *The New Great Migration: Black Americans' Return to the South, 1965–2000.* Washington, DC: Center on Urban and Metropolitan Policy, Brookings Institute.

———. 2005. *The Electoral College Moves to the Sun Belt.* Washington, DC: The Brookings Institution.

———. 2009. "The Great American Migration Slowdown: Regional and Metropolitan Dimensions." Washington, DC: Center on Urban and Metropolitan Policy, Brookings Institute.

Frey, William H. 1987. "Migration and Depopulation of the Metropolis: Regional Restructuring or Rural Renaissance?" *American Sociological Review* 52 (2): 240–57.

———, and Kao-Lee Liaw. 1998. "Immigrant Concentration and Domestic Migrant Dispersal: Is Movement to Nonmetropolitan Areas 'White Flight'?" *Professional Geographer* 50 (2): 215–32.

Friedman, Thomas. 2005. *The World Is Flat: A Brief History of the 21st Century.* New York: Farrar, Straus and Giroux.

Fry, Richard, and Paul Taylor. 2012. *The Rise of Residential Segregation by Income.* Washington, DC: Pew Research Center.

Fuguitt, Glenn V. 1985. "The Nonmetropolitan Population Turnaround." *Annual Review of Sociology* 11: 259–80.

Garand, James C., Catherine T. Parkhurst, and Rusanne Jourdan Seoud. 1991. "Bureaucrats, Policy Attitudes, and Political Behavior: Extension of the Bureau Voting Model of Government Growth." *Journal of Public Administration Research and Theory* 1 (2): 177–212.

Garkovich, Loraine. 1989. *Population and Community in Rural America*. New York: Greenwood Press.

Gauthier, Ann H. 2007. "The Impact of Family Policies on Fertility in Industrialized Countries: A Review of the Literature." *Population Research and Policy Review* 26 (3): 323–46.

Gelman, Andrew, and Jennifer Hill. 2007. *Data Analysis Using Regression and Multilevel/Hierarchical Models*. Cambridge, MA: Cambridge University Press.

Gelman, Andrew, David Park, Boris Shor, Joseph Bafumi, and Jeronimo Cortina. 2008. *Red State, Blue State, Rich State, Poor State: Why Americans Vote the Way They Do*. Princeton, NJ: Princeton University Press.

Gerber, Alan S., Donald P. Green, and Christopher W. Larimer. 2008. "Social Pressure and Voter Turnout: Evidence from a Large-Scale Field Experiment." *American Political Science Review* 102 (1): 33–48.

Gershkoff, Amy R. 2009. "The Marriage Gap." In *Beyond Red State, Blue State: Electoral Gaps in the Twenty-First Century American Electorate*, eds. by Laura Olson and John C. Green. Upper Saddle River, NJ: Pearson Prentice Hall, 24–39.

Gerson, Kathleen. 1987. "Emerging Social Divisions among Women: Implications for Welfare State Politics." *Politics & Society* 15 (2): 213–21.

Gey, Benny. 2006. "Explaining Voter Turnout: A Review of Aggregate-Level Research." *Electoral Studies* 25 (4): 637–63.

Gilliam, Franklin D. 1985. "Influences on Voter Turnout for U.S. House Elections in Non- Presidential Years." *Legislative Studies Quarterly* 10 (3): 339–51.

Gimpel, James G. 1999. *Separate Destinations: Migration, Immigration, and the Politics of Places*. Ann Arbor: University of Michigan Press.

———. 2010, February. "Immigration, Political Realignment, and the Demise of Republican Political Prospects." *Backgrounder*. Washington, DC: Center for Immigration Studies.

———, and Jason E. Schuknecht 2001. "Interstate Migration and Electoral Politics." *Journal of Politics* 63 (1): 207–31.

———, Francis E. Lee, and Joshua Kaminski. 2006. "The Political Geography of Campaign Contributions in American Politics." *Journal of Politics* 68 (3): 626–39.

———, and Kimberly A. Karnes. 2009. "TheRural-Urban Gap." In *Beyond Red State, Blue State: Electoral Gaps in the Twenty-First Century American Electorate*, eds. Laura Olson and John C. Green. Upper Saddle River, NJ: Pearson Prentice Hall, 74–91.

Glaeser, Edward L., and Bryce A. Ward. 2006. "Myths and Realities of American Political Geography." *Journal of Economic Perspectives* 20 (2): 119–44.

Glaeser, Edward L., and Jacob Vigdor. 2012. "The End of the Segregated Century: Racial Separation in America's Neighborhoods, 1890–2010." Civil Report 66. New York: Manhattan Institute for Policy Research.

Glaser, James. 1994. "Back to the Black Belt: Racial Environment and White Racial Attitudes in the South." *Journal of Politics* 56 (1): 21–41.

Goodsell, Willystine. 1937. "Housing and Birthrates in Sweden." *American Sociological Review*. 2 (6): 850–59.

Goren, Paul. 2005. "Party Identification and Core Political Values." *American Journal of Political Science* 49 (4): 882–97.

Goss, E. P. (1985). "General Skills, Specific Skills and the Migration Decision." *Journal of Regional Analysis and Policy* 15 (2): 17–26.

Greeley, Andrew M., & Joe L. Spaeth. 1970. "Research Note: Political Change among College Alumni." *Sociology of Education* 43 (1): 106–13.

Green, Donald. 1998. "On the Dimensionality of Public Sentiment toward Partisan and Ideological Groups." *American Journal of Political Science* 32 (3): 758–80.

———, Bradley Palmquist, and Erik Schickler. 2002. *Partisan Hearts and Minds: Political Parties and the Social Identities of Voters*. New Haven, CT: Yale University Press.

Grigg, D. B. 1977. "E. G. Ravenstein and the 'Laws of Migration.' " *Journal of Historical Geography* 3 (1): 41–54.

Griliches, Zvi. 1992. "The Search for R&D Spillovers." *Scandinavian Journal of Economics* 94: 29–47.

Hackworth, Jason. 2007. *The Neoliberal City: Governance, Ideology, and Development in American Urbanism*. Ithaca, NY: Cornell University Press.

Hajnal, John. 1965. "European Marriage Patterns in Perspective." In *Population and History: Essays on Historical Demography*. eds. D.V. Glass and D.E.C. Eversley, 101–143. London: Arnold.

Hamilton, Reeve. 2010, August 30. "Five Years Later, Houstonians Conflicted about Katrina." *Texas Tribune*. http://www.texastribune.org/texas-politics/texas-political-news/five-years-houstonians-conflicted-about-katrina/. Accessed December 10, 2012.

Hammond, John L. 1986. "Yuppies." *Public Opinion Quarterly* 50 (4): 487–501.

Hanson, Russell, and John Hartman. 1994. *Do Welfare Magnets Attract?* Madison, WI: Institute for Research on Poverty.

Hawley, George. 2013. "Local Political Context and Polarization in the Electorate: Evidence from the 2004 Presidential Election." *American Review of Politics*. 34 (1): Article 1.

Hegstrom, Edward. 2005, December 4. "Shadows Cloaking Immigrants Prevents Accurate Count." *Houston Chronicle*. http://www.chron.com/news/houston-texas/article/Shadows-cloaking-immigrants-prevent-accurate-count-1525589.php. Accessed December 10, 2012.

Hernstein, Richard J., and Charles Murray. 1994. *The Bell Curve: Intelligence and Class Structure in American Life*. New York: Simon and Schuster.

Hershkowitz, Sara. 1987. "Residential Segregation by Religion: A Conceptual Framework." *Tijdschrift voor Economische en Sociale Geografie* 78: 44–52.

Hewitt, Hugh. 2006. *Painting the Map Red: The Fight to Create a Permanent Republican Majority*. Washington, DC: Regnery.

Hicks, J. R. 1932. *The Theory of Wages*. London: MacMillan.

Highton, Benjamin, and Arthur L. Burris. 2002. "New Perspectives on Latino Voter Turnout in the United States." *American Politics Research* 30 (3): 285–306.

Hillygus, D. Sunshine, and Todd G. Shields. 2008. *The Persuadable Voter: Wedge Issues in Presidential Campaigns*. Princeton, NJ: Princeton University Press.

Hoeffel, Elizabeth M., Sonya Rastogi, Myoung Ouk Kim, and Hasan Shahi. 2010. *The Asian Population: 2010*. Washington, DC: United States Census Bureau.

Hood III, M. V., and Irwin Morris. 1998. "Give Us Your Tired, Your Poor, . . . But Make Sure They Have a Green Card: The Effects of Documented and Undocumented Migrant Context on Anglo Opinion toward Immigration." *Political Behavior* 20 (1): 1–15.

Hood III, M. V., and Seth C. McKee. 2010. "What Made Carolina Blue? In-Migration and the 2008 North Carolina Presidential Vote." *American Politics Research* 38 (2): 266–302.

Huckfeldt, Robert. 1983. "Social Contexts, Social Networks, and Urban Neighborhoods: Environmental Constraints on Friendship Choice." *American Journal of Sociology* 89 (3): 651–69.

———. 1986. *Politics in Context: Assimilation and Contact in Urban Neighborhoods.* New York: Agathon Press.

———, Jeanette Morehouse, and Tracy Osborn. 2004. "Disagreement, Ambivalence, and Engagement: The Political Consequences of Heterogeneous Networks." *Political Psychology* 26: 65–96.

Hunt, Jennifer. 2004. "Innis Lecture: Are Migrants More Skilled Than Non-Migrants? Repeat, Return, and Same-Employer Migrants." *Canadian Journal of Economics* 37 (4): 830–49.

Hunt, Larry L., Matthew O. Hunt, and William W. Falk. 2008. "Who Is Headed South? Migration Trends in Black and White, 1970–2000." *Social Forces* 87 (1): 95–119.

Hunter, James D. 1991. *Culture Wars: The Struggle to Define America.* New York: Basic Books.

Irhke, David. 2011. "Moving, Moving On, Moving Out—What's the Story?" *Random Samplings: The Official Blog of the U.S. Census Bureau.* http://blogs.census.gov/2011/05/23/moving-up-moving-on-moving-out-whats-the-story/. Accessed May 23, 2011.

Jackman, Mary R. and Marie Crane. 1986. "'Some of my best friends are black . . .' Interracial Friendships and White Racial Attitudes." *Public Opinion Quarterly.* 50 (4): 459–86.

Jacobson, Gary C. 2012. "The Electoral Origins of Polarized Politics: Evidence from the 2010 Cooperative Congressional Election Study." *American Behavioral Scientist* 56 (12): 1612–30.

Jennings, M. Kent. 1987. "Residuals of a Movement: The Aging American Protest Generation." *American Political Science Review* 81: 365–81.

———, and Richard G. Niemi. 1981. *Generations and Politics: A Panel Study of Youth and Their Parents.* Princeton, NJ: Princeton University Press.

———, and Gregory B. Markus. 1984. "Partisan Orientations over the Long Haul: Results from the Three-Wave Political Socialization Study." *American Political Science Review* 78: 1000–1018.

Johnston, Richard. 2006. "Party Identification: Unmoved Mover or Sum of Preferences?" *Annual Review of Political Science* 9: 329–51.

Jones, Dale E., Sherri Doty, Clifford Grammich, James E. Horsch, Richard Houseal, Mac Lynn, John P. Marcum, Kenneth M. Sanchagrin, and Richard H. Taylor. 2002. *Religious Congregations and Membership in the United States: 2000.* Nashville, TN: Glenmary Research Center.

Judis, John B., and Ruy Teixeira. 2002. *The Emerging Democratic Majority.* New York: Lisa Drew/Scribner.

Kaplan, Greg, and Sam Schulhofer-Wohl. 2010. "Interstate Migration Has Fallen Less Than You Think: Consequences of Hot Deck Imputation in the Current Population Survey." No. w16536. Washington, DC: National Bureau of Economic Research.

Karlgaard, Rich. 2004. *Life 2.0: How People across America Are Transforming Their Lives by Finding the Where of Their Happiness.* New York: Crown Business.

Kaufmann, Eric. 2010. *Shall the Religious Inherit the Earth: Demography and Politics in the 21st Century.* London: Profile Books.

Keeter, Scott, Juliana Horowitz, and Alec Tyson. 2008. "Young Voters in the 2008 Election." *Pew Research Center.* http://pewresearch.org/pubs/1031/young-voters-in-the-2008-election. Accessed December 14, 2012.

Keith, Bruce E., David B. Magleby, Candice J. Nelson, Elizabeth Orr, Mark C. Westlye, and Raymond E. Wolfinger. 1992. *The Myth of the Independent Voter.* Berkeley: University of California Press.

Kelly, Nathan J., and Jana Morgan. 2008. "Religious Traditionalism and Latino Politics in the United States." *American Politics Research* 36 (2): 236–63.

Key, V. O. 1949. *Southern Politics in State and Nation.* Knoxville: University of Tennessee Press.

King, Gary. 1996. "Why Context Should Not Count." *Political Geography* 15 (2): 159–64.

Kinsella, Chad I. 2011. "The Little Sort: A Spatial Analysis of Polarization and the Sorting of Like-Minded People." PhD diss., University of Cincinnati.

Kleiner, Morris M. 1982. "Evidence on Occupational Migration." *Growth and Change* 13 (3): 43–48.

Klineberg, Stephen. 2008. *An Historical Overview of Immigration in Houston, Based on the Houston Area Survey.* Report for the Center for Houston's Future. http://has.rice.edu/downloads/?ekmensel=c580fa7b_8_0_1748_6. Accessed December 10, 2012.

Kosman, J. 1993. "Toward an Inclusionary Jurisprudence: A Reconceptualization of Zoning." *Catholic University Law Review* 43: 59–108.

Krassa, Michael A. 1990. "Political Information, Social Environment, and Deviants." *Political Behavior* 12 (4): 315–30.

Krugman, Paul. 1991. "Increasing Returns on Economic Geography." *Journal of Political Economy* 99 (3): 483–99.

Kuhn, David Paul. 2008, November 5. "Exit Polls: How Obama Won." *Politico.* http://www.politico.com/news/stories/1108/15297.html. Accessed February 4, 2012.

Kulu, Hill, and Andres Vikat. 2008. "Fertility Differences by Housing Type: An Effect of Housing Conditions or of Selective Moves?" *Demographic Research* 17 (26): 775–802.

Kulu, Hill, and Paul J. Boyle. 2009. "High Fertility in City Suburbs: Compositional or Contextual Effects?" *European Journal of Population* 25 (2): 157–74.

Landale, Nancy S., and Avery M. Guest. 1985. "Constraints, Satisfaction, and Residential Mobility: Speare's Model Reconsidered." *Demography* 22 (2): 199–222.

Landale, Nancy S. and Stewart E. Tolnay. 1991. "Group Differences in Economic Opportunity and the Timing of Marriage: Blacks and Whites in the Rural South, 1910." *American Sociological Review.* 56(1): 33–45.

Last, Jonathan V. 2012, December 10. "A Nation of Singles." *Weekly Standard.* http://www.weeklystandard.com/articles/nation-singles_664275.html. Accessed December 13, 2012.

Layman, Geoffrey C., Thomas M. Carsey, and Juliana Menasce Horowitz. 2006. "Party Polarization in American Politics: Characteristics, Causes, and Consequences." *Annual Review of Political Science.* 9: 83–110.

Lazarsfeld, Paul F., Bernard Berelson, and Hazel Gaudet. 1944. *The People's Choice.* 3rd ed. New York: Columbia University Press.

Lee, Everett S. 1966. "A Theory of Migration." *Demography* 3: 47–57.

Lees, Loretta, Tom Slater, and Elvin Wyly. 2008. *Gentrification.* London: Routledge.

Lehrer, Evelyn L. 2004. "The Role of Religion in Union Formation: An Economic Perspective." *Population Research and Policy Review.* 23: 161–85.

Lesthaeghe, Ron J., and Lisa Neidert. 2006, March. "The 'Second Demographic Transition' in the U.S.: Spatial Patterns and Correlates." Population Studies Center Research Report No. 06–592, Ann Arbor, MI.

Levine, Phillip, and Daniel Zimmerman. 1995. "An Empirical Analysis of the Welfare Magnet Debate Using the NLSY." *National Bureau of Economic Research Working Paper Series.* Paper No. 5264, Cambridge, MA.

Lewis, W. Arthur. 1954. "Economic Development with Unlimited Supplies of Labor." *Manchester School of Economics and Social Studies* 22: 139–91.

Lichter, Daniel T. and Kenneth M. Johnson. 2009. "Immigrant Gateways and Hispanic Migration to New Destinations." *International Migration Review* 43 (3): 496–519.

———, Diane K. McLaughlin, George Kephart, and David J. Landry. 1992. "Race and the Retreat from Marriage: A Shortage of Marriageable Men?" *American Sociological Review* 57 (6): 781–99.

———, and Nancy S. Landale. 1995. "Parental Work, Family Structure, and Poverty among Latino Children." *Journal of Marriage and Family* 57 (2): 346–54.

Lieberson, Stanley. 1980. *A Piece of the Pie: Black and White Immigrants since 1980.* Berkeley: University of California Press.

Lipton, S. Gregory. 1977. "Evidence of Central City Revival." *Journal of the American Institute of Planners* 43: 136–47.

Liu, Ben-chieh. 1975. "Differential Net Migration Rates and the Quality of Life." *Review of Economics and Statistics* 57 (3): 329–37.

Livingston, Gretchen, and D'Vera Cohn. 2012. *U.S. Birthrate Falls to Record Lows: Decline Is Greatest among Immigrants.* Washington, DC: Pew Research Center.

Long, Larry. 1973. "Migration Differentials by Education and Occupation: Trends and Variations." *Demography* 10 (2): 243–58.

———. 1988. *Migration and Residential Mobility in the United States.* New York: Russell Sage Foundation.

———, and Diana DeAre. 1988. "U.S. Population Redistribution: A Perspective on the Nonmetropolitan Turnaround." *Population and Development Review* 14: 433–50.

———, and Alfred Nucci. 1997. "The 'Clean Break' Revisited: Is U.S. Population Again Deconcentrating?" *Environment and Planning A* 29: 1355–66.

Loomis, Charles P., and Horace H. Hamilton. 1936. "Family Life-Cycle Analysis." *Social Forces* 15: 225–31.

Lopez, Mark Hugo. 2008. *The Hispanic Vote in the 2008 Election.* Washington, DC: Pew Hispanic Center.

Lottes, Ilsa L., and Peter J. Kuriloff. 1994. "The Impact of College Experience on Political and Social Attitudes." *Sex Roles* 31 (1/2): 31–54.

Lyons, Jeffrey. 2011. "Where You Live and Who You Know: Political Environments, Social Pressures, and Partisan Stability." *American Politics Research* 39 (6): 963–92.

MacKuen, Michael, and Courtney Brown. 1987. "Political Context and Attitude Change." *American Political Science Review* 81 (2): 471–90.

MacRae Jr., Duncan. 1955. "Occupation and the Congressional Vote." *American Sociological Review* 20 (3): 332–40.

Malthus, Thomas. 1798. *First Essay on Population.* London.

Marks, Carol. 1989. *Farewell—We're Good and Gone: The Great Black Migration.* Bloomington: Indiana University Press.

Marshall, Alfred. 1890. *Principles of Economics.* London: Macmillan.

Martin, Ron, and Peter Sunley. 2003. "Deconstructing Clusters: Chaotic Concept or Policy Panacea?" *Journal of Economic Geography* 3 (1): 5–35.

Mason, Lilliana. 2013. "The Rise of Uncivil Agreement: Issue versus Behavioral Polarization in the American Electorate." *American Behavioral Scientist* 57 (1): 140–59.

Massey, Douglas S. 2007. "Borderline Madness: America's Counterproductive Immigration Policy." In *Debating Immigration*, ed. Carol M. Swain. Cambridge, UK: Cambridge University Press, 129–138.

Massey, Douglas, and Nancy A. Denton. 1988. "Suburbanization and Segregation in U.S. Metropolitan Areas." *American Journal of Sociology* 94 (3): 592–626.

———. 1993. *American Apartheid: Segregation and the Making of the Underclass.* Cambridge, MA: Harvard University Press.

Massey, Douglas, and Rene M. Zenteno. 1999. "The Dynamics of Mass Migration." *Proceedings of the National Academy of Sciences of the United States of America* 96 (9): 5328–35.

Massey, Douglas, and Chiara Capoferro. 2010. "The Geographic Diversification of American Immigration." In *New Faces in New Places: The Changing Geography of American Immigration*, edited by Douglas Massey, 25–50. New York: Russell Sage Foundation.

May, Caroline. 2012, November 7. "Obama Wins Fastest Growing Racial Group in America by 47 Points." *Daily Caller.* http://dailycaller.com/2012/11/07/obama-wins-the-fastest-growing-racial-group-in-america-by-47-percentage-points/. Accessed December 15, 2012.

McCarty, Nolan, Keith Poole, and Howard Rosenthal. 2006. *Polarized America: The Dance of Ideology and Unequal Riches.* Cambridge, MA: MIT Press.

———. 2009. "Does Gerrymandering Cause Polarization?" *American Journal of Political Science* 53 (3): 666–80.

McDonald, Ian. 2011. "Migration and Sorting in the American Electorate: Evidence from the 2006 Cooperative Congressional Election Study." *American Politics Research* 39 (3): 512–33.

McDonald, Michael P. 2006, December. "Rocking the House: Competition and Turnout in the 2006 Midterm Election." *The Forum* 4 (3).

McHugh, Kevin E., Patricia Gober, and Neil Reid. 1990. "Determinants of Short- and Long- Term Mobility Expectations for Home Owners and Renters." *Demography* 27 (1): 81–95.

McKee, Seth C. 2008. "Rural Voters in Presidential Elections, 1994–2004." *The Forum* 5 (2): Article 2.

McKee, Seth C., and Daron R. Shaw. 2003. "Suburban Voting in Presidential Elections." *Presidential Studies Quarterly* 33 (1): 125–44.

McLanahan, Sara. 2004. "Diverging Destinies: How Children Are Faring under the Second Demographic Transition." *Demography* 41 (4): 607–27.

McVeigh, Rory, and Juliana M. Sobolewski. 2007. "Red Counties, Blue Counties, and Occupation Segregation by Race and Sex." *American Journal of Sociology* 113 (2): 446–506.

Medina, Jennifer, and Sabrina Tavernise. 2011, October 27. "Economy Alters How Americans Are Moving." *New York Times.* http://www.nytimes.com/2011/10/28/us/americans-migration-patterns-shifting.html?_r=0. Accessed November 18, 2012.

Meyers, Adam S. 2013. "Secular Geographic Polarization in the American South: The Case of Texas, 1996–2010." *Electoral Studies.* 32 (1): 48–62.

Michalos, Alex C. 1996. "Migration and the Quality of Life: A Review Essay." *Social Indicators Research* 39 (2): 121–66.

Miller, Warren E. 1956. "One-Party Politics and the Voter." *American Political Science Review* 50 (3): 707–25.

Miller, William L. 1977. *Electoral Dynamics in Britain Since 1918.* New York: St. Martin's Press.

Mills, Bradford, and Gautam Hazarika. 2001. "The Migration of Young Adults from Non- Metropolitan Counties." *American Journal of Agricultural Economics* 83 (2): 329–40.

Mollenhorst, Gerald, Beate V lker, and Henk Flap. 2008. "Social Contexts and Personal Relationships: The Effect of Meeting Opportunities on Similarity for Relationships of Different Strength." *Social Networks* 30: 60–68.

Monson, Renee A., and Jo Beth Mertens. 2011. "All in the Family: Red States, Blue States and Postmodern Family Patterns, 2000 and 2004." *Sociological Quarterly* 52: 244–67.

Morrill, Richard. 1995. "Racial Segregation and Class in a Liberal Metropolis." *Geographical Analysis* 27 (1): 22–41.

Mulder, Clara H. 2006. "Home-Ownership and Family Formation." *Journal of Housing and the Built Environment* 21: 281–98.

———, and Michael Wagner. 2001. "The Connection between Family Formation and First Time Home Ownership in the Context of West Germany and the Netherlands." *European Journal of Population* 17: 137–64.

Murray, Charles. 2012. *Coming Apart: The State of White America, 1960–2010.* New York: Crown Forum.

Mutz, Diana C. 2002. "The Consequences of Cross-Cutting Networks for Political Participation." *American Journal of Political Science* 46 (4): 838–55.

Nelson, Paul B., Alexander Oberg, and Lise Nelsen. 2010. "Rural Gentrification and Linked Migration in the United States." *Journal of Rural Studies* 26 (4): 343–52.

Noah, Timothy. 2012, November 29. "No, Romney Didn't Win the Middle Class." *New Republic*. http://www.tnr.com/blog/plank/110584/romney-didnt-win-the-middle-class. Accessed December 5, 2012.

Nord, Stephen, and Yuan Ting. 1991. "The Impact of Advance Notice of Plant Closings on Earnings and the Probability of Unemployment." *Industrial and Labor Relations Review* 44 (4): 681–91.

Nuño, Stephen A. 2007. "Latino Mobilization and Vote Choice in the 2000 Presidential Election." *American Politics Research* 35 (2): 273–93.

Odland, John. 1988. "Migration and Occupational Choice Among Young Labor Force Entrants: A Human Capital Model." *Geographical Analysis*. 20(4): 281–296.

Ohls, James C., Richard C. Weisberg, and Michelle J. White. 1974. "The Effect of Zoning on Land Values." *Journal of Urban Economics* 1: 428–44.

Olson, Laura R., and John C. Green. 2009. "The Worship–Attendance Gap." In *Beyond Red State, Blue State: Electoral Gaps in the Twenty-First Century American Electorate*, eds. Laura Olson and John C. Green. Upper Saddle River, NJ: Pearson Prentice Hall, 40–52.

Pantoja, Adrian D., and Gary M. Segura. 2003. "Fear and Loathing in California: Contextual Threat and Political Sophistication among Latino Voters." *Political Behavior* 25 (3): 265–86.

Papademetriou, Demetrios G., Madeleine Sumption, Aaron Terrazas, Carola Burkert, Steven Loyal, and Ruth Ferrero-Turrión. 2010. *Migration and Immigrants Two Years after the Financial Collapse: Where Do We Stand?* Washington, DC: Migration Policy Institute.

Parrado, Emilio. 2011. "How High is Hispanic Fertility?" *Demography*. 48 (3): 1059–1080.

Parrado, Emilio A. 2011. "How High Is Hispanic/Mexican Fertility in the United States? Immigration and Tempo Considerations." *Demography* 48 (3): 1059–80.

Pashigian, B. Peter. 1977. "Occupational Licensing and the Inter-State Mobility of Professionals." *Journal of Law and Economics* 22 (1): 1–25.

Pekkala, Sari, and Hannu Tervo. 2002. "Unemployment and Migration: Does Moving Help?" *Scandinavian Journal of Economics* 104 (4): 621–39.

Peterson, Paul E., and Mark C. Rom. 1990. *Welfare Magnets*. Washington, DC: Brookings Institution.

Pew Research Center. 2012. "Young Voters Supported Obama Less, but May Have Mattered More." www.people-press.org/2012/11/26/young-voters-supported-obama-less-but-may-have-mattered-more/. Accessed December 14, 2012.

Pierce, Russell. 2012. "Immigration Statistics Show SB 1070 is Working." *Townhall*. http://townhall.com/columnists/russellpearce/2012/04/03/immigration_statistics_show_sb_1070_is_working/page/full/. Accessed April 18, 2013

Piore, Michael J. 1979. *Birds of Passage: Migrant Labor in Industrial Societies*. London: Cambridge University Press.

Plissner, Martin. 1983. "The Marriage Gap." *Public Opinion* 53 (February–March)

Poole, Keith T., and Howard Rosenthal. 1997. *Congress: A Political-Economic History of Roll-Call Voting*. New York: Oxford University Press.

———. 2001. "D-Nominate after 10 Years: A Comparative Update to Congress: A Political-Economic History of Roll-Call Voting." *Legislative Studies Quarterly* 26 (1): 5–29.

Porter, Michael. 1998. "Clusters and the New Economic Concentration." *Harvard Business Review* 76: 77–90.

————, and Paul D. Umbach. 2006. "College Major Choice: An Analysis of Person-Environment Fit." *Research in Higher Education* 47 (4): 429–49.

Pulsinelli, Olivia. 2012, August 7. "Houston Leading Southern City for Population Growth." *Houston Business Journal.* http://www.bizjournals.com/houston/news/2012/08/07/houston-leading-southern-city-for.html. Accessed December 9, 2012.

Putnam, Robert D. 1966. "Political Attitudes and the Local Community." *American Political Science Review.* 60 (3): 640–54.

Putnam, Robert D., and David E. Campbell. 2010. *American Grace: How Religion Divides and Unites Us.* New York: Simon and Schuster.

Rae, Nicol C. 1989. *The Decline and Fall of Liberal Republicans.* New York: Oxford University Press.

Raley, R. Kelly, and Megan M. Sweeney. 2009. "Explaining Race and Ethnic Variation in Marriage: Directions for Future Research." *Race and Social Problems* 1 (3): 132–42.

Ranis, Gustav, and J.C.H. Fei. 1961. "A Theory of Economic Development." *American Economic Review* 51: 533–65.

Ravenstein, E. G. 1885. "The Laws of Migration." *Journal of the Statistical Society of London* 48 (2): 167–235.

————. 1889. "The Laws of Migration: Second Paper." *Journal of the Royal Statistical Society* 52: 241–305.

Ridout, Travis. 2009. "Campaign Microtargeting and the Relevance of the Televised Political Ad." *The Forum* 7 (2): Article 5.

Robinson, Tony, and Stephen Noriega. 2010. "Voter Migration as a Source of Electoral Change in the Mountain West." *Political Geography* 29: 28–39.

Robinson, William S. 1950. "Ecological Correlations and the Behavior of Individuals." *American Sociological Review* 15: 351–57.

Rogers, Andrei, and Sameer Rajbhandary. 1997. "Period and Cohort Age Patterns of US Migration, 1948–1993: Are American Males Migrating Less?" *Population Research and Policy Review* 16 (6): 513–30.

Rogerson, Peter A. 1987. "Changes in U.S. National Mobility Levels." *Professional Geographer* 39: 344–51.

————, and Ikuho Yamada. 2009. *Statistical Detection and Surveillance of Geographic Clusters.* Boca Raton, FL: Chapman and Hall/CRC Press.

Romero, Simon. 2003, September 23. "Energy of Africa Draws the Eyes of Houston." *New York Times.* http://www.nytimes.com/2003/09/23/business/energy-of-africa-draws-the-eyes-of-houston.html?pagewanted=all&src=pm. Accessed December 10, 2012.

Rosenbloom, Joshua L., and William A Sundstrom. 2004. "The Decline and Rise of Interstate Migration in the United States: Evidence from the IPUMS, 1850–1990." In *Research in Economic History.* Vol. 22, 289–325. Bingley, UK: Emerald Group.

Rossi, Peter. 1955. *Why Families Move: A Study in the Social Psychology of Urban Mobility.* Glencoe, IL: Free Press.

Rothbart, Myron, and Oliver P. John. 1993. "Intergroup Relations and Stereotype Change: A Social-Cognitive Analysis and Some Longitudinal Findings." In *Prejudice, Politics, and the American Dilemma,* eds. Paul M. Sniderman, Philip E. Tetlock, and Edward G. Carmines. Stanford, CA: Stanford University Press, 32–59.

Rupasingha, Anil, and Stephan J. Goetz. 2004. "County Amenities and Net Migration." *Agricultural and Resource Economics Review* 33 (2): 245–54.

Sailer, Steve. 2008. "Value Voters." *American Conservative* 7: 16–20.

————. 2012, November 19. "The GOP's Other Problem: Marriage Gap Huge in 2012—But Marriage Is Starting to Disappear." *Vdare.com.* http://www.vdare.com/articles/the-gop-s-other-problem-marriage-gap-huge-in-2012-but-marriage-declining. Accessed November 22, 2012.

Sandler, Lauren. 2012, November 19. "Tell Me a State's Fertility Rate, and I'll Tell You How It Voted." *The Cut*. http://nymag.com/thecut/2012/11/states-conservative-as-their-women-are-fertile.html. Accessed November, 22 2012.

Sassler, Sharon, and Robert Schoen. 1999. "The Effects of Attitudes and Economic Activity on Marriage." *Journal of Marriage and the Family* 61 (1): 147–59.

Schachter, Jason. 2001, May. *Why People Move: Exploring the March 2000 Current Population Survey*. Current Population Report. Washington, DC: United States Census Bureau.

Schelling, Thomas C. 1971. "Dynamic Models of Segregation." *Journal of Mathematical Sociology* 1 (2): 143–86.

Schoen, Robert, and James R. Kluegel. 1988. "The Widening Gap in Black and White Marriage Rates: The Impact of Population Composition and Differential Marriage Propensities." *American Sociological Review* 53 (6): 895–907.

Seabrook, Nicholas. 2009. "The Obama Effect: Patterns of Geographic Clustering in the 2004 and 2008 Presidential Election." *The Forum* 7 (2): Article 6.

Segura, Gary M., Dennis Falcon, and Harry Pachon. 1997. "Dynamics of Latino Partisanship in California: Immigration, Issue Salience, and Their Implications." *Harvard Journal of Hispanic Politics* 10: 62–80.

Seitz, Shannon. 2009. "Accounting for Racial Differences in Marriage and Employment." *Journal of Labor Economics* 27 (3): 386–437.

Sherkat, Darren E. 2000. " 'That They Be Keepers of the Home': The Effect of Conservative Religion on Early and Late Transitions into Housewifery." *Review of Religious Research* 41 (3): 344–58.

Sjaastad, Larry A. 1962. "Costs and Returns on Human Migration." *Journal of Political Economy* 70 (5): 80–93.

Slater, Tom. 2006. "The Eviction of Critical Perspectives from Gentrification Research." *International Journal of Urban and Regional Research* 30 (4): 737–57.

Sokhey, Anand Edward, and Paul A. Djupe. 2009. "The Generation Gap." In *Beyond Red State, Blue State: Electoral Gaps in the Twenty-First Century American Electorate*, eds. Laura Olson and John C. Green. Upper Saddle River, NJ: Pearson Prentice Hall, 109–128.

Sousa, David J. 1993. "Organized Labor in the Electorate, 1960–1988." *Political Research Quarterly* 46 (4): 741–58.

Sowell, Thomas. 2002. *A Conflict of Visions: Ideological Origins of Political Struggles*. New York: Basic Books.

Speare, Alden. 1974. "Residential Satisfaction as an Intervening Variable in Residential Mobility." *Demography* 11: 173–88.

Stark, Oded, and David Levhari. 1982. "On Migration and Risk in LDCs." *Economic Development and Cultural Change* 31 (1): 191–96.

Stark, Oded, and David E. Bloom. 1985. "The New Economics of Migration." *American Economic Review* 75 (2): 173–78.

Steenbergen, Marco R., and Bradford S. Jones. 2002. "Modeling Multilevel Data Structures." *American Journal of Political Science* 46: 218–37.

Stinner, William F., and Mollie Van Loon. 1992. "Community Size Preference Status, Community Satisfaction and Migration Intentions." *Population and Environment* 14 (2): 177–95.

Stonecash, Jeffrey M., Mark D. Brewer, and Mack D. Mariani. 2003. *Diverging Parties: Social Change, Realignment, and Party Polarization*. Boulder, CO: Westview Press.

Tajfel, Henri. 1978. "Social Categorization, Social Identity, and Social Comparison." In *Differentiation between Social Groups*, ed. Henri Tajfel. New York: Academic Press, 61–76.

Taueber, Karl E., and Alma F. Taueber. 1965. "The Changing Character of Negro Migration." *American Journal of Sociology* 70 (4): 429–41.

Therialt, Sean M. 2005. *Party Polarization in Congress.* Cambridge, UK: Cambridge University Press.

Thompson, Chuck. 2012. *Better off without 'Em: A Northern Manifesto for Southern Secession.* New York: Simon and Schuster.

Thompson, Warren S. 1938. "The Effect of Housing upon Population Growth." *Milbank Memorial Fund Quarterly* 16 (4): 359–68.

Thornton, Arland, William G. Axinn, and Daniel H. Hill. 1992. "Reciprocal Effects of Religiosity, Cohabitation, and Marriage." *American Journal of Sociology* 98 (3): 628–51.

Tiebout, Charles M. 1956. "A Pure Theory of Local Expenditures." *Journal of Political Economy* 64 (5): 416–24.

Tolbert, Caroline, and Rodney Hero. 2001. "Dealing with Diversity: Racial/Ethnic Context and Social Policy Change." *Political Research Quarterly* 54: 571–604.

Tolnay, Stewart E. 2003. "The African American 'Great Migration' and Beyond." *Annual Review of Sociology* 29: 209–32.

United States Census Bureau. 2010. "Census Bureau Releases Estimates of Same-Sex Married Couples." http://www.census.gov/newsroom/releases/archives/2010_census/cb11-cn181.html. Accessed December 14, 2012.

Urban Research Center of Houston. 2009. *The Houston Area Survey Central Findings from Year 28.* http://has.rice.edu/downloads/?ekmensel=c580fa7b_8_0_1748_6. Accessed December 10, 2012.

Van Ommeren, Jos N., Piet Rietveld, and Peter Nijkamp. 1998. "Spatial Moving Behavior of Two-Earner Households." *Journal of Regional Science* 38 (1): 23–41.

Vobecká, Jana, and Virginie Piguet. 2011. "Fertility, Natural Growth, and Migration in the Czech Republic: An Urban–Suburban–Rural Gradient Analysis of Long-Term Trends and Recent Reversals." *Population, Space and Place* 18: 225–40.

Vos, Allison E. 2009. "Falling Fertility Rates: New Challenges to the European Welfare State." *Socio-Economic Review* 7 (3): 485–503.

Voss, Paul, Scott McNiven, Roger Hammer, Kenneth Johnson, and Glenn Fuguitt. 2004. *County- Specific Net Migration by Five-Year Age Groups, Hispanic Origin, Race, and Sex, 1990- 2000.* Madison: Center for Demography and Ecology, University of Wisconsin.

Wacquant, Loïc. 2008. "Relocating Gentrification: The Working Class, Science and the State in Recent Urban Research." *International Journal of Urban and Regional Research* 32 (1): 195–208.

Walker, James. 1994. "Migration among Low-Income Households: Helping the Witch Doctors Reach Consensus." Discussion Paper No. 1031–94. Madison, WI: Institute for Research on Poverty.

Warner, Mildred, and Robert Hebdon. 2001. "Local Government Restructuring: Privatization and Its Alternatives." *Journal of Policy Analysis and Management* 20 (2): 315–36.

Weigel, David. 2012, September 24. "Poll: Outside the South, Obama's Doing Well with the 'White Working Class.' " *Slate.* http://www.slate.com/blogs/weigel/2012/09/24/poll_outside_the_south_obama_s_doing_well_with_the_white_working_class_.html. Accessed December 6, 2012.

Weiner, Terry S., and Bruce K. Eckland. 1979. "Education and Political Party: The Effects of College or Social Class?" *American Journal of Sociology* 84 (4): 911–28.

Weisberg, Herbert F. 1987. "The Demographics of a New Voting Gap: Marital Differences in American Voting." *Public Opinion Quarterly* 51 (3): 335–43.

Weiss, Michael J. 1988. *The Clustering of America: A Vivid Portrait of the Nation's 40 Neighborhood Types—Their Values, Lifestyles, and Eccentricities.* New York: Harper and Row.

Wellman, Barry, Anabel Quan Haase, James Witte, and Keith Hampton. 2001. "Does the Internet Increase, Decrease, or Supplement Social Capital?" *American Behavioral Scientist.* 45 (3): 436–55.

White, Michael. 1987. *American Neighborhoods and Residential Differentiation.* New York: Russell Sage Foundation.

Wilcox, W. Bradford, and Nicholas H. Wolfinger. 2006. "Then Comes Marriage? Religion, Race, and Urban America." *Social Science Research* 36 (2): 569–89.

Williamson, Thad. 2008. "Sprawl, Spatial Location, and Politics: How Ideological Identification Tracks the Built Environment." *American Politics Research.* 36 (6): 903–933.

Winters, John V. 2011. "Human Capital and Population Growth in Nonmetropolitan U.S. Counties: The Importance of College Student Migration." *Economic Development Quarterly* 25: 353–65.

Withers, Suzanne Davies, and William A. V. Clark. 2006. "Housing Costs and the Geography of Family Migration Outcomes." *Population, Space and Place* 12: 273–89.

Withers, Suzanne Davies, William A.V. Clark, and Tricia Ruiz. 2008. "Demographic Variation in Housing Cost Adjustments with US Family Migration." *Population, Space and Place* 14 (4): 305–25.

Wong, Vanessa. 2011, December 11. "Population in Richest Zip Codes Keeps Growing." *Bloomberg Businessweek.* http://www.businessweek.com/lifestyle/population-in-richest-zip-codes-keeps-growing-12072011.html. Accessed December 5, 2012.

Wright, Erik Olin. 1997. *Class Counts: Comparative Studies in Class Analysis.* Cambridge, UK: Cambridge University Press.

Zimmer, G. Basil. 1973. "Migration and Changes in Occupational Compositions." *International Migration Review* 7: 437–48.

Zukin, Sharon. 1987. "Gentrification: Culture and Capital in the Urban Core." *Annual Review of Sociology* 13: 129–47.

Index

For Product Safety Concerns and Information please contact our EU
representative GPSR@taylorandfrancis.com
Taylor & Francis Verlag GmbH, Kaufingerstraße 24, 80331 München, Germany